# The Uruk Phenomenon

The role of social ideology in the expansion of the Uruk culture during the fourth millennium BC

Paul Collins

BAR International Series 900
2000

Published in 2016 by
BAR Publishing, Oxford

BAR International Series 900

*The Uruk Phenomenon*

© P Collins and the Publisher 2000

The author's moral rights under the 1988 UK Copyright,
Designs and Patents Act are hereby expressly asserted.

All rights reserved. No part of this work may be copied, reproduced, stored,
sold, distributed, scanned, saved in any form of digital format or transmitted
in any form digitally, without the written permission of the Publisher.

ISBN 9781841710969 paperback
ISBN 9781407352442 e-format
DOI https://doi.org/10.30861/9781841710969
A catalogue record for this book is available from the British Library

BAR Publishing is the trading name of British Archaeological Reports (Oxford) Ltd.
British Archaeological Reports was first incorporated in 1974 to publish the BAR
Series, International and British. In 1992 Hadrian Books Ltd became part of the BAR
group. This volume was originally published by Archaeopress in conjunction with
British Archaeological Reports (Oxford) Ltd / Hadrian Books Ltd, the Series principal
publisher, in 2000. This present volume is published by BAR Publishing, 2016.

BAR titles are available from:

BAR Publishing
122 Banbury Rd, Oxford, OX2 7BP, UK
EMAIL  info@barpublishing.com
PHONE  +44 (0)1865 310431
FAX  +44 (0)1865 316916
www.barpublishing.com

# CONTENTS

| | | |
|---|---|---|
| | ACKNOWLEDGEMENTS | iii |
| 1. | INTRODUCTION | 1 |
| 2. | SOCIAL IDEOLOGY AND ARCHAEOLOGY | 3 |
| 2.1. | Social Ideology | 3 |
| 2.2. | Ideology, complex society, and archaeology | 4 |
| 2.3. | Theories of social transformation and ideology | 8 |
| 3. | FACTORS EFFECTING THE EMERGENCE OF A SOCIAL IDEOLOGY | 10 |
| 3.1. | Physical environment | 10 |
| 3.1.1. | South Mesopotamia | 11 |
| 3.1.2. | North Mesopotamia | 12 |
| 3.2. | Social organization | 12 |
| 3.2.1. | The family | 12 |
| 3.2.2. | Too many chiefs? | 13 |
| 3.2.2.i. | South Mesopotamia | 14 |
| 3.2.2.ii. | North Mesopotamia | 15 |
| 3.2.3. | The ideology of third millennium Babylonia | 15 |
| 3.2.3.i. | Kingship | 15 |
| 3.2.3.ii. | Religious belief | 16 |
| 3.2.4. | Summary | 18 |
| 3.3. | Communication | 19 |
| 3.4. | Population movement/growth | 20 |
| 3.4.1. | Population and technology | 21 |
| 3.4.1.i. | Agricultural developments | 22 |
| 3.4.1.ii. | Ceramic production | 22 |
| 3.4.1.iii. | Metals | 22 |
| 4. | CHRONOLOGY 4000-3000 BC | 24 |
| 4.1. | Geographical regions | 25 |
| 4.1.1. | Southern Plain (Babylonia) | 25 |
| 4.1.2. | Northern regions | 25 |
| 4.1.2.i. | Middle Euphrates | 25 |
| 4.1.2.ii. | Upper Euphrates | 27 |
| 4.1.2.iii. | Habur | 27 |
| 4.1.2.iv. | North Jazira | 27 |
| 4.1.3. | Iran | 28 |
| 5. | SOCIETY AND MATERIAL | 29 |
| 5.1. | Monumental building | 31 |
| 5.2. | Uruk Sites | 31 |
| 5.3. | Settlement layout | 39 |
| 5.4. | Organization of monumental architecture | 40 |
| 5.4.1. | Platforms | 40 |
| 5.4.2. | Orientation | 41 |
| 5.4.3. | Standard units of measurement | 41 |
| 5.4.4. | Building Materials | 42 |
| 5.4.4.i. | Stone and gypsum | 42 |
| 5.4.4.ii. | Mud brick | 42 |
| 5.4.4.iii. | Bitumen | 43 |
| 5.4.5. | Decoration | 43 |
| 5.4.5.i. | Buttresses and niches | 43 |
| 5.4.5.ii. | Cone mosaic | 43 |
| 5.4.5.iii. | Paint decoration | 45 |

| | | |
|---|---|---|
| 5.5. | Domestic architecture | 45 |
| 5.6. | Associated indicators of a common ideology | 46 |
| *5.6.1.* | *Pottery and food* | 46 |
| *5.6.2.* | *Images of ideology* | 48 |
| 5.6.2.i. | Seals and sealings | 49 |
| 5.6.2.ii. | Sculpture | 50 |
| 5.6.2.iii. | Prestige vessels | 51 |
| 6. | FACTORS EFFECTING AND AFFECTING THE SPREAD OF A SOCIAL IDEOLOGY | 52 |
| 6.1. | Management, administration and economy | 52 |
| *6.1.1.* | *Seals and sealings* | 52 |
| *6.1.2.* | *Tags, tablets and bullae* | 54 |
| 6.2. | Trade and economy | 57 |
| *6.2.1.* | *Trade* | 57 |
| *6.2.2.* | *Economy* | 58 |
| 6.3. | Urbanization | 59 |
| 6.4. | Warfare | 60 |
| 7. | SUMMARY AND CONCLUSIONS | 62 |
| 7.1. | The background to a social ideology | 62 |
| 7.2. | The social ideology | 63 |
| 7.3. | Uruk organization | 64 |
| 7.4. | The nature of power within the Uruk world | 64 |
| 7.5. | The Uruk expansion | 65 |
| 7.6. | The end of the Uruk phenomenon | 66 |
| 7.7. | The legacy of the Uruk phenomenon | 66 |
| 7.8. | Theoretical review | 67 |
| 7.9. | Future research | 68 |
| | REFERENCES | 69 |
| | ILLUSTRATIONS | 87 |

## ACKNOWLEDGMENTS

This book is based on my doctoral dissertation entitled 'Social Ideology and the Uruk Phenomenon' (University of London 1999). I would like to thank all the numerous scholars whose support and encouragement have made the work possible. First and foremost, I am greatly indebted to Dr. Harriet Crawford for supervising the work over many years and patiently offering invaluable advice and criticisms. The work has also benefited enormously from the comments and suggestions of my examiners Dr. Karen Wright and Professor Roger Moorey. I am grateful to them both for encouraging publication.

Further thanks are due to Professor Fekri Hassan for illuminating discussions and helpful advice. My own continuing education students at Birkbeck College and Oxford University have contributed to the rich debate about the puzzles of the Uruk phenomenon for which I am very grateful.

Other people have offered support in many different ways. Thanks are due to the staff of the British Museum's Education Service, especially John Reeve and George Hart, and the Western Asiatic Department, in particular Dr. John Curtis.

The help and encouragement of all my friends, particularly my erstwhile colleagues of the BM's Information Service, has been invaluable.

Finally, the greatest debt is to my parents and family. Without their constant support this work would never have been completed.

Any errors in the text are entirely my responsibility.

# THE URUK PHENOMENON

"What happened? Fourth millennium specialists have a tendency to hide under their desks if they think that someone might ask them this question." (Johnson 1987: 126).

## 1. INTRODUCTION

It has long been recognised that urban society and states arose first on the southern alluvial plains of Mesopotamia during the fourth millennium BC. This Uruk culture represents a development which emerges around 4000 BC in the form of a fusion of elements from regional traditions, resulting in a much more homogeneous material culture, so that sites can be recognized with little difficulty as Uruk. The common features that emerge relate to a dramatic development in the forms of social interaction and control. From around 3600 BC, this transformation was achieved over an area not matched again for over another millennium. Essentially, the area forms an arc running from Susa to the southern alluvial plain of Sumer, along the Euphrates and through north Syria to Brak, with connections onto Nineveh (Fig. 1.).

An understanding of the period has been influenced by a reliance on excavations in southern Mesopotamia which, although producing spectacular results, were limited in terms of space (primarily the site of Warka), nature (ceremonial buildings), and time (the major material dating to the second half of the fourth millennium BC). The picture that emerged of the region, essentially based on surface surveys, was one of increasing urbanisation and four tier hierarchies of settlement associated with monumental architecture, art, and accounting systems which would develop into writing. However, in the last thirty years knowledge of developments in north Mesopotamia has revolutionised perceptions of this period and it is now clear that a long tradition of complex society, including monumental architecture and accounting systems, existed parallel with the developing southern culture.

With a few exceptions, (e.g., Fangipane 1993a,1997; Lupton 1996; Oates 1993; Stein 1994, 1996), the appreciation of the importance of the new material from north Mesopotamia has been diluted by a continuing emphasis on the south with its eventual move into history which appears to give a more accessible entry into ancient Mesopotamian civilisation.

Studies have approached the problem of the genesis of the southern 'Sumerian' civilisation and the emergence of city-states from a variety of directions, including: the growth of urbanism (Adams 1981; Adams and Nissen 1972); the development of complex administration (Johnson 1987); social and political stratification (Zagarell 1986); interregional trade (Wright and Johnson 1975); economic exploitation of less developed areas (Algaze 1989; 1993); warfare (Wright *et al* 1975); and, the more traditional prime movers, agricultural intensification and population growth (Smith and Young 1972) and climatic change (Hole 1994). Many theories thus explain the developments of the mid to late fourth millennium by emphasising the south as a 'core' which expands into a northern periphery through colonisation and/or warfare primarily to acquire raw materials unavailable on the alluvial plain.

The authors of these studies claim not that their particular topic represents the only factor, or *prime mover*, in the emergence of the state but rather the *principal mover*. All, however, recognise that a systems approach must be adopted where any number of variables are interlinked. Systems science, which identifies and investigates a range of phenomena and network of concepts, is again finding increasing favour as a method of inquiry by those concerned with building models not only of the past but also the future (e.g., Rowland 1995; Kauffman 1996). In investigating the rise of state society the process of interaction of *movers* is too complex to be reduced to simple themes or models (Yoffee 1979). However, the greater the number of movers identified, the greater our understanding of the forces which led to the appearance of urbanisation and statehood.

This work identifies 'social ideology' as an example of a crucial mover in the emergence of complex society and one which helps to help explain the developments visible in the archaeological record of fourth millennium BC Mesopotamia. It is argued that these developments were the result of an expansion in the exploitation of resources (flora and fauna); acquisition of rare materials, such as stones and metals, probably played a role but not as the primary basis for the resulting pattern. The shape this expansion took was conditioned by a unique ideology which had developed during the fourth millennium within the communities of the southern alluvial plain. It was the expansion of this southern ideology that created the Uruk phenomenon (and in a manner suggested here of total opposites to the military empire of Agade c. 2350 BC, see chapter **6.4.**).

To understand the Uruk phenomenon we are restricted to an analysis of the archaeological record; there is no writing of a later period which clearly refers back to it and provides a basis for its description (contemporary texts are limited in their content and are difficult to understand although examples like the professions list from Warka might help in offering a view of a hierarchically based society, institution or administration). This then poses the problem of what methodology might be employed to investigate the ideology. Despite its limitations, there is sufficient archaeological material to provide the basis for interpretations and this is worthwhile because the evidence is important in understanding the role of social ideologies in the development of complex societies in general.

Ideas derived from the critique of ideology have been applied to the analysis of prehistoric materials (e.g., Miller and Tilley 1984), and may be used in the analysis of fourth millennium Mesopotamia. This approach is grounded on the assumption that the prehistoric record can be interpreted not as a mere passive reflection of a past society but as an active process of representation which acted to constitute as well as to reflect social relations. Thus whatever the immediate uses made of artefacts such as buildings and seals, all artefacts are also forms through which a society creates representations of itself and thereby makes itself. They provide an important element in the everyday world in which the human operates whether as individuals and/or as social groups and thus help to create history.

While the material world may be understood as an active form of intervention, rather than a mere passive reflection, there is not necessarily a direct relationship between the social ideology it provides and the elements of social organisation. For example, evidence from burials or ritual may show an ideal view such as egalitarianism, but this may be contradicted by evidence of a hierarchy of people controlling resources. A particular type of evidence may thus represent the interests of a particular group which may mask other groups. This poses a problem since different sources of evidence may well provide entirely contradictory images of the same society. It has been usual to investigate the past by looking at social inequalities and hierarchies of power and organisation. Here it is proposed that an investigation of the 'ideal view' provides one of the most powerful explanations for both historical stasis and change. The reconstruction of such a social ideology cannot be approached, as was done up to the first half of this century, by generalisations, direct ethnographic analogies or retrojections. Here it will be investigated in terms of cognitive archaeology (Renfrew & Bahn 1991; Renfrew 1994a, 1994b) where it is argued that, although the archaeological record is biased through patterns of survival, it is possible to recognise a communal approach to relations between humans (demonstrated by common religious beliefs, measurement, planning, and depiction etc.).

The Uruk settlements are to be considered as artefacts, that is, 'artificial' creations of the Uruk world. The kinds of order they represent were instrumental in the organisation of society. However, this Uruk world collapsed at the end of the fourth millennium BC. External developments possibly resulted in contradictions emerging in the ideological basis of the culture that unified the various elements and justified its continuance. This resulted in a reconfiguration of the social ideology and a political system developed in southern Mesopotamia which was already present to limited degree in the north.

The resultant interpretation, although superficially similar to some of the accounts of the Uruk period (expansion of a religion, imperialism, world trade system), has implications very different from those assumed in these interpretations. Although many of the details of power and social relations are far from clear, an overall pattern may be discerned, signifying a process which may account for the various characteristic traits of the Uruk world.

## 2. SOCIAL IDEOLOGY AND ARHAEOLOGY

### 2.1. Social Ideology

Humans stand apart from animals in their ability to express self-knowledge through language and symbolism. An individual's concept of the world in which they live is a product of the capacity to produce and interpret symbols, and to create an often elaborate image of time and relationships; behaviour may be profoundly affected by a particular understanding of the past and present events which are part of their lives. Because of the importance for the individual of symbolic images, together with any behaviour based on them, it is not easy to clearly separate the level of the individual human from the social world of which they are part. Boulding (1956) defines a society not as collection of individuals but rather as a collection of individual 'social role(s)' - a social system may therefore be viewed as a set of such roles tied together with and by channels of communication. However, the interrelationship between the social role and the individual cannot be ignored as any understanding of the role will be affected by those who occupied it in the past. An ideology, therefore, represents an often unspoken language of symbols and ideas which may express either an entire social system or a specific collection of roles within that system.

In traditional sociological terms, an ideology may be defined as, "shared ideas or beliefs which serve to justify the interests of dominant groups. Ideologies are found in all societies in which there are inequalities between groups. The concept of ideology connects closely with that of power, since ideological systems serve to legitimise the differential power which groups hold." (Giddens 1989: 727). Power is therefore a medium of cohesion and may be assigned to charismatic individuals or institutions embodied by individuals as in kingship. It may be available to representative collectives or interests held by various groups within a society. This classic definition of the term, however, illuminates only one form of the concept - representation of specific social roles. Alternatively, an ideology will not represent a formally conceived set of ideas or beliefs but rather an implicit outlook of social ordering. Power need not be conceived of as merely the coercive abilities of particular individuals, institutions or groups, but may be considered as a more overarching and pervasive principle that both constrains as well as generates social forms, but is often strongly standardising in its effects (Foucault 1981: 92-95). When people come together in a society, a new entity is born out of their mutual agreement and this entity in turn changes the nature of the individuals who compose it. People outside society are a different kind of thing from people who have association. This new organic whole, cannot be reduced to the cells that compose it, since their nature depends upon their participation in this whole. While elements of this social ideology may form a system of beliefs which a group may manipulate to reinforce its social position, the underlying set of values on which the group has built their own will not represent or reflect the interests of one section of society but it will be equally powerful in directing and defining a society's approach to their world. Although an ideology is built from individual perceptions of the universe, shared systems may only be visible at the social level. The science of archaeology is rarely able to distinguish the individual. However, the collective concepts of a group will be reflected by identifying the content, dimensions, and homogeneity of value systems, images representing a particular view of history, and symbols of power and identity. A problem lies in how far this often very unclear material may be used to identify an ideology of a society. We therefore have to look for distribution patterns, scale, and context. It is here suggested that a social ideology may develop through a number of shared factors which will influence the acceptance of particular concepts (chapters 3 and 6).

The adoption of these concepts by members of a community has recently been explained in terms of analogies with genetic transmission (Dawkins, 1989, 1991; Dennett, 1995; Wilson, 1998). Although basically conservative, cultural transmission, (fashion, consciously recognised as such or not), can give rise to a form of evolution, e.g., language seems to 'evolve' by non-genetic means. There has thus been proposed the idea of replicators of the mind which have been dubbed by different authors variously as mnemotype, idea, idene, sociogene, concept, culturgen and culture type but perhaps most famously 'memes' (Dawkins 1989) - tunes, ideas, catch phrases which propagate by leaping from brain to brain, that is, by imitation. If an idea catches on it has 'propagated' itself. The survival value of any meme results from its psychological appeal. Just as not all genes replicate successfully, some memes are more successful than others. Some memes can achieve short-term success in spreading rapidly, but do not last long. Other ideas continue to propagate because of the potential permanence of written records. Memes are subject to continuous mutation and blending (in the style of the game Chinese whispers) but shared concepts have a common core. Clearly, if this core of understanding did not exist, then almost any statement concerning agreement about an idea would be meaningless. Like society, (which is the product of shared memes), the memes are not conscious, purposeful agents. But, also like society, blind natural selection makes them behave as if they were purposeful. This is because a meme will be associated with other particular memes. It is possible, therefore, to "regard an organised church, with its architecture, rituals, laws, music, art, and written tradition, as a co-adapted stable set of mutually-assisting memes." (Dawkins 1989: 197). Ideas which may appear to have been planned in advance, e.g., religious concepts, are self perpetuating because of their psychological impact. Ritual and architecture become linked with the 'god' meme because they reinforce each other. Selection favours memes that exploit their cultural environment to their advantage. Memes have, however, no foresight. They are unconscious, blind, replicators. The fact that they may or may not replicate means that those that do tend towards the evolution of qualities which can be called selfish, thus short-term selfishness appears to dominate and thus actively influences social organisation and progression (Plotkin 1994: 215-27).

The concept of memes is an attractive one but there are problems with how to identify them and, even if that should prove possible, whether they will be preserved in some form in the archaeological record. Dennett would like to envisage memes as "complex ideas that form themselves into distinct memorable units - such as the ideas of the arch, wheel, wearing clothes" (Dennett 1998: 344) but this has been shown to be too flexible an approach with any definition of a 'memorable unit' open to personal choice (Lake 1998). Even Dawkins has suggested that, while the meme is a useful analogy, the idea "can be taken too far if we are not careful" (Dawkins 1986:196). Wilson (1998) argues that one should look for the meme in the brain. Since culture is created by the communal mind, and each mind in turn is the product of the genetically structured brain, genes and culture are linked, but only tortuously. Some individuals inherit genetic rules enabling them to survive and reproduce better in the surrounding environment and culture than individuals who lack those rules. "By this means, over many generations, the more successful rules have spread through the population along with the genes that proscribe those rules. The quicker the pace of cultural evolution the looser the connection between genes and culture" (Wilson 1998:140). Thus society creates culture and is created by it. "Through constant grooming, decorating, exchange of gifts, sharing of food and fermented beverages, music and storytelling, the symbolic communal life of the mind takes form, unifying the group into a dreamworld that masters the external reality into which the group has been thrust" (Wilson 1998:143). What then is the basic unit of culture? Wilson associates this with neural activity in the brain. Concepts and symbols are labelled by words. Complex information is thus organised and transmitted by language composed of words. A meme is the same as the "nodule of semantic memory and its correlates in brain activity" (Wilson 1998: 149). Brains are sufficiently alike for certain memories to fit more easily than others. This explains why there are apparently common developments in different parts of the world, and complex society throws up monumental building and writing. Humans answer needs in a similar fashion constrained by their biology. How they reach those high level denominators varies depending on environment. It is clear, therefore, that if one accepts this definition of a meme, it will not be visible in the archaeological record. It is, however, a useful theory for helping to explain the spread of versions of an acceptable world view between individuals or groups. It also explains why culture is not naturally conservative and why internal tensions arise that might promote change.

## 2.2. Ideology, complex society, and archaeology

Ideology as a possible catalyst in the rise of the state has only recently begun to be explored. Its role has been considered for China (Wheatley 1971), Egypt (Hassan 1992), the Indus Valley (Miller 1985; Atre 1989; Maisels 1991, 1999), and, to a lesser extent, Mesopotamia (Adams 1966) but has generally been regarded by most researchers as a by-product of factors such as trade, population growth, or organised and intensified agriculture (based on the limited definition of ideology as related to specific social roles).

The most important investigations of the role of ideology in the emergence of a civilization relate to the Indus Valley or Harappan culture, the mature phase of which is dated between roughly 2500 BC and 1900 BC (Ehrich 1992). The debate over whether the Harappan culture was a state society (e.g., Kenoyer 1994; Chakrabarti 1995: 14; Possehl 1998: 281-7) does not concern us here. Increasingly scholars recognize that it represents a unique experiment in the development of an urban, literate culture (Allchin and Allchin 1982; Chakrabarti 1995) and was not reliant on stimulus from Mesopotamia. Reinterpretations of the archaeological material however continue to emphasize the dynamic role of an ideology in its creation.

Today more than one thousand sites associated with the development of the Harappan culture are known although few have been archaeologically explored. The three largest sites investigated in detail - Mohenjo-Daro, Harappa, and Kalibangan - show what has been described as a 'typical' layout of the Harappan city, that is an isolated western citadel and a lower city whose architectural features are oriented toward the cardinal points with roads running north-south at intervals. Mohenjo-Daro, which provides some of the best evidence, appears to have been built as a complete settlement on an artificial platform as a defense from flooding within a relatively short period of time. Its construction and design must have been devised by master builders and administrators who were thoroughly familiar with the vagaries of the river. The private houses as well as monumental structures were mostly built of baked bricks. Many domestic structures had wells of their own and bathrooms with paved floors. Pottery pipes carried waste water to the covered baked-brick drains running along the streets. The bricks were all standardized (1:2:4) and measures of length were based on an Harappan foot and cubit. Weights of polished cubes of stone were also highly standardized.

The archaeological evidence has been interpreted in various ways. Piggott (1950: 140), for example, suggested a "rigorously authoritarian rule" and a "rigid and highly evolved bureaucratic machine capable of organizing and distributing surplus wealth and defending it" (Wheeler quoted in Piggott 1950: 154). The emphasis was on cultural unity over some 1.25 million square kilometers. However, rather than emphasizing 'sameness' and 'isolation' recent research has identified regional 'polities' and interaction (Possehl 1998: 274-5). The so-called cultural unity of the Indus civilization is now seen to have been overstated (Shaffer 1982)

Nonetheless, homogeneous features of the Harappa culture certainly existed - the techniques of house construction, water supply, and effluent discharge, as well as the existence of a common system of weights and measures, and a common technology in the production of ceramics across a vast area over more than three hundred years. How was this achieved? Jansen (1993: 48) suggests that the inhabitants of the 'cities' exhibited an extraordinary conservative and traditional social behavior, and constitute "the actual backbone of the Indus civilization." Indeed, he has come to believe that Mohenjo-Daro was a physical manifestation intended to symbolize the Harappan ideology and way of life. Urbanization was a defining characteristic of this culture. Yet the town planning between sites "differed according to the demands of the local environment and the original function of the settlement. Several common features were maintained as a matter of natural adherence to some inherently accepted norms but no rigidity was to be observed." (Atre 1989: 50). It is, therefore, "more prudent to talk of coordination than imposition" (Sarcina 1979: 446).

Fairservis (1967: 43) thinks that such coordination was not beyond the powers of an elaborated village administration. Thus the evidence suggests that a 'great tradition' marked by both urban and rural elements evolved out of hybrid 'little communities': village and city alike shared a common culture. Harappan society thus consisted of groups bound together by ties of kinship and ideology. Similarly, Possehl (1993: 289-90) suggests a decentralized institution without centralized leadership with multi-regional politics, perhaps based on older tribal organizations.

It is possible that a leader, or leaders received tribute but there is no evidence for the figure of a king, no cult of personality. Miller (1985) therefore rejects the traditional models of a redistributive élite of priest-kings and interprets the evidence as indicative of an order in the settlements that opposes the natural environment. He suggests that Harappan society was authoritarian, non-ranked and puritanical, and considers the caste composition of contemporary Hindu society to be more a polar opposite than a direct analogy.

Thus a central theme within the study of the Indus Valley civilization is that it represents a social ideology, a way of life in a holistic sense. "This ideology was more than a simple religion; it is better understood as a *genre de vie*. . . . The ideology crossed the segmented, regional political boundaries, reaching into every Harappan family. Other forms of solidarity, such as trade, ecological interdependence, and intermarriage, would have augmented the ideological basis" (Possehl 1998: 289).

The rise of the unified Egyptian state is another relevant example from the ancient world which demonstrates the creative power of ideology. Many elements of the well-known Egyptian iconography and ideology of historic times (e.g., the divine pharaoh smiting his enemy) survived from the Predynastic and Early Dynastic periods. While the meaning of these symbols may have been modified or changed over time, "in their content and style the pieces are the product of a great codifying of traditions that took place immediately prior to the beginning of the 1st Dynasty." (Kemp 1989:46). The early rulers of Egypt adopted, adapted and united ideas and symbols from throughout the country. The Egypt state was rapidly built on the foundations of a single ideology which, with numerous local adaptations, was to prove incredibly cohesive and successful. From at least the Middle Kingdom (c.2000-1800 BC), Egyptian texts relate that the Pharaonic Kingdom resulted from the 'unification of the Two Lands' of Upper and Lower Egypt (Quirke and Spencer 1992: 70). Traditionally, the country was united about 3100 BC, when Upper Egypt conquered Lower Egypt. Today, Egyptologists recognise that the process of unification was probably a slow phenomenon not completed until the end of the Archaic period, c.2700 BC (Spencer 1993). The country emerged from a number of chiefdoms and states united by alliances and warfare during the late Predynastic period centred on Nagada and Hierakonpolis (Hoffman 1980; Kemp 1989). Clearly the modern concept of the state can only be applied very imperfectly to these early political organisations, where the characteristic functions of state power might be exercised at irregular intervals or with little obvious differentiation between political organisation and the kind of activities based on kinship, religion, and status. Despite the problems of defining the early Egyptian state, most interpretations of the rise of Dynastic Egypt see ideology in terms of both masking and reflecting élite power and wealth.

Recently, the central feature of an ideology which rose with the Egyptian state has been identified as "the emergence of a power mystique that binds people from different kinship groups (lineages) into a very large society over a vast territory" (Hassan 1992:319). Thus, it is argued that the emergence of the centralised Egyptian state rested on a link between the king and supernatural forces. The ruler was believed to be the son, brother and husband of a goddess and as such became divine; he was, in effect, the god Horus. This was the central part in the evolution of a 'kingship mythology'. Egypt evolved from a series of local chiefdoms into a unified state with the aid of a wealth of symbols and rituals which commanded widespread respect or rapidly came to 'colonise' the minds of the nation. That such political and social changes can happen rapidly, rather than in a slow, smooth evolutionary process (as suggested takes place in nature by those whom Eldredge (1995) calls 'Ultra-Darwinians'), is demonstrated by developments in the Olmec and Benin cultures (Coe 1989; Darling 1988) and argued to exist in biological evolution by the theory of 'punctuated equilibrium' (Eldredge & Gould 1972). In Predynastic Egypt, therefore, ideology may have acted to mask local social stratification but it was in terms acceptable to the population and appears to have been a major driving force behind the emergence of leaders from local chiefs to divine king and political unification of the land.

The lack of focus on the role of ideology within Mesopotamian studies appears to stem from a strong reaction away from the *Tempelwirtshaft* models of the early Sumerian state. Based solely on a detailed study of the Ba'u (or Baba) temple archive in Lagash (twenty-fourth century BC) this model argued that the city temple, and by association the god, 'owned' all the land (Deimel 1931). The inhabitants were thus ruled by a religious ideology where the temple was the dominant economic and political force. Recently, however, major flaws in this model have been demonstrated by the work of Diakonoff (1974; 1982) and Gelb (1979; *et al* 1991) who show that a substantial amount of land in Early Dynastic Sumer (c.2800-2350 BC) was owned not by temples but by families and individuals. However, the surviving monuments of historic Mesopotamia stress an ideology (albeit one which is heavily biased by the archaeological record) based on the importance of the temple, emphasising the divinely appointed ruler with the community focused on, and identified with, a particular god or goddess, their temple and symbols. The effects of such a politico-religious ideology in Mesopotamia may be seen in the coronation oath of Middle and Neo-Assyrian monarchs where their duty is to extend the territory of the land of the national god, Ashur (Kuhrt 1995:365).

In the Egyptian and Mesopotamian examples, the use of symbolism, often embedded in theology and the past, reflects an ideology - an idealised image of society defining its place in the universe and justifying any actions of the community. Such a phenomenon is well known from other areas and times. For example, for the ancient Greeks, each polis had myths of heroes and patron gods which were important for creating the group's political identity. There was also the notion of a Golden Age of unity (possibly memories of the Mycenaean civilisation) expressed by the concept of Hellenism (Ferguson 1991). Public ritual has been and continues to be an important method by which a society might be unified and reinforced. Such manipulation of the psychology of a community may, for example, rest on the acceptance of the majesty and mystery of an élite, often embedded in theology and enhanced in powerful symbolic terms. The importance of Mayan ideology, for example, has recently been proposed by Schele and Miler (1986) where the élite may have identified themselves through a complex series of bloodletting rituals or, as in Aztec society, the exchange of prestige items by an élite over vast geographical areas (Conrad and Demarest 1984). This may also involve the identification of a common enemy, whether real or imagined. Even modern states rely on what is often anachronistic yet politically valid forms of ritual and symbolism to maintain the position of the governing aristocracy. A society's ideology can therefore stand "as the infrastructure and justification for developing political domination" (Earle 1991:1). In its wider form, a social ideology (and an individual's recognition of their being part of that ideological community) will also act as a unifying force. The form of that ideology will determine how it is 'exploited' or develops to represent specific social and political groups within a society. This, in turn, may ultimately decide how long the ideology survives.

Since the first translation of Mesopotamian cuneiform documents in the last century, much effort has been directed towards understanding the speculative thoughts and belief systems of the ancient inhabitants. All too often, however, such studies are flawed by "the nature of the available evidence, and the problems of comprehension across the barriers of conceptual conditioning" (Oppenheim 1977:172). Conclusions based on explanatory works of Mesopotamian scholars, as well as a heavy reliance on myths and legends preserved in texts from different periods, tend to create the illusion of a standard 'Mesopotamian' religious and political framework, apparently unaffected by social changes. Important studies, such as those of Henri Frankfort (1948) and Thorkild Jacobsen (1946; 1976), attempted to provide histories of Mesopotamian religious ideology which emphasised change as well as continuity but, although the deficiency of such broad approaches to speculative thought during historic periods was recognised by the authors, all too often such generalisations were projected into the prehistoric past. When attempts are made to record prehistoric ideas, it is all too easy to interpret prehistory with one eye on history. This happens regardless of which part of the world one is discussing, and many studies fall into the trap of drawing inferences about periods where writing is non-existent from better documented periods. For example, Mesopotamian studies are replete with 'sacred marriage' rituals, used as an explanation of fourth millennium BC glyptic and sculptural art although the first evidence for such practices date to the end of the third millennium BC (e.g., Schmandt Besserat 1992). Confident statements in terms of prehistoric beliefs can stretch to the point where pottery figurines from possible shrines at Gilat and Ein Gedi in Israel are described as part of the cult of "a deity resembling Dumuzi the Mesopotamian god of fertility and fields, before whom milk was libated" (Gonen 1992:64). Such general approaches have also been adopted for discussions of political history and there has been a tendency to view Mesopotamian culture as continuous; bigger and better 'empires' followed one another, to be broken by 'dark ages', after which progress again marched on.

During the 1960s and 1970s archaeologists became aware that many of the statements about past symbolic and belief systems were too generalised and, therefore, defective. From this recognition emerged 'new' or processual archaeology which emphasised material aspects of life. Theories produced by the processual exponents were based upon a methodology rooted in Darwinian adaptation and selection, and may be described as 'functionalist'. While economic and social aspects of the past were emphasised, all too often belief and communication systems of early societies were ignored. Because Near Eastern archaeology is historically rooted in the fields of art history, linguistics, and ancient history, the impact of this processual approach was less severe than in the fields of European and American prehistory where it first developed. Nonetheless, the advances in our understanding of the 'ancient mind' have not been promoted by an emphasis on a methodology where past human society is believed to be shaped purely by economic, ecological and political adaptation.

Within most processual studies of the transformation of societies towards more complex forms, the role of ideology as a guiding force is usually considered secondary to economic forces, emerging only to legitimise the systems of domination, in other words, it is interpreted functionally in relation to the economic base. The "material culture may be 'active' but this is a fairly passive end-product of functional needs" (Hodder 1991:64). Thus, it is argued, an ideology serves to create social cohesion which would otherwise break apart when any group wished to, for example, end alliance networks and concentrate production within their local community. Or, ideology can also be seen as a method by which élites can reflect their material wealth by transforming surplus into, for example, ritual feasting and monumental building works; major buildings like Stonehenge, the temples of Malta, or the statues of Easter Island can be built by chiefdom societies (Renfrew 1972, 1984; see chapter **3.2.** for a discussion of chiefdoms).

Belief and communication systems were therefore ignored in what was considered by some archaeologists as 'palaeopsychology' (e.g., Binford 1987). However, as part of a shift in philosophical thinking, processual archaeology has recently been rejected by some archaeologists in favour of a hermeneutic approach. The emphasis on the material aspects of past cultures was countered by ‚post-processual* archaeology which attempted to focus upon the symbolic and cognitive aspects in the archaeological record, often to the point where empirical evidence was ignored in an attempt to 'enter the mind' of a long-dead person. As the leading exponent of this move from the materialistic emphasis of the processual archaeologists, Ian Hodder has argued that ideology can have a central role in the development of complex societies since it "is an aspect of symbol systems ... a framework within which, from a particular standpoint, resources are given value, inequalities are defined and power legitimated" (Hodder 1991:72). In this sense, ideology can be seen, not just as a reflection of economic and political developments, even if intertwined and developing together, but also as a potential guiding force, directing a group in a particular direction. As such it is possible to avoid "objectivism (social action happens with mechanical inevitability, through processes of which actors are ignorant) and subjectivism (social action is produced solely by skilled actors)" (Hodder 1991).

The philosophical debate between the followers of processual and post-processual archaeology, as represented most robustly by Binford and Hodder, has done little to add to the consideration of ancient belief and communication systems and their role in the emergence of complex society. This lacuna has been recognised by Renfrew who rejects Hodder's 'anti-processual' stance in favour of what he terms 'cognitive' archaeology (Renfrew & Bahn 1991; Renfrew 1994a, 1994b). This can be defined as "the study of all aspects of ancient culture that are the product of the human mind: the perception, description, and classification of the universe (cosmology); the nature of the supernatural (religion); the principles, philosophies, ethics, and values by which human societies are governed (ideology); the ways in which aspects of the world, the supernatural, or human values are conveyed in art (iconography); and all other forms of human intellectual and symbolic behaviour that survive in the archaeological record" (Flannery and Marcus 1998: 36-7). While recognising the important role ideology plays in shaping human actions, archaeologists are, clearly, always constrained by the surviving evidence. Renfrew argues that it is possible to recognise in the evidence a communal approach to relations between human beings (which may be demonstrated by common religious beliefs, measurement, planning, and depiction). Individuals who live together in a community (however that may be structured) share in some sense the same world view. This can be described as a common cognitive map or social ideology, a set of shared ideas which forms the basis of a group's approach to everyday existence. Of course there are different levels to that map. Special interest groups will posses their own version which fits into the overarching world view. The Mesopotamian historical record, as indicated above, appears predominately to represent evidence of interest groups - temples, palaces. While distinguishing various social groupings is not always easy in the archaeological record - the most informative evidence is often provided by cemetery sites but no fourth millennium examples have so far been located in southern Mesopotamia - any evidence is often mistakenly projected onto society as a whole and it is this problem that will be dealt with in the next chapter.

## 2.3. Theories of social transformation and ideology

Just how society is transformed and changed has been the preoccupation of sociologists, historians and archaeologists since the last century. The nineteenth century witnessed the advancement of a number of theoretical approaches to the problem which have continued to influence researchers.

Emile Durkheim (1915; 1982), for example, emphasised the constraining nature of social influences on an individual's actions. Recognisable social structures represent sufficiently stable forms to leave evidence of their existence comparable to structures in the material environment. In this way society constrains our activities in a parallel way.

> When I perform my duties as a brother, a husband, or a citizen and carry out the commitments I have entered into, I fulfil obligations which are defined in law and custom and which are external to myself and my actions. . . . Similarly, the believer has discovered from birth, ready fashioned, the beliefs and practices of his religious life; if they existed before he did, it follows that they exist outside him. The system of signs that I employ to express my thoughts, the monetary system I use to pay my debts, the credit instruments I utilise in my commercial relationships, the practices I follow in my profession, etc. - all function independently of the use I make of them. Considering in turn each member of society, the following remarks could be made for each single one of them. (Durkheim 1982 (1895): 50-1).

If social structures are so powerful and constraining how does change ever occur? Durkheim explained change by exploring divisions of labour, in other words, the growth of ever more complex distinctions between different occupations. He argued that increasingly specialised labour gradually replaces religion as the main foundation of social cohesion since people become more and more dependent on one another, needing goods and services that those in other occupations supply. Religious beliefs and relationships between dependent groups reaffirm people's adherence to core social values in the face of change and disruption. The ideas and values of the society will shape the pattern of relationships across a society and therefore determine the way in which it develops.

This is contrary to theories developed by Marx (1963) who considered that the main source of social change was not human ideas or values developing to fit new social roles but rather economic influences. These are linked to conflicts between social classes which provide the motive power of historical development. Marxist ideas have heavily influenced interpretations of social developments with the emphasis on factors such as trade, economy, class divisions, and conflict, as 'prime movers'. Conflict of another kind is suggested by Merton (1957) whose 'dysfunctions' are aspects of social activity which tend to produce change because they threaten social cohesion.

Investigators have, therefore, tended to emphasis either consensus (shared ideas and values between dependent groups) or conflict (disputes between groups) to explain social transformation and the emergence of complex society. Renfrew (1972) combined these approaches by regarding society and culture as a system. Different activities (including the artefacts and material culture) of a society, influenced by settlement patterns, production of different crops, materials etc. (Renfrew and Bahn 1991: 421), change as a result of positive feedback where one or more element of the system favours more of the same. Growth occurs and may effect other elements within the system and potentially lead to new forms of society or culture. Such a view can be criticised because it appears mechanistic and ignores individuals or even small numbers of humans. It is, however, possible to reinstate the individual by recognising the importance of cultural transmission or fashion as an engine of change. Fashions in dress and diet, ceremonies and customs, art and architecture, engineering and technology, all evolve in historical time. Essentially a new fashion represents something that is used by those 'in the know' and not by those who lag behind. Difference is the key. Some concepts may be adopted by society and others rejected, determined by the acceptability of a collection of ideas (or, to adopt Dawkin's terminology, memes). Those ideas which are transmitted across the whole of society thus become the norm. This is a process of continual building and taking apart. Conflict is followed by consensus - a fashion adopted by a minority (not necessarily the most important group in society) may or may not be adopted by the majority (or the most important group in society) before a new fashion emerges. As a result, culture does not move in any particular direction since there is both positive and negative feedback within the system. There is no *inevitable* Spencerian style evolution of society. Ideas influenced by changes in trade, economy, communication, or politics may find favour in the minds of a large number of individuals but will be most visible in a style of art, architecture or clothes. For example, the impact of American culture, politics and economic strength can be readily recognised in the spread of the baseball cap. It is important to recognise, however, that the presence of a baseball cap does not automatically imply the acceptance of an American cultural ideology. The fashion for baseball caps may restrict the availability of other hats, and a hat wearer, regardless of ideological considerations, may be 'forced' to wear a baseball cap in the absence of any other style of dress. Therefore, to identify an ideology rather than the fashion, especially in the archaeological record where evidence is always limited and biased by object deposition and survival rates, it is necessary to identify a number of ideological indicators and examine their distribution, scale and context, e.g., the baseball cap could be investigated alongside the spread of the $ and McDonald symbols.

With the passage of time cultural change may appear as a smooth, inevitable evolution, but in reality change is erratic and can take place in bursts of activity as certain memes prove more popular than others. If one follows, for example, the ideas of Durkheim, or Merton's concept of latent functions (consequences of activity of which participants are unaware), religion is a mechanism for solidifying group identity. This suggests that society itself in some way 'drives' its members to act in a certain way, adopting various fashions (ideas, dress, architecture), because it 'needs' religion to hold it together. However, society is 'blind and deaf', it has no purpose or will-power, only human individuals have these. In this way individuals can to a limited extent attempt to direct cultural transmission and social transformation. However, if an individual's idea is not adopted, society will move in a particular direction having adopted and adapted other ideas. As such humans are not the creatures of society, but its creators and actively make and remake social structure during the course of everyday activities. However, "the extent to which people act with a clear idea of their ends, knowing what effects they are aiming at, is easily exaggerated. Most human action is tentative, experimental, directed not by a knowledge of what it will lead to but rather by a desire to know what will come of it" (Collingwood 1993: 42).

## 3. FACTORS EFFECTING THE EMERGENCE OF A SOCIAL IDEOLOGY

Accepting that an ideology may be viewed as a driving force, propelling a society in a particular direction (even if that is represented by stasis) as well as reflecting current beliefs of a community, inevitably leaves the problem of how to identify such a closely interacting system of cause and effect within the archaeological record. When considering the prehistoric period, and taking into account the dangers of using later ideas preserved by writing, it may be useful to create a theoretically level playing field representing a social ideology from which a recognisable political / economic / religious ideology may emerge. It is suggested, therefore, that ideology, as a unifying force between individuals or groups of humans, may be brought about by one, or more likely, a combination of deeply held beliefs based on a number of shared criteria:

**3.1. Physical environment**
**3.2. Social organisation**
**3.3. Communication**
**3.4. Population movement and/or growth**

In addition there are a number of crucial factors which may encourage the transmission of an ideology, but are also important factors for determining its development and form and these will be examined in chapter 6:

**6.1. Management, administration and economy**
**6.2. Trade and economy**
**6.3. Urbanization**
**6.4. Warfare**

No doubt there are other kinds of criteria which may act as a driving force towards a common cognitive map, but this simplistic listing will serve to begin the analysis. It is often difficult to tease out distinctions between these factors. For example, the difference between an economy as a concept separate from trade, or political as opposed to religious allegiance, particularly where societies make no distinction between 'spiritual' and 'secular' as in the modern Western world. One should be wary of imposing modern concepts onto societies where such distinctions did not exist.

Similar criteria have been used by researchers in different fields for investigating complexity, particularly using computer-aided simulations. Among the most ambitious of such projects involves research into models which suggest that deep laws exist behind complexity. Mathematical theories, that use conceptions such as chaos, self-criticality and adaptive landscapes, are used to suggest some of the essential elements (Kauffman 1996). These abstractions help to explain the way complex systems might build themselves up, persist for a while and then disintegrate. Chaos theory says that extremely complicated, outwardly indecipherable patterns can be determined by small, measurable changes within the system. If there is any basis to these suggestions, they will only be demonstrated by vast amounts of empirical data. As such, these models cannot be applied directly to archaeological and historical material as any interpretation is inevitably based on incomplete evidence. Nonetheless, the criteria of this chapter and chapter **6** will point towards alternative explanations of complexity.

### 3.1. Physical Environment

One of the most important factors in any human's relationship with the world is the physical environment in which they live. It is probably the primary factor from which all other ideological criteria will emerge. The environment provides a stage and an interactive habitat with potentials and constraints. This is not to suggest that separate individuals will arrive at the same attitude to life (and death) by living in the same physical landscape but rather that it will fashion a response from a shared experience. The possibility of identifying the root of an ideology is remote since it will probably lie deeply embedded among other criteria. A possible example of environmental influence on a belief system may be evident in the different concepts of an afterlife among the ancient

Egyptians (a paradise involving a carbon copy of the Nile valley) and the inhabitants of Mesopotamia (a dour, shadowy existence, eating mud and dust). This example is of course a gross generalisation, since these beliefs are based on a whole series of interlocking historical and ideological developments, and the only evidence concerning the Mesopotamian beliefs comes from a limited number of poetic compositions. However, in a theoretically undifferentiated landscape where access to water, fertile soil, and natural resources are all equal it is likely that human inhabitants, dispersed evenly across the land but in contact with each other, would share the same cognitive map.

### 3.1.1. South Mesopotamia

Naturally, in the real world no such uniform environments exist, and even in such a superficially undifferentiated area as the plains of southern Mesopotamia there were a number of specialised subsistence zones (Adams 1966; Wheatley 1971). Distances between these different ecological regions would, however, have often been small and any geographical barriers generally unimportant. Interaction between those engaged in different subsistence pursuits was, as a result, very close and most communities must have been self sufficient in subsistence specialisation, indeed the possibility of surpluses was essential to provide the reason for specialisation and contact with other groups. It was the effective exploitation of these various eco-niches which would have been a major factor in the evolution of a symbiotic interdependence between different sections of society. This interdependence would also have recognised certain over-arching factors. That is, the crucial importance of access to water to utilise the potentially fertile soil as well as the more immediate concerns of drinking supplies and washing/waste disposal. In addition, the hostile natural forces (high temperatures in summer, sand and dust storms, wild animals) would have acted to produce a common attitude to the environment - this is certainly reflected in the historic period where natural forces were held to be divine elements which needed appeasing though offerings and prayers (Leick 1991: 30 'Demons').

The modern appearance of the southern plain provides no reliable guide to the past. The shifting nature of the environment, resulting from changes in water flow patterns due to flooding, water shortages and channel siltation, as well as changes in productive fields through salinisation, were dangers the inhabitants of the region faced on a daily basis. Of major significance, therefore, was the need for a dependability of production in such a unstable landscape. This could be achieved through diversification. Although closely connected, the various modes of production encouraged specialised occupations.

There is no evidence to suggest that the basic agricultural products of the various eco-niches in the late prehistoric period would have been significantly different from those identified by third millennium texts, particularly the important archive from Girsu (Powell 1990). The main activity was based on cereal culture. In areas adjacent to permanent watercourses, orchard and garden crops, especially the date, were grown. An important feature of the region was the pasturing of cattle by sedentary herdsmen on rough land and cereal stubble; and the grazing of migratory herds by nomadic pastoralists on semiarid steppe. The geography of the plain therefore suggests a mosaic of arable land interspersed with areas better suited to pastoral pursuits (Rowton 1973). The southern swampland was also essential in providing building materials (mud, palms, reeds), game, wildfowl and fish.

Our understanding of agricultural production in Mesopotamia is based on the wealth of documents from the later third millennium. These are biased towards the large public institutions and emphasise large scale land management and the maximisation of agricultural production - a direct result of demands from cities, their associated élites and large populations. Historical Mesopotamia, therefore, presents a picture of agricultural activity where, to adopt a modern concept, the countryside interacted with, and was directed by, the urban sector. What is lacking from the archaeological record, however, is substantial evidence for the steps which led from small Ubiad period farming communities to the complex urban life of the late fourth millennium. According to Wittfogel (1955, 1957) it was the need for organised large-scale irrigation works necessary to produce food surpluses that led to the emergence of a stratified society and a focus of a community in urban form around an administrative élite. His arguments in favour of a 'prime mover' focused on irrigation are now generally rejected as significant in the move towards complex social organisation (e.g. Maisels 1990:211; Postgate 1992:173). It was only in the middle of the third millennium that "the multiple, small shifting canals" of late Uruk, Jemdet Nasr and Early Dynastic times were "consolidated into a much reduced number of larger and more permanent courses" (Adams and Nissen 1972: 38). Indeed, the irregular changing river regime of Mesopotamia probably ensured an impermanence in both land conditions and human attachments with nothing more than a few areas of stable land. For example, Adams (1981: 62) demonstrates the shift of a major branch of the Euphrates during the fourth millennium which led to a large scale transformation of the settlement pattern. Nissen (1988; 1993a; 1993b) argues that during the fifth and fourth millennia the previously waterlogged Mesopotamian plain began to dry allowing permanent settlement (based on the not universally accepted interpretation of Nützel (1976; but see Hole 1994) that the Gulf was more than 2 m higher in the fourth millennium). It was, according to this interpretation, the emergence of an increasingly stable environment in a society where land was the primary means of production which has emphasised the importance of agriculture on the processes of social change. Nissen also contends that the drying conditions and thus shrinkage of the irrigation systems "led to an abandonment of the marginal areas and a flocking of the population to or close to the nodes" (Nissen 1993b: 94), that is, the main branching, and thus controlling points of the irrigation system. Even with the availability of habitable land, the shifting environment of Mesopotamia ensured the necessity to maintain links across a broad area. Crop failure in one area could be offset by contact elsewhere. The unstable character of the landscape would have produced an ideology which would have reflected the wide variety of subsistence strategies and the necessity to integrate. How this was achieved will be discussed in the next section.

The southern alluvial plain, which has been the focus thus far in discussing the physical environment, is often treated as a homogeneous entity (albeit one with various local differences). There has thus been a tendency to interpret changes in Lower Mesopotamian as a single unified development. There is however, increasing evidence to suggest a distinction between the upper and lower sections of the alluvium. From at least ED I (c. 2900 BC) these two regions followed markedly different courses of political and socio-economic development possibly based on geomorphological differences between the areas (Steinkeller 1993: 107; also Gelb 1991). "The distinctive ecology of Akkad [the northern half of the plain] favored - as it does now - a dimorphic approach to society. In that way the pastoral populations and settled farmers and urban dwellers together created a unique settlement pattern in the northern alluvium" (Zarins 1990: 55). The distinction between the settlement pattern of the upper and lower plain is evident in the surveys which investigate the region from as early as the Ubaid period (Adams and Nissen 1981; chapter **3.4**). How this created a distinction in the ideology between the two areas is unknown since the evidence for the fifth and fourth millennia (and to a large extent also the third millennium) is dominated by the material culture of the lower half of the alluvium and will form the basis of the analysis here.

### 3.1.2. North Mesopotamia

A clearer distinction can be drawn between the environmentally more secure north Mesopotamia and the less stable southern plain. North of the alluvium, the region is distinguished from the south by dry farming methods and by the fact that the area is more unambiguously divided into many more distinct geographical zones. The regions are also smaller than the southern plain and relatively self contained. Three areas are chosen to distinguish the various physical environments of the north amplified by recent survey work which has identified discrete cultural units for each region in the fourth millennium (Frangipane 1993a; Lupton 1996: 6-7; chapter ***4.1.2.***): (i) where the Euphrates river emerges from the Taurus mountains, the Karababa basin forms a series of fertile terraces and acts as an extension of the north Syrian Jazira; (ii) further east, the North Jazira area of northern Iraq is a broad undulating plain stretching from the region of the headwaters of the Khabur east to the river Tigris. These areas lie within the dry-farming agricultural zone; (iii) the third region is the mid-Euphrates valley, west of the Syrian Jazira, the area of the modern Tabqa Dam. Here erratic rainfall means there is in a requirement for irrigation to supplement dry farming. Contact is possible between these regions although it is more difficult in the Karababa basin. Wheat was the main produce of the historical period, indeed "surpluses generated by early agriculturists in northern Mesopotamia have been consistently underestimated" (Moorey 1994: 3). Cattle and sheep rearing were also very important features of the economy (Oates 1968). On the basis of the differences in the physical environment we would expect to find evidence of different, though perhaps related ideological developments.

These ideas, it must be noted, are not a return to Montesquieu's (1989 (1748)) explanation of history in terms of differences in climate and geography. He regarded humans as a part of nature, and the explanation of historical events was sought in the facts of the natural world, that is, natural causes and not human reason. However, there is clearly an intimate relation between any culture and its natural environment, but what determines its character is not the facts of that environment in themselves, but what humans are able to get out of them.

## 3.2. Social organisation

### 3.2.1. The family

Human interaction starts at its most basic level with the family. The family context provides the means by which continuity is achieved across the generations. Extended families and kin groups provide additional ways in which a particular approach to the world is reflected over a wide geographical area and through time. The importance of, and relationship between, individual family members vary between cultures but "in most traditional societies there are large kinship groupings which go well beyond immediate family relationships" (Giddens 1989:384). The clan, for example, represents kin groups where all members claim descent from a common ancestor. Groups of related people may recognise one member of their society as particularly important and delegate responsibility for certain activities or decisions to that person - a chief (the usefulness of this term will be discussed below). The reasons for the chief's position will vary in time and place (e.g., eldest, strongest, related directly to an ancestor). However, the way in which a society may be structured has been viewed as central in understanding the emergence of complex state organisation, especially among researchers who emphasise conflicts between classes, and the role of politics and economics (Marxist approaches).

A social ideology will be closely conditioned by family structure and kinship patterns. It has been demonstrated that people respond very powerfully to the order in which they were born and thus to the roles they assume in family dynamics (Sulloway 1996). Those born later, who identify least with the roles and beliefs of their parents, tend to become more innovative and accepting of political and scientific revolutions than do most of the first born. Indeed, Todd (1985) has recognised that different areas of the modern world are dominated by particular social ideologies because they share common family forms, e.g., similar attitudes to marital stability, inheritance, infanticide etc. It is not a case of the family structure growing to fit the ideology since new social approaches, such as communism, appear to thrive where certain social ideologies (familial approaches to the world) exist. He has thus identified seven family structures. While this theory might appear as a deterministic, historicist model, it in fact demonstrates that, as far as ideology is concerned, human history is meaningless. While the family acts as the infrastructure of an ideology, determining the system, it is varied in form and is not determined by any particular rationale. The family structure reproduces through each generation in unconscious imitation which ensures the continuation of anthropological systems. There appears to be no connection between ecological factors and family types although the environment will inevitably shape the way in which a particular family structure can operate. While interesting, this theory inevitably gives no guide to the past since family structures can not be related to 'types' of ideologies. The model does, however, demonstrate that in a relatively large area, similar family structures not only encourage but potentially create a common social ideology. This is reflected most readily, in the past as in the present, by particular political structures.

The family structure of southern Mesopotamia has been a subject of discussion since a number of sites revealed a similar form of architecture. Dating from the sixth millennium nucleated settlements appear in the archaeological record such as with the tripartite buildings at Tell es-Sawwan (Breniquet 1992). Similar structures also occur from the early Ubaid period at 'Oueili (Huot 1989). A continuity of building traditions is demonstrated even more clearly in the later Ubaid buildings at Tell Abada (Jasim 1985), Kheit Qasim (Forest 1983) and Tell Madhhur (Killick and Roaf 1979). Here large houses have tripartite plan with T-shaped or central halls which shows its finest development in the large buildings of Late Ubaid Eridu and Late Uruk Warka (see chapter 5.2.1.ii and 5.2.1.iv). Each of the T-units in the Ubaid domestic structures contains its own hearth. From this Forest (1984: 85) suggests that the layout of the buildings reflects the presence of a number of related generations. The occupants are therefore not a nucleated family but rather an extended one. Maisels (1990: 166; 1999: 156) prefers to interpret this arrangement as an 'augmented and stratified' household that includes dependants who are non-kin; that is, augmented households structured around a dominant family. Such organisation can also be demonstrated at sites of third millennium BC date. For example, at Abu Salabikh the layout of buildings "suggests that at the beginning of the Early Dynastic I period we should envisage a city composed of large, self-contained compounds, and socially of corresponding groups of persons" (Postgate 1983: 59). It will be argued that the architecture and organisation of sites of the Uruk culture reflects a similar social structure which forms the basis for economic and political order (chapters 5 and 7).

### 3.2.2. Too many chiefs?

It has been claimed that theories of the emergence of complex society and state formation often "fall at the first hurdle through their author's failure to distinguish chiefdom from the true state" (Maisels 1990: 199). The terms chiefdom and state are used by social anthropologists to refer to parts of a hierarchy of culture change (tribe, chiefdom, state) (Service 1972). The fundamental distinction between the terms is that chiefdom societies are organised by kinship groups in a hierarchy of lineages, the status of which are determined by their position in the hereditary linkage to the chief who holds the highest 'standing'. By contrast a state may be defined by the presence of a "unique power centre manifesting sovereignty, characterised by *ultimate control* of the population which are its subject" (Maisels 1990:199). There is no evolutionary necessity implied by this hierarchy and all chiefdom societies do not evolve into states. Indeed it has been convincingly demonstrated that the classic evolutionary approach to the transformation in social organisation, i.e., bands becoming tribes then chiefdoms and finally states, is merely a reflection of nineteenth century evolutionism (Yoffee 1993a. Also: Rindos, 1985; Upham 1987; Spencer 1987).

However, Renfrew and Bahn (1991:157) argue that, while it would be wrong to assume inevitable evolution, the categories provide a useful framework to help organise data when attempting to explain why some societies become more complex and others do not. Indeed, the social structure of a group, however that may be formed, will influence the way in which contact is made between members of that group and with other, perhaps differently structured groups. An evolutionary typology is, therefore, helpful to define, however vaguely, differences in social and political structure (Earle 1987; 1991). These differences are most apparent in the nature of tribute/taxation, ownership, labour mobilisation and social classes (Kristiansen 1991). This should not imply that societies all posses a standard 'check-list' of characteristics that has to be present or absent, but rather that there exists a set of interrelated variables. As a result, anthropologists have used subdivisions to create various schemes where the main defining characteristics are (i) scale of development, (ii) basis of finance, and (iii) structure (Earle 1991). These three schemes for understanding variability within chiefdoms may be explained as: (i) simple chiefdoms (population of perhaps a thousand) against complex chiefdoms (integrated populations in the tens of thousands) (Wright 1984; Earle 1987, 1991); (ii) staple payment (redistribution of food and goods as payment for services, e.g., providing feasts) against wealth payment (symbolic objects bestowed on supporters) (Earle 1991; Stein 1994); and (iii) group oriented (a group defined by corporate labour constructions) against individualising chiefdoms (élites defined by status symbols) (Earle 1987, 1991).

Over recent years the links between the economy and political control of a society have been much debated (Earle 1987). It is clear that the emergence of a leader or wider élite must rest to a large extent on their ability to control or direct basic resources through a society as a means to finance new institutions (Earle 1991). The élite, together with their non-producing retinue, depend on their ability to mobilise and direct a 'surplus' extracted from the common producers. This control may be sanctioned by economic, social, political, or religious rules. However, the leader's ability to extract a 'surplus' rests on dominating labour, the limiting factor in production in non-industrial societies. The ability to gather a sufficient following is based on the elite's ability to solve or resolve problems, meet the needs of their followers, and the resulting prestige they acquire. There is, however, no reason why followers cannot 'vote with their feet' to a more successful, prestigious leader. In return for labour, the élite might offer access to land and its productive resources as well as access to both ritual and élite patronage. In the rise of the state, economic and ideological power were the essential forms of control because they could be controlled across generations. This gave the necessary stability on which a polity could be based.

The sources of power open to a leader were numerous. These are summed up in Mann's (1986) IEMP model, an account of a complex interrelating of ideology, economy, military and political forces. It has been assumed that the hierarchy of a society based on kinship will only lead to a state organisation if the hierarchy is broken by someone who is able to exclude others from power. For example, was it the power of one person or a group to restrict access to the supernatural powers that established legitimacy? Domination then, would depend on an interlocking and overlapping of the different sources of power so as it can be concentrated, thus overcoming the limiting characteristics of the individual power sources.

According to such traditional models of social stratification, power, institutional or individual, evolved from a balancing act between a dependent population and an emerging aristocracy. As stratification evolved, the aristocracy manipulated the network of social power to increase the dependency of the commoners and alter the balance in the interests of the élites. The major limit to the élite source of power - agricultural production - was labour. The maintenance of this control of labour required the ruling élites to retain authority through a recognised respectability. This could be achieved and advertised through religious duties, political competition and exchange in prestige items. In turn, this could lead to the emergence of common 'international' ideologies which acted to bind élites over a wide geographical area often at the expense of the local groups they dominated, such as in Aztec society (Conrad and Demarest 1984). While many factors may merge into a complex political power base, it is clear that leaders attempt to justify their position using sources of power and influence (prestige) inaccessible to others. For example, special wealth objects, often from abroad, may be a feature where they symbolically encapsulate the élite's position (Earle 1991).

Such are the standard interpretations of stratified society and ultimately the emergence of the state societies. How far can these models be applied to prehistoric Mesopotamia?

### 3.2.2.i. South Mesopotamia

Several pieces of evidence suggest the development of social complexity in Mesopotamia as early as Ubaid 2/3: south and central Mesopotamia has a two level settlement pattern hierarchy with sites like Eridu, Ur and Uqair apparently acting as centres (Adams 1981; Wright and Pollock 1986). Also during the Ubaid period, architecture and associated artefacts suggest economic differentiation and possible leaders, for example, associated with the large, walled Building 'A' at Tell Abada were a number of 'prestige' stone artefacts such as mace heads, carved stone vessels, stone palettes, and tokens (Jasim 1985:174); and specialised 'temple' buildings are found, e.g., at Eridu (Safar et al 1981), Uqair (Lloyd and Safar 1943), and Warka (Schmidt 1974).

Wright (1984:68) has suggested that Ubaid Mesopotamia consisted of a number of ideologically related chiefdoms based on the presence of architectural complexity and monumentality, common ritual vessels, grave goods and, at Susa, communal burial. The most obvious archaeological indicators of chiefdom societies are traditionally those developed from the study of Polynesian and American cultures. The recognisable features postulated by this general model are: warfare; long distance exchange of goods as status markers; exaggerated symbolism of social ranking, and an unstable political system which cycles between consolidation and collapse (Earle 1991). The model bases socio-political organisation on an economic system of wealth distribution - the manufacture or procurement of special products such as craft goods or exotic materials (Earle 1987, 1991; D'Altroy & Earle 1985). These are exchanged for staples and redistributed among the élites as badges of rank or rewards for service. Wealth finance thus leads to centrally located specialists, pronounced differentiation in élites with foreign connections, competition and warfare.

However, as Stein (1994) has pointed out there is an absence of this traditional evidence for chiefdom organisation in Mesopotamia and to explain this he makes a connection between economic organisation and ritual elaboration based on staple, rather than wealth, finance - the mobilisation of surplus staples such as cereals to support the élite (Earle 1987). According to Stein's thesis,

Ubaid Mesopotamia consisted of small, localised chiefdoms based on: "economic differentiation; centralised storage facilities for staples; rural production of surpluses; either village-based craft production, or high proportions of local, as opposed to long-distance exchange; and either ritual, kinship-based, or coercive modes of surplus mobilisation" (Stein 1994:41). There is, for example, no evidence of wealth finance and social stratification marked by exotic materials in the Ubaid cemeteries at Ur and Eridu. The evidence from Susa might suggests otherwise (Hole 1989) but the major problem is the limited samples of burials and how far the surviving examples relate to the real world (Chapmen *et al*. 1981; Hodder 1982a & b). Maisels (1999: 157) rejects Stein's need for 'chiefs' arguing that "stratification was internal to the household, the settlement and the settlement cluster" (chapter *3.2.1.*) although it is likely that some households (e.g., Abada 'A' building) were more important/wealthier than others. Such groups would have had access to specialized roles within the wider community, e.g., priest, and been responsible for larger numbers of workers.

Indeed, Adams (1981: 62-63) has argued that the dispersed pattern of settlements during the Ubiad period does not suggest groups centred on rivers or irrigation. In this way, the power base of a community leader or influential families lay not with control of access to water, land and labour beyond the most local level. The pattern may rather suggest local tribal allegiances, related to an ecological zone centred on places with ceremonial and market roles. A centre like Warka, for example, would service a large area. Control of labour by an élite or larger households across ecological zones could be achieved by a common ideological map. "The ability to mobilise labour presupposes the existence of a cohesive, bounded community with formal institutions whose ideological power crosscuts kin lines to extend over the entire community" (Stein 1994: 42). In this way, internalised ideologies could be used to emphasise group membership. The mobilisation of staple finance did not lead to the more obvious signs of social stratification

Further interaction between and within regions could be achieved by an element of the population which is generally invisible in the archaeological record, the nomadic or transhumant groups. As has already been pointed out (chapter **3.1.**) the plain was a mosaic of arable land interspersed with areas better suited to pastoral pursuits (Rowton 1973). This must have fostered close interactions and interdependencies between nomadic and sedentary parts of the population. Indeed, the populations may have not been distinct. Adams (1974; 1981) has argued that the distinctiveness of the Mesopotamian settlement patterns owes much to the flexible and fluid alternation between transhumant (or nomadic) pastoral and more sedentary, agricultural way of life. Herders could be a source of news for the sedentary population as well as transporting small amounts of goods over long distances.

3.2.2.ii. North Mesopotamia

It has been argued that the evidence from north Mesopotamia suggests that during the fifth and fourth millennia distinct regional centres emerged, interconnected by a small range of ceramics, each exhibiting a hierarchically structured settlement system (Lupton 1996: 35). This reflects the divisions apparent in the geography of the region (chapter *3.1.2.*). Power relations shifted from "a socio-political strategy based largely on access to land and to the labour necessary to farm it, to a strategy where the acquisition, possession and display of prestige items was increasingly important" (Lupton 1996: 38). Prestige goods such as those recovered from the rich tombs of early Uruk level X Tepe Gawra included objects of lapis lazuli, gold (de Jesus 1980: 82) and silver (*ibid*.: 64) and demonstrate international trade as well as high (local?) craftsmanship as exemplified by the electrum wolf's head from tomb 114 (Tobler 1950). It is generally assumed that the élite owners of prestige items also controlled other aspects of the political economy, attested, it is suggested, "by the discovery of a complex array of stamp seals and sealings at many of the more important sites in the region, including Arslantepe, Tell al Hawa and Nineveh" (Lupton 1996: 38). Thus a distinction between north and south is identified where the northern social structure was more independent of the sort of communal relations that is suggested here existed in the south. Different avenues where thus available to be exploited by the local northern authorities including the emergence of élite exchange systems of exotic status enhancing goods, as Flannery (1968) first argued for interaction between the Olmec and the Oaxaca valley of Mexico where prestige goods were imbued with political meaning and used in local power relations.

This distinction between north and south Mesopotamia may be dependant on archaeological discovery. The changing view of the way Babylonia was structured in the third millennium BC, e.g., the role of temples discussed below (chapter *3.2.3.*), might suggest that the overall pattern between the different areas may not have been as extreme as the evidence currently suggests.

### *3.2.3. The ideology of third millennium Babylonia*

3.2.3.i. Kingship

Although it is far from necessary to reconstruct Ubaid Babylonia using a chiefdom model, by the third millennium textual, architectural and sculptural evidence clearly shows the emergence of an office which may be described as a king. The emergence of this figure is traditionally associated with the expansion of population resulting from irrigation works, the development of stratified society and the increasing incidence of inter-city conflicts (Jacobsen 1957: 96-98). The rulers then vie with the temples for power. The *Tempelwirtshaft* model has been shown to be flawed (chapter *2.2.*) and so the "traditional picture of Babylonia dominated by its temples may not reflect any historical reality, but just the pattern of archaeological discovery" (Kuhrt 1990: 126). The importance of irrigation proposed by Wittfogel (1957) has been also been challenged (chapter *3.1.1.*). It is clear, therefore that a reassessment of state development is necessary. As has already been noted (chapter **1**) the origins of state society lie in the fourth millennium. To place this period in context it will be necessary to show the contrast between the Ubaid organisation of chapter *3.2.2.* and the ideology of kingship and religion in the third millennium BC.

As society on the southern plain became focused within an urban setting at the end of the fourth millennium (chapter **6.3.**), the increasing emphasis on the control of larger cities and their rural hinterlands must have required a greater body of administrators. The development of administrative tools accompanied and drove this development and was thus self perpetuating (chapter **6.2.**). This in effect, reduced the immediate control by a leading figure or figures as their responsibilities were delegated to others. This development is reflected in the ideas developed by Weber (1978) and his study of bureaucracy - the rule of 'experts', whose decisions are taken without reference to those affected by them, and sometimes without reference to those whom they notionally serve. By the end of the third millennium BC, it is clear that temple personnel were a separate body from other institutions, but the connection between a ruler and the divine remained close; he was theoretically the representative of the god in all matters. The earliest substantial evidence of this relationship is preserved in a large archive of cuneiform texts written c.2400 BC. Consisting of some 1,500 documents, the archive forms part of the accounts of the temple of the goddess Bau in the town of Girsu (modern Tello) in the city-state of Lagash. However, it is now clear that the land referred to in these documents belonged not to a 'temple-state' as reconstructed by Deimel (1931) but was the property of the city-ruler and his family (Foster 1981).

Thus it is possible to revise the traditional view of southern Mesopotamia in the third millennium from a temple based 'priest-king' to a city-based oligarchy where the dominant economic institutions were the royal domain and private households. Steinkeller (1993) has suggested that this was a system that arose in northern Babylonia as Semitic people entered the area in the early third millennium (as a contrast to the assumed temple based society further south which he associated with the 'native' Sumerian population). He argued that the novelty of the organisation was reflected by an earlier presence of a Sumerian linguistic group in the upper half of the plain as suggested by the presence of place-names with Sumerian genitival compounds (Steinkeller 1993: 111). There are clearly major problems in associating a particular socio-political organisation with language groups, particularly were it survives only in written form (chapter **3.3**). But in the light of the new interpretation of city-state organisation, the presence of Sumerian names throughout the plain may not only suggest a linguistically unified region in the fourth millennium, an important element for a social ideology (chapter **3.3**), but also reflect a common form of political and economic life.

Although the temple no longer needs to be viewed as the prime economic mover in third millennium Babylonian society it nonetheless played a central role in the ideology of kingship and power. All royal monuments and inscriptions demonstrate that the rulers were acutely aware of their responsibilities towards their gods - their position depended upon it (the safety of the state from the wrath of gods depended on their acting on behalf of the population in constructing temples and providing offerings). The major source of information concerning the ideology of early historic Mesopotamia comes from royal inscriptions and representations; our evidence is, therefore, biased in favour of a small section of the population albeit probably the most important politically and socially. The vast majority of all royal inscriptions commemorate the dedication of a structure or object by the ruler to a god. Surviving building inscriptions from the Pre-Sargonic period (i.e., before c.2350 BC) are on specially made artefacts that were ceremonially buried in foundations or under floors, set into walls or carved onto door sockets. The dangers of drawing too many generalisations from this fragmentary record is confirmed by the type of evidence surviving in the archaeological record. Clay, an inexpensive material, does not record inscriptions concerning deities but rather political-military matters or social and administrative questions (Cooper 1986). Offerings were part of the ruler's duty in the hope of receiving the deity's blessing. When politics moved beyond an individual city state, a ruler sent offerings to Nippur, home of the supreme Sumerian deity Enlil, and thus received divine blessing for international events, for example, the confirmation of Lugalzagesi of Umma or Sargon of Agade as overlord of many Sumerian cities (Cooper 1986: 94, Um 7.1; Sollberger and Kupper 1971: IIA1a).

As the major player in third millennium society, the actions and concerns of a ruler will reflect an ideology, albeit of a specific role. Identity, at least among the major players in third millennium society, was with the city (chapter 3.2.3.ii.). This may have encouraged a similar response by those in rural communities that supplied the city's needs and received in return protection and administrators. It was the development of political allegiance based on family/tribal groupings and the emergence of a strong ideology during the Uruk period which initiated this process (chapter **7**).

### 3.2.3.ii. Religious belief

History might suggest that one of the most powerful forms for creating a common ideology is one based on religious belief. This need not suggest a proselytising cult with associated missionary fervour although it can never be ruled out (the expansion of the Arabs in the seventh century AD can only be explained by the unifying force of Islam). Modern nations usually recognise one particular 'national' religion which forms the basis of moral, political and social notions of acceptability and religious beliefs are often the basis for interpreting the past and thus forging a common ideology.

By the time of adequate textual evidence in the mid-third millennium BC it is clear that there existed a belief in a countrywide pantheon of gods. Royal inscriptions demonstrate political alliances and divisions among the numerous competing city states, each attempting to control access to trade, booty and land, e.g., the Umma - Lagash dispute (Cooper 1983). Yet all seem to recognise Nippur as the seat of the supreme god Enlil. This is all the more extraordinary considering that each city held claim to a unique deity. (Cooper 1986). It has been suggested that these local deities reflect a prehistoric stage of religion in which different communities each had their own deity in the form of a standard or symbol, that is fetishism. These different local traditions came together to form a unified pantheon in the attempts at political unification that culminated in the 'empire'' of Akkad (c.2350 BC) and Ur III (c.2100 BC). Such a notion relies heavily on nineteenth century ideas of social development. After Darwin published *The Origin of the Species* anthropologists began to apply the notion of evolution to religion. Scholars like Tyler (1871), Freud (1918) and Frazer (1922) envisaged a model of progress where religion 'developed' from fetishism to theriomorphic polytheism to anthropomorphic polytheism to monotheism. Today few historians of religion accept these simplistic patterns of religious development which should be set aside as ethnocentric (Smart 1969).

It has been suggested that a conference took place to allocate each city with a particular deity when the Sumerians arrived on the southern plain (Lambert 1975) but this immediately raises the dangers of connecting race, culture and language and is rejected below (chapter **3.3.**; Jones 1997). Jacobsen (1976) sees the various city gods as representing powers in the basic economies characteristic of the region in which their cities were situated. Thus in the "south are gods closely related to marsh life and its primary economies, fishing and hunting: Enki, Nanshe, Dumuzi-abzu. Along the lower Euphrates deities of orchardmen alternate with deities of cowherders: Ningishida, Ninazu, Damu, Ningublaga, Nanna, Ninsuna. Farther north, in a half-circle around the central grassland of the Edin lie the cities of the sheepherders with their chief deities Dumuzi the shepherd. to the north and east lie the cities of farmers: Ninlil, Ninshebargunu, Nidaba, Enlil, Ninurta." (Jacobsen 1976: 25). The pantheon that appears in the third millennium texts is not fixed but changes to reflect political developments. Families of gods within each city state include many deities not found elsewhere. Gudea's inscriptions provide the most detailed evidence of this arrangement (e.g., Falkenstein 1966). Political control of an area could also catapult an obscure city god to national or international status (e.g., the god of Babylon, Marduk, rose to prominence after his city came to dominate southern Mesopotamia in the second millennium). This again demonstrates the inextricable nature of politics and religion.

Often such reconstructions of religious developments have been projected onto the conveniently blank record of prehistoric religious practice, occasionally illuminated by a few objects. It is thus impossible to determine whether the individual gods that appear in the texts of the third millennium have their origin as separate cults or rather they represent, like the apparent multiplicity of Hindu deities today, the all-pervasive nature of a divine force, each aspect occupying a different space in human experience. The pantheon may therefore have been a means of perceiving divinity that already existed in the fourth millennium BC, a unified system of beliefs corresponding to the closely tied culture of the river valleys. With the move towards urbanism at the end of the fourth millennium BC, deities began to be associated with particular localities as a method of identity. This is demonstrated by sealings dated from the Uruk III-Early Dynastic I period known as 'city-seals' where divine symbols appear to represent intimate formal relationships between city states rooted in a religious ritual framework (Matthews, R.J. 1993). The importance of Nippur as the home of the god Enlil may have emerged during the third millennium, reflecting its geographical position in the centre of the southern Mesopotamian plain. Recourse to this metaphor was a regular feature of the historical period when the land was divided between equal-ranking city-states, e.g., mid-third millennium BC and Isin-Larsa Period c.2000-1800 BC. The late fourth millennium city lists from Warka place Nippur second although it is difficult to see any pattern or meaning behind these texts (Matthews, D. 1993: 39; Englund and Nissen 1993).

From the earliest period probably one of the most important factors for facilitating contact between settlements across the southern plain was an overarching religious affiliation. The focus for communication was the temple. As Postgate (1972) has noted, the flat Babylonian plain (and to a lesser extent Assyria) presents little in the way of natural features with any particular numinous qualities. As a result it would seem unlikely that a Mesopotamian temple preceded any settlement, or grew independently of an ordinary community. However, as a focus for a community (which may have been more extensive than just the settled population) cult centres may have acted as ceremonial centres which attracted pilgrimages and offerings. In a region such as the southern Mesopotamian plain, which is largely undifferentiated physically, contact between centres would have been relatively easy by water and the cultic/administrative centres may have acted to *standardise* human reactions to that environment. Certainly in the historic period there is clear evidence of pilgrimages, offerings and ritual journeys of the god's image by boat to visit other temples (Black &

Green 1992: 45). However, it was the role of the temple as 'wealthy neighbour' which provides the best evidence for the communal approach to survival. Small scale offerings (labour and agricultural products) and redistribution (agricultural produce and land) provided the basis for this contact. It was the responsibility of central authorities in relation to subsistence to maintain and improve a system of relationships within and also outside their boundaries.

In historical times it appears that every sizeable settlement possessed its own temple. The temple owed its existence to the community and not vice versa. Naturally, therefore, the size of the temple depended on the size of the settlement it served. During the third millennium, it is clear that some temples found themselves the symbolic focus of the city, its hinterland and also of an entire state. So-called 'city seals', dating to the Jemdet Nasr and Early Dynastic 1 periods, demonstrate use of the city god's symbol as a 'flag' for identifying the city-state (Matthews, R.J. 1993). The temples represented the state, and the self- esteem of the state and its rulers ensured a concentration of communal effort in these buildings. Most surviving royal inscriptions commemorate either the construction or renovation of temples by kings and governors who were proud to commemorate in writing and images their achievements. The importance placed on the royal search for the best materials is reflected in the story of Enmerkar's refurbishment of the Eanna complex in the Early Dynastic period c.2600 BC (Cohen, 1973).

At all periods the Mesopotamian temple was an integral part of the community which it served. In economic terms, the temple could not survive without the co-operation of the community, and in return, the temple was able (and probably expected) to provide certain services to the settlement or group of settlements which it served. The temple secured the survival of the state by looking after the god in an appropriate manner but was also involved in day-to-day human affairs such as finance and organisation of festivals, scribal education, 'wealthy neighbour', and the organisation of private ceremonies, e.g., burials and oath taking. As has been suggested (chapter 3.2.3.ii), the third millennium priests enjoyed the economic fruits of ritual prerogative but they were not directors of Mesopotamian states. However, gods and temples were subject to a hierarchy like humans. The more important gods resided in larger temples, while lesser, perhaps more localised village deities, lived either in small temples or in shrines. Temples constructed of permanent materials were an important source of financial investment (private chapels/wall plaques etc.). The priesthood were probably largely dependent on the rulers and nobles for financial support although they could own private land. Thus while society was segmented, temple and community were interdependent on each other, together forming a whole. It was this interdependence that sustained, at least in part, a religious system which had no over-arching ecclesiastical structure. The Mesopotamian religious scene appears to mirror historic Hinduism where there "is no dividing line between sacred and secular, no area of belief or custom that is alien to religious influence" (Hopkins 1971: 1).

In the case of religious architecture power theoretically rests not with individuals or groups but rather with the divinity. Of course certain members of society may benefit materially from their association with the deity and cult but one should be wary of interpreting this association only in terms of cynical manipulation of the group. Conspicuous consumption as well as efficiency of production can be seen as the basic factors in shaping the political as well as the economic behaviour of human beings. But this need not mean that temples were the dominant political movers. Like Hindu temples today, the temple was the focus for a community's identity and only reflected the power and position of members of the community through their support of the institution (Golzio 1983).

### 3.2.4. Summary

An approach to life on the alluvial plain of southern Mesopotamia was dominated by natural forces: extremes of both environmental and atmospheric phenomena. Underlying the needs to offset disaster through flooding, changes in the river regime, desert storms etc., it was necessary for the inhabitants to maintain contact over a broad area. This would have generated common methods of interaction and a shared approach to the world. The institutions through which this contact was achieved appear to have been ceremonial/market centres which focused local communities. The settlement pattern of these centres in the early fourth millennium is not based on a linear riverine system but were sited as central places for areas based on multiple forms of subsistence and organised around tribal or kin-based regionalisation sharing common ideologies. Distinctions in the socio-politico-economic pattern of the upper and lower plain in the early third millennium may not have existed in the fourth millennium as suggested by the presence in the historical period of settlement names in the upper (Semitic) region containing Sumerian (lower plain) elements (Steinkeller 1993). Thus the inhabitants of the whole alluvium were united by the very variegated nature of the physical and socio-political landscape which acted as the midwife to a common ideology and held everything together.

In contrast, northern Mesopotamia was a homogeneous region of rain-fed agriculture (it was easily absorbed, for example, into the large military structures of the Old, Middle and Neo-Assyrian periods). It thus differs from the south in both physical and climatic environment. Despite the apparent unity, there are distinct geographical units which are reflected in the settlement pattern and socio-political organisation of the fourth millennium BC. The focus for communities may have been centred on political élites who expressed their power through acquisition, exchange and display of exotic materials.

## 3.3. Communication

Cross-ecological groupings, in both north and south Mesopotamia, could only be effectively achieved through at least some elements of a common approach to the world. This requires at its most basic level recognisable forms of communication, which may take many forms: spoken, symbolic and written. Interaction among humans, and their interaction across information systems forms the basis of this chapter.

A common spoken language might appear to be an essential element of information sharing. The ability to communicate and understand a language will encourage contact and the transmission of technological, political and theological concepts. From the middle of this century there has been much discussion concerning the use of language in society for representing the universe and indeed influencing the way in which that universe is viewed. Ethnolinguistic or sociolinguistic studies have attempted to correlate language with the thoughts and belief systems of the speakers. The study of the role of language as an important factor in cultural change (ethnography of communication) derives from the work of Sapir (1949) and Whorf (1956). As part of American cultural anthropology, this work relates different languages to the definition of community and culture and treats language as a feature of social order and internal cohesion. This is a shift away from the nineteenth century approach of descriptive theory and historical analysis, which emphasised the relationship between distinct languages, towards an anthropological emphasis on seeing the world through the eyes of those being studied. The work of Whorf, in particular, focuses upon language, culture and cognition where meaning was both culture bound and subconsciously structured at the same time. Thus a "society's culture consists of whatever it is one has to know or believe in order to operate in a manner acceptable to its members, and to do so in any role that they accept for one of themselves" (Goodenough 1957: 167).

Language codes of any society, what to say to whom and how to say it in any given situation, represents part of a cultural and social knowledge which are an essential feature of successful communication. The extent of knowledge of these codes appears to relate to the social status, but also related psychological conditions such as 'grades of interaction' (Williams 1992). This variation in social structure is conveyed in speech so that when reference is made to competence to convey meaning it is a social meaning that is involved. Roles are thus signalled by speech.

The social variation within the community gives rise to different language codes which have a potential to indicate a shared history, values, and obligations. Language is one and the same as well as a mirror of society. However, to participate in a speech 'community' is not the same as being a member of that community since membership depends upon the shared knowledge of rules of conduct and interpretation of speech (Hymes 1977: 50). Not all languages are equal in the sense of their functional potential. That is, while language has the potential to serve all functions it is only communication which activates that potential. Here communication appears as the driving force of 'progress' (Williams 1992).

The earliest Mesopotamian texts in which a language may be identified are written in Sumerian (Nissen 1993a; Nissen *et al* 1993). Many writers have fallen into the trap of assuming that a given pottery form, or an archaeological assemblage, can be equated directly with a group of people and hence supposedly with a particular language or language group (Jones 1997). This has led to questions concerning the origin of the Sumerians and various attempts have been made to locate a Sumerian 'homeland'. However, it should be emphasised that 'Sumerian' refers to a language, not to people or groups of people. There is of course no reason why language and culture should not go together; they often do. For example, even in modern mixed cultures, languages will change at an artificial frontier and with it a whole way of life and systems of belief and religion. Conversely, groups of people with very different cultures may speak the same language or "within an area where the way of life is essentially the same, different languages may be spoken" (Renfrew 1987:76). Indeed it is suggested that many of the earliest cuneiform texts which can be read (Jemdet Nasr period) preserve elements of a language other than Sumerian in names of cities, deities and professions (Landsberger 1944). In addition, the occurrence of names and words with the nominative ending -*um*, is evidence of the presence of a Semitic language or languages related to Akkadian (Krispijn 1991-92: 15).

It is always a serious mistake to equate race and language. Even with skeletal material (all but absent for the fourth millennium BC) there is no scientifically acceptable way of assigning it to a particular 'race'. However, even with the absence of skeletal remains, scholars have resorted to considering representations, particularly the often crude votive figurines, of the third millennium to identify typical 'Sumerian' features. And so it is possible to read that "the Sumerian and Elamite have a high thin nose whose bridge joins the cranium without much curvature of the bridge, a square jaw and round chin, thin pursed lips, a long head with a large brain capacity." (Langdon 1920: 145). Even costume has been used to demonstrate specific Sumerian people, with the sheep's fleece garment often worn by the worshipers described as a 'national dress' (Langdon 1920: 146). If language, race and culture are distinct concepts the starting point for any consideration of the 'Sumerian problem' must be the study of the language. Here, however, we are constrained by the Sumerian language's relationship, or lack of relationship, with any other known language or group (Thomsen 1984).

What emerges, therefore, is the possibility of *at least* three languages being spoken in southern Mesopotamia at the end of the fourth millennium. (How many were not recorded?) That Sumerian was written down, however, might suggest that the people speaking this language were either in the majority or that the speakers formed a separate élite group. The former may be more likely based on the presence of place-names with Sumerian genitival compounds found in the north of the plain (Steinkeller 1993: 111) suggesting that the entire alluvium was a linguistically unified region in the late fourth millennium (chapter 3.2.3.i.).

Language is not the only form of communication. Mead (1934) emphasised the centrality of symbols in human social life. Rather than examine whole societies he concentrated on studying small-scale social processes but demonstrated how essential the knowledge of symbols is for effective communication. A symbol is something that stands for something else. Symbols have meaning but these meanings are known only to those who share knowledge of the meaning. For example, the exchange of prestige items between élite groups formed a central aspect of Maya and Aztec societies (Conrad and Demarest 1984). The ability to recognise the symbols and signals that these objects represented is similar to the use of language codes. Since we are constrained by our lack of written evidence (let alone evidence of how the language was spoken) in late fourth millennium BC Mesopotamia, it would seem sensible to look for the symbolic indicators of communication. Although the meaning of symbols will be lost to us, the presence of similar objects in particular contexts will suggest channels through which societies ideas flowed (albeit for a limited section of that society due to the restricted activity of archaeologists). This material: cylinder seals and sealings, prestige ceramics, accounting devices and especially forms of architecture, is examined in chapters 5 and 6.

## 3.4. Population movement and/or growth

For southern Mesopotamia, major demographic changes can be traced for the fourth millennium based on are a number of extensive surveys in Sumer and Akkad, the Kur River basin and the plains of Susiana, Deh Luran, Izeh, and Ram Hormuz (Adams 1962; Johnson 1973; Adams & Nissen 1972; Wright 1979; Adams 1981; Alden 1982; Wright 1987). The evidence is inevitably very irregular with inherent limitations resulting from site siltation, erosion and interpretation errors based on the problem of contemporanity of sites/materials. In addition, many areas remain unexplored. However, the evidence provides a broad picture of change.

Although the population of the Ur-Eridu region declined after the Early Uruk period (see chapter 4), there is a considerable increase in the total number of sites on the Sumerian plain, with a wide range in the size of settlements during the Early and Middle Uruk periods. There is a distinct difference in the pattern between north and south of Babylonia: the north (Nippur-Adab region) is characterised by fewer, larger, well scattered sites;

whereas, in the south, only two sites, one of which is Warka, reach more than 20 ha. although a greater number sites in the 5-10 ha range cluster around the larger sites. It is estimated that a similar area of land was under cultivation in both areas (Adams 1981). The Late Uruk period witnessed dramatic urban expansion on the southern plain. Four ranks of settlement may be identified, and Warka apparently reached an area of about 100 ha., far greater than anything to the north. Around Warka total settlement area increased by 121% (Potts 1994: 61-62, Table 2.2). The presence of one large settlement in the south appears to have inhibited the development of middle-ranking sites in a radius of some 30 km.

Using the conventional settlement figures derived from the survey of the Sumerian plain there appears to be a shift in proportions of the settled population living in the Nippur-Adab and Warka regions from the earlier to the later Uruk period which suggests that large numbers of the people living in the northern region moved south. Pollock (1999; Table 1.) has 'corrected' these using a model developed by Dewer (1991). The adjusted figures suggest that populations of the entire alluvium grew, although the Warka area expands more substantially (Pollock 1999: Fig. 3.13). In the Warka region all settlements increased during the fourth millennium while in the Nippur-Adab region small sites expanded, followed by a substantial decline in the Jemdet Nasr period, whereas the population living in communities of more than 7 hectares remained relatively steady. If these numbers are a more accurate reflection of reality it is clearly very unlikely that the growth in the south was the result of immigration from the north.

|  | Nippur-Adab region |  | Warka region |  |
| --- | --- | --- | --- | --- |
| Period | Convent-ional | Corrected | Convent-ional | Corrected |
| Early-Middle Uruk | 374 | 88 | 198 | 81 |
| Late Uruk | 194 | 112 | 477 | 210 |
| Total | 568 | 200 | 675 | 291 |

Table 1. Settled area (ha.) during the Uruk period (Pollock 1999: 71, Table 3.1)

There is simply an explosion of sedentarism and urbanisation. This may have been due to a substantial influx of people from elsewhere and/or settling down or previously nomadic or semisedentary people (Adams and Nissen 1972: 11; cf. Johnson 1988-89) but there is no direct evidence to support or refute this.

The surveys outside the Sumerian plain may provide evidence for a source of this rapid population rise. While settlement in the Kish and Diyala regions grew in the Uruk period, nearly all the settlements were abandoned at the end of the Ubaid period in the Hamrin basin. The population of Susiana expanded from the Early to Middle Uruk periods, when Susa itself covered ca. 25 ha.. In Late Uruk, the settlement area of Susiana dropped by 58% to ca. 53 ha., this consisting mainly of Susa, Abu Fanduweh and Choga Mish. The Deh Luran plain also declined at this time by 66%, a total of only 3 ha.. In the Izeh plain only one Middle Uruk settlement has been identified, and none at all in Late Uruk. The Ram Hormuz plain and most of Luristan seem also to have been completely deserted at this time (Potts 1994: 62, Table 2.2).

From the very end of the fourth millennium (Jemdet Nasr) to Early Dynastic I there was a doubling of settlement in the Uruk region. Uruk itself reached 200 hectares, five times the size of any other Mesopotamian settlement. There was also abandonment and new settlement at the end of the Jemdet Nasr (Postgate 1986) which may have been due to the centripetal effects large urban centres like Uruk. Sites like Adab (50 ha.) and Shurrupak (25 ha.) develop at this time.

In the Susa III period the depopulation of Susiana continued. The total settlement area fell by more than half to 31 sites which were, as in Sumer, generally new foundations. Susa, remained the largest settlement on the plain, but shrank to between 11 hectares (Alden 1982: 618). Choga Mish was abandoned. In contrast with events in Susiana but similar to the pattern in Sumer, the Deh Luran plain witnessed a population increase in Susa III times (Wright 1987: 148). The Kangavar Valley of northern Luristan and the Kur River basin also saw a rise in population and urbanisation during the Late Uruk (Young 1986: 218; Alden 1982: 620).

By the third millennium it is clear that southern urban centres have consolidated in two areas of population density reflecting the historic cultural/political regions of Sumer and Elam.

In northern Mesopotamia recent survey work and analysis has demonstrated developments in a number of ecological and cultural zones (Lupton 1996, chapter *3.1.2.*). In the Early Uruk period the area of the Karababa basin demonstrates a highly centralised three-tier settlement system characterised by the central dominant regional centre of Samsat (10 ha. though possibly larger) with three other sites between 2 and 3 ha. (Lupton 1996: 24). Five sites, smaller than 1 ha., lay around Kurban Höyük in west. Six sites were scattered in the east. There is no evidence of a settled population in the Tabqa Dam area in the Early Uruk. In contrast, the North Jazira area survey (Lupton 1996: 24 based on Wilkinson 1990) revealed 77 sites dominated by Tell al Hawa which was possibly larger than 33 ha.. A three tier settlement pattern was evident.

By the Late Uruk period the settlement pattern of the Karababa basin is a simplified version of the Early Uruk with a 3-tier settlement structure of 12 sites of which Samsat remained the dominant centre. Kurban Höyük grew from 2 to 4 ha.. The Tabqa region is heavily populated for the first time (see chapter *5.2.2.*). To the east, the number of smaller sites in the North Jazira rose from 32 to 41 sites although Tell al Hawa apparently became smaller at c.20 ha. although it continued to act as the central place (Lupton 1996: 56).

In the post-Uruk period the Karababa area witnessed a 50% increase in settlement density with an increase in small villages or hamlets (Lupton 1996: 84). The 3-tier settlement pattern endures and Samsat continues to dominate the region without any obvious reduction in size. However many sites are abandoned in the Tabqa dam area and only four sites exist (2 of which were occupied in the Late Uruk - Tell Habuba and Tell Hadidi) ranging from 1 to 3 ha.. A change in the settlement pattern also took place in the North Jazira where 30 sites were identified of which 11 were occupied in the Late Uruk period. Tel al Hawa continued to dominate the area and grew to 24 hectares, possibly as a result of the abandonment of the western and south-western parts of the plain (Lupton 1996: 88).

### 3.4.1. Population growth and technology

The growth of human population (and with it the technology employed) is not a law of nature but an outcome of prevailing social relations (Hassan 1988). The elaboration of societies throughout Mesopotamia with the exploitation of a wider range of resources during the fifth and fourth millennia had a profound impact on population expansion and on the processes of settlement and urbanisation (chapters 5 and 6.3).

What then were the causes of these dramatic changes in population? Partly it is simply because it becomes evident in the archaeological record as a result of urbanisation (chapter **6.3.**). This, however, cannot account for the entire picture since there were not enough people abandoning regions to account for a growth in the magnitude observed throughout Mesopotamia. Indeed, in south-west Iran, the evidence for mobile groups actually increases at the same time as settled population grows in this and neighbouring regions (Wright 1987).

The growth in population is probably to be equated with a wider exploitation of resources across the region (see below). New materials, and with them new techniques of manufacture and procurement, were developed. Inevitably this led to transformations in the social order as specialists in the new technologies emerged. As agriculture became more efficient larger numbers of people were available for agricultural work as well as in the increasing industrial production of textiles and ceramics in what was probably an economic 'boom'.

The unprecedented rate of technological change and rapid developments of production, services and communication in the modern world tend to blur their impact on developments of a social ideology. A similar spurt of technological change in the fourth millennium BC, albeit less intense, inevitably had a direct impact on human life.

### 3.4.1.i. Agricultural developments

Lamberg-Karlovsky (1989) has suggested that the Late Uruk expansion was the result of earlier dramatic increases in population in Sumer leading to a crises in agricultural production, which in turn inspired new management technologies and colonisation. There is no evidence in the archaeological record for such a crisis and any technological developments to counter it. The first clear indication of the existence of ploughs in Mesopotamia appears with the Uruk IV pictographs (Green and Nissen 1987: 176, no. 33) and is of a type which remained standard in ancient Mesopotamia using locally available clay, stone and timber. However, earlier indicators of ploughs exist: plough marks have been reported in fifth millennium BC (Susa I) at Tepe Sharafabad in Khuzistan (Wright *et al* 1980: 275) and may be related to the domestication of bovids. This would inevitably lead to different approaches in land management, potentially allowing more land to be cultivated and thus provide a greater agricultural surplus. As part of a positive feedback system this may have played a part. In addition, the domestication of other animals during the fourth millennium such as the donkey would have allowed the movement of bulk commodities

### 3.4.1.ii. Ceramic production

Nissen (1988:46f) proposes that the spread of Ubaid pottery style was a result of a technological change, that is the introduction of the tournette. First recognised in the south, it quickly appeared in the North and East. The fast wheel and mould manufacture may have had a similar effect in the Uruk period when ceramic styles come to exhibit pronounced differences from the Ubaid period: painted decoration disappears virtually entirely whereas the variety of vessel shapes increases sharply. The Middle to Late Uruk period is characterised by a repertoire of shapes which were increasingly standardised (chapter **4.1.**). This indicates not only a new range of materials being stored or transported but also a revision in the messages being carried by the pottery forms and decoration.

These new forms of pottery are depicted on seals and sealings of the later fourth millennium from the southern alluvium. Bowls, dishes, jars (with looped appendages, as if for transport), drinking-vessels, stands, and stemmed dishes all appear. Although details are limited by scale, scenes appear to show banquets and offerings. Figures squatting before jars or lines of figures with their arms outstretched towards a jar set between them, are interpreted as pottery production and, by implication, some form of mass-production (Frankfort 1939: 36-7; Amiet 1980: 103 n. 13; Baudot 1979; chapter *5.6.2*). Seal impressions from Susa have been interpreted as showing the preparation and loading of a domed pottery kiln (Crawford 1991: 129), although bread ovens or granaries are alternative explanations (Moorey 1994: 142).

The glyptic evidence appears to reflect the emergence of industrial production during the Uruk period though whether this took place within a strongly centralized and administered economy or a more decentralized, household-based organization will be discussed in chapter **6.1.** There is no clear evidence for industrial ceramic manufacture before about the middle of the fourth millennium. In Khuzistan and adjacent regions 'mass-produced' pottery has been identified in the Middle Uruk period (Alden 1988: 146). Identical manufacturing techniques and comparable organisation of potters was evident on the alluvium and the so-called 'colonies' in Syria (Sürenhagen 1974-5). Such extensive production of a restricted repertoire may have appeared in response to growing concentrations of population and perhaps of centralisation of craft activities.

Differing socio-economic structures between north and south Mesopotamia (chapter *3.2.2.*) does not seem to have reduced industrialisation in any one region.

### 3.4.1.iii. Metals

Because metalwork can be melted and reused examples rarely survive from any period in Mesopotamia. In addition because the southern Mesopotamian plain has no metal deposits or easily accessible sources it was always an expensive commodity and therefore more likely to be limited in quantity. As a result any technological developments in metalwork production are likely to have arisen close to the natural sources, i.e., in the mountains surrounding the Mesopotamian plains, e.g., a hoard of 22 arsenical copper daggers (some hilts were inlaid with silver), spearheads, and an ornament from level VIA at Arslantepe linked to Trans-Caucasian influence (Frangipane 1985: 220-4: Frangipane 1996: 69). For basic subsistence, however, metal was not vital - stone and baked clay tools were the primary farming implements in southern Mesopotamia - and there was, therefore, no incentive to increase any supplies of metal (principally copper). However, by the middle and late fourth millennium socio-economic developments in Mesopotamia produced a demand for metalwork and associated technological advances throughout the region. This technology of metalwork manufacture appears in the south during the Late Uruk but there are difficulties in the proposed identification of workshops at Warka (Lenzen 1960: 10, pls. 39, 3b, 4a-d; Nissen 1988: 82, fig. 32) in the absence of industrial debris and working tools. Good metallurgical evidence of cast copper objects comes from Susa dating from the Uruk period (Tallon 1987: i. 315-16, fig. 49) but it is located nearer to highland sources than sites on the alluvium as demonstrated by a coppersmith's workplace at Tepe Ghabristan, perhaps contemporary with Susa II-III containing 20 kilos of copper ore (Moorey 1994: 257).

It is important to emphasise that the evidence of fourth millennium Mesopotamian metalwork (both precious and base metals) is based principally on material from the sites of Warka and Tepe Gawra (3.2.2.ii.). These may not be typical of the region as a whole (coming from tombs in the case of Gawra and ceremonial deposits at Warka) and often context and date are very uncertain (*cf.* Forest 1983). Nonetheless, there is good evidence for an expansion in metal production in the second half of the millennium. Copper is found at numerous sites, e.g., Hacinebi produced a lot of copper evidence from raw materials to finished products, crucible fragments and moulds (Stein 1998), and a small copper chisel is reported at Jerablus (Peltenburg 1998), raw materials and fragments are also present at Brak (Oates 1998). The origin of the raw material is unknown although sources in Anatolia are possible. In addition there was a "surprising widespread use (and preservation) of silver objects" (Prag 1978: 36). At Warka a huge range of metal is represented (Moorey 1994: (gold) 222, (silver) 235, (base) 257; Lindemeyer and Martin 1992) and archaic texts from Uruk III levels refer to copper from Dilmun (Oman?).

Widespread knowledge of metal technologies is therefore apparent as well as a demand for finished products. The ultimate purpose and destination of these objects is unclear, though larger institutions was certainly one, for example, some of the larger cylinder seals used by high ranking administrators (chapter *6.1.1.*) sometimes have knobs dowelled into the top which are in the shape of animals cast in copper and provide some of the earliest evidence for the use of the lost-wax technique of metal casting.

The important exploitation of new foods is covered in chapter *5.6.1*.

## 4. CHRONOLOGY 4000-3000 BC

A reconstruction of developments and associated ideologies of fourth millennium BC Mesopotamia is dependent on the chronological relationships established between northern and southern sites. It is very clear that during the fourth millennium BC southern style artefacts appear at northern sites. However, their precise dating is hampered by problems in their chronological relationship to similar objects on the southern plain. Of central importance in reconstructing this chronology is a recognition that the entire period is heavily dependent on the interpretation of the, possibly specialized, site of Warka where the only complete sequence for the fourth millennium has been revealed (*4.1.1.*). In addition, there are no Carbon 14 absolute dates from the south and, as a result, the relationship of southern and southern style material is poorly defined because of a heavy reliance on stylistic comparisons.

This chapter will attempt to draw chronological parallels between sites and regions, although this will inevitably be a continual process of refinement as excavations continue to be published and material analyzed (Algaze *et al* 1998).

In the debate over chronological relationships, much time has been devoted to the terminology employed to distinguish the various chronological and cultural markers. There is little consistency in their usage. The cultural tradition of south Mesopotamia during the fourth millennium is widely referred to as 'Uruk' although this can been criticized as implying the dominance (ecnonomic/political/cultural) of the site of Warka/Uruk. Although the site of Warka appears to have been the largest settlement on the Babylonian plain, and acted as the 'central place' for the lower half of the region (Adams and Nissen 1972; Adams 1981), it cannot be assumed that this reflects a primary political, cultural or economic role - few other sites of the fourth millennium date in southern Mesopotamia have been sufficiently investigated by excavation.

The problems for defining the traditions of north Mesopotamia are even more complicated because it is a less homogeneous region, both physically and culturally, than the southern alluvium (chapter *3.1.2.* and 3.2.2.ii.). The term 'Gawran' has been applied to the northeast ceramic traditions but this is a poor name for a period - Gawra's chronology is based on type fossils which are very particular and it is difficult to find comparisons and connections between them and ceramics from North Syrian, Jaziran, and Upper Euphrates sites (Rothman 1988; Lupton 1996:19; chapter 4.1.2.iv.). Nineveh is also of questionable chronological value (Gut 1995). A recent conference on the fourth millennium (Algaze *et al* 1998) proposed a purely chronological terminology 'Late Chalcolithic 1-5' with local 'Late Chalcolithic' used to refer to northern cultural traditions. Oates (1998), however, prefers to retain the term Uruk "as more chronologically informative than the much vaguer 'chalcolithic'." She uses the expression 'northern Uruk' to distinguish periods at Tell Brak before the appearance of southern (Uruk) inspired material (Oates and Oates 1994; Oates 1998). An alternative approach has been to use the presence of Uruk style material at northern sites as a chronological marker, simply referring to 'pre-contact' and 'contact' (Lupton 1996).

To avoid confusion the terminology adopted for this thesis will be:

Uruk = cultural traditions of south Mesopotamia
local Chalcolithic = non-Uruk cultural traditions

For chronology I will retain the familiar Early, Middle and Late Uruk as a convenient method of dividing the period in question. Although these terms as used here simply imply a range of years, the alternative of using dates would be cumbersome and imply a greater precision in absolute chronology than is currently available. There is no implication in this terminology of either southern dominance or the preeminence of the site of Warka/Uruk. On a more general level, local Chalcolithic sites where Uruk material appears will be designated as belonging to a 'contact period' with the time before the Uruk presence termed 'pre-contact'. A few C-14 dates that do exist provide potential absolute reference points although these can act only as a general guide and cannot be used to resolve specific chronological problems.

With the end of the Uruk phenomenon, towards the end of the fourth millennium, new traditions emerge which are variously termed Jemdet Nasr (south), Ninevite V (north east), Early Bronze Age I (north west and Levant). I shall use the term post-Uruk.

## 4.1. Geographical regions

### 4.1.1. Southern Plain (Babylonia)

The traditional type sequence comes from the eponymous site of Warka/Uruk. This ceramic sequence is based on excavations of the area known as Eanna where levels XIV to III are dated to the fourth millennium. These have been variously named and subdivided by researchers (e.g. Johnson 1973; Nissen 1993b) and demonstrates how the use of ceramics as markers of cultural phases is at best tenuous. Here I adopt the widely used convention of dividing the sequence into Early (levels XIV-IX), Middle (levels VIII-VI) and Late (V-IV) followed by the post-Uruk (Jemdet Nasr) phase (level III) (Ehrich 1992). This should not be taken to imply there were three major cultural changes; Nissen (1993b) argues for only two clear divisions in the material which he calls Early and Late. There are no abrupt breaks and gradual change makes any of these divisions very subjective. However, what is normally taken to distinguish the Late Uruk are the surviving remains of a series of monumental buildings in levels VI-IV. Level III represents a break in the architectural sequence with the destruction of the level IV buildings (Strommenger 1980b, Nissen 1972) and the digging of pits containing evidence of burning which has been interpreted as either ritual purification (Lenzen 1955:13) or food preparation (Barrelet 1974). The buildings are dated by stratigraphy, styles of decoration, ceramics and other associated objects such as seals, sealings, and other recording devices, but unfortunately the finds do not come from secure contexts (Finkbeiner 1986: 33). Likewise small finds of this period from an area to the east of Eanna, the Anu Ziggurat, are dated by style, not from their stratigraphy: hence a cylinder seal in the intermediate level D-C is said to belong to the initial stage of cylinder seal engraving, while seal impressions from the postholes of level C are stylistically similar to impressions from Eanna IV (Dunham 1980:131-45). The last casing of the Anu Ziggurat (A1-A3) is considered to be contemporary with Eanna III based on ceramic evidence.

Because so much of the Warka material relies on stylistic comparisons, fine distinctions cannot be drawn on this evidence alone. A much clearer stratigraphic sequence was recovered at Nippur (Hansen 1992) where the ceramics were compared with the Eanna sequence (Table 2).

Similarly, recent excavations on the Acropolis mound at Susa have revealed a sequence which may be tied to the Nippur/Warka material (Stève & Gasche 1971; Le Brun 1978; chapter *4.1.3.*). Although this has provided a scheme against which to compare ceramics from other sites it should be stressed that differences in styles of material between and within sites may be temporal or functional, this makes acute variances in time scales and relationships between sites difficult to assess. It is also true here, as elsewhere, that stylistic changes in ceramics may not directly reflect political/historical change if at all.

### 4.1.2. Northern regions

North of Babylonia the region can be divided ceramically (as well as physically, chapter *3.1.2.*) into three regional varieties (Frangipane 1993: 155) perhaps suggesting three culturally and politically distinct areas:

1. North Syria to West of Euphrates (Amuq, Qoueiq, Hama - closely linked to Arslantepe): red slipped burnished vessels and necked jars with plain rims and collars and rims modelled or channelled on the wheel; also found at Brak and Nineveh 3. Braidwood noted that much Amuq Phase G pottery had 'an almost "factory-made" look' (Braidwood and Braidwood 1960: 259).
2. Balikh and Habur valleys: these two regions demonstrate significant contact as well as with the other northern areas - small proportion of red-slip (at Hamman and Leilan) corrugated necks (Leilan and Tell Brak, the latter revealing wide links with a greater diffusion of red-slipped wares and shapes related to Tepe Gawra).
3. Upper Tigris. Alongside sites with a close Syro-Anatolian characteristic e.g. Nineveh 3, there is also local development, e.g., Tepe Gawra, with closest relations being with northern most section of the Euphrates (Norsuntepe, Korucutepe). Incised and stamped pottery were circulated more broadly, e.g., Tell Brak and Sakce Gozu. The introduction of a Late Uruk pottery from the south appears to have stimulated the development of a local painted style of Ninevite 5 in the early third millennium.

Such a division is confirmed by Lupton (1996: 19, Fig. 2.4) and Rova (1996: 15-19). The chronological details are:

#### 4.1.2.i. Middle Euphrates

With the building of the Tabqa Dam and the creation of Lake Assad on the Euphrates in Syria, a series of surveys and rescue excavations revealed a number of sites dated from the mid to late fourth millennium. It is not clear if a lack of settlement in the early fourth millennium reflects a real gap in the settlement of the Tabqa region or if the sites were simply not recognized. However at Tell Sheikh Hassan and Mureybit there is a settlement hiatus between

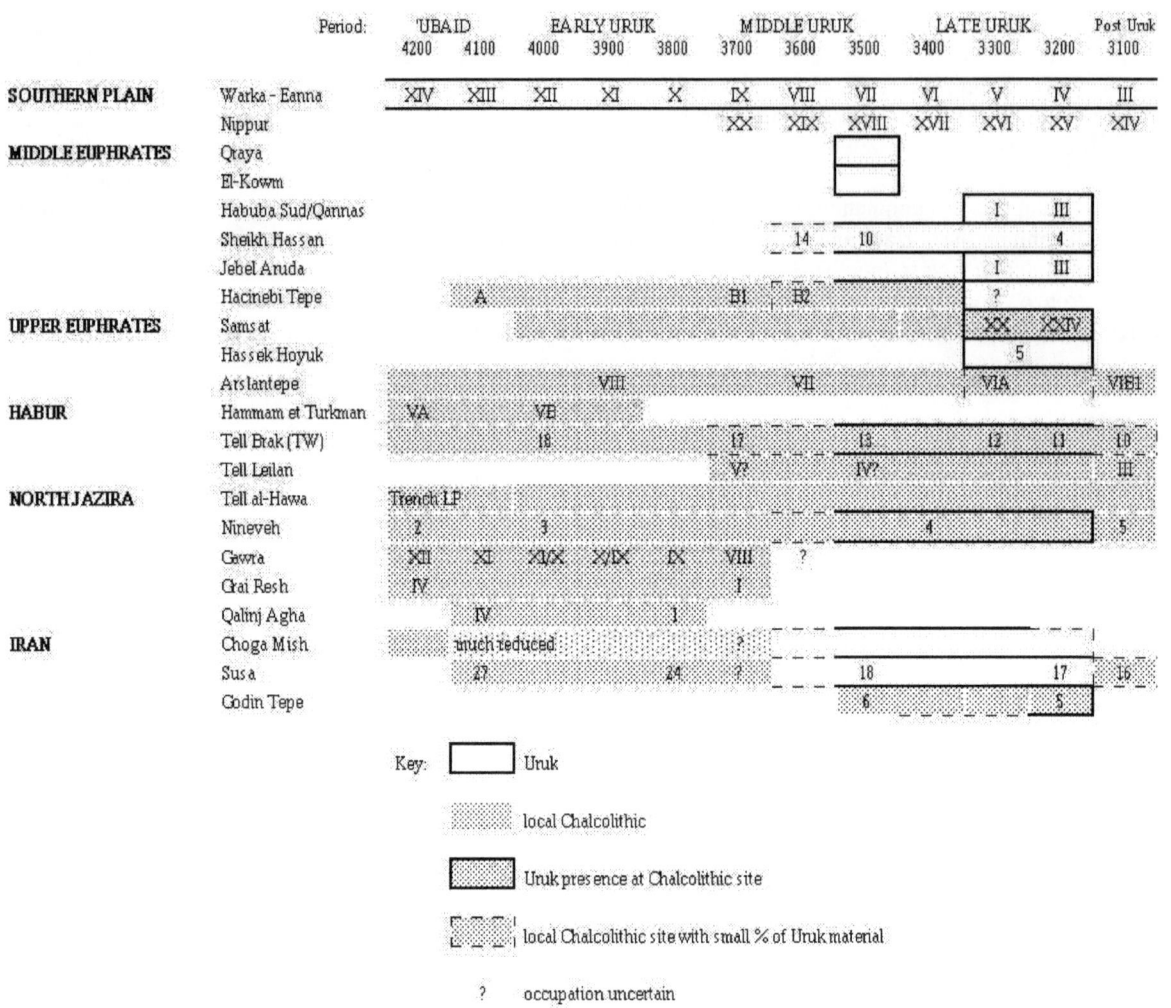

Table 2. Chronology of principle fourth millennium BC sites.

the Neolithic and latter half of the fourth millennium (Lupton 1996: 17) and, since most of the later sites were founded on virgin soil, there were possibly no pre-existing settled indigenous people. The sites produced grit-tempered ceramics of southern form, either independently or alongside chaff-tempered ceramics belonging to a northern tradition, e.g., Amuq F type assemblages (Braidwood and Braidwood 1960: 234, 264-75). While the Amuq F Chaff-faced Simple Ware disappears in Amuq G at Judeidah and Hama K (Ingholt 1940:22-23), where wheel made, mineral tempered Plain Simple Ware dominates together with the appearance of cylinder seals with southern Mesopotamian Late Uruk/JN parallels, this pattern does not appear to have temporal consistency between sites.

Although at Habuba Kabira there are three building levels, a short period of occupation is implied by the apparent lack of change seen in the material culture at the site (Strommenger 1979: 65; Sürenhagen 1986a:17) although the plan of the site did develop (Vallet 1998b; see below chapter 5.3.2.i.). Because of this continuity, Habuba has been viewed as a virtual 'single period' site. Unfortunately, the ceramics found on other Tabqa sites which were clearly occupied during this phase have as yet not been fully published. Preliminary reports on some of the pottery are available from Jebel Aruda (Kalsbeck 1981) and Tell al Hajj (Bridel et al. 1974). References to the Habuba-like ceramics on the other Tabqa contact period sites are: Tell Habuba Kabira level 1 (Strommenger 1979; 1980a), Tell Hadidi stratum 1, Mureybit Op. W15, Tell Qannas (Finet 1979: Fig. 23) and Tell Sheikh Hassan levels 4-5. Consequently, most reference is made to the detailed study of the ceramics found at Habuba Süd (Sürenhagen 1974/75):

Sürenhagen (1986b) analyzed the evidence for the appearance of southern style pottery which may be compared with the Eanna sequence at Uruk. He identified six common ceramic types at Habuba Kabira Süd, in Eanna VII and VI and Susa Acropolis 18 and 17B which he suggested would represent the same stage at all sites: mass-produced BRBs, reserve slip ware, water bottles with bent spouts, straight or sinuous-sided conical cups, conical bowls with pouring lips, and large ovoid storage jars with rounded bases and cylindrical necks.

Despite Sürenhagen's conclusions, the ceramics he analyzed would be equally at home in Eanna V and IV and the period of southern influence seems to best fit this later date. The drooping spout has been used to place Tabqa sites into the Late Uruk period and, for many researchers, the appearance of numerical tablets at some Tabqa sites confirms this as they do not appear in Eanna until level IV (although the dating of tablets is fraught with difficulties, see chapter *6.1.2.*). In addition cone mosaic decoration (Eanna V-III) is known at a number of Tabqa sites (chapter **5.4.**). Recent excavation in area TW at Tell Brak has shown that the horizon dominated by true southern ceramic types is indeed restricted to the Late Uruk period which in turn immediately precedes a 'Jemdet Nasr' post-Uruk horizon (Oates & Oates 1993).

A single C-14 determination from Habuba of 5085 ± 65 bp (Oates 1983: 272) calibrated to 3900 BC, appears much too early to correlate with other C-14 samples taken from levels in sites that produced similar material (Boehmer 1991). Two samples from Jebel Aruda (GrN 7989) 4495 ± 35 bp and (GrN 8463) 4490 ± 35 pb are calibrated to 3360-3210 and 3350-3200 BC (van Driel and van Driel-Murray 1979: 24). Similarly samples from the Late Uruk levels at Sheikh Hassan produced calibrated dates of 3350-3250 BC (Zaccagnini 1993: 19).

### 4.1.2.ii. Upper Euphrates

Arslantepe VIA has pottery forms and types reminiscent of Habuba Süd, Jebel Aruda and Hassek Höyük (Amuq F) although the vast majority of the ceramics were still manufactured in local fashion and has an Amuq G inventory. For the most part, they attest to influence from the south rather than any direct presence at the site. The C-14 samples taken from VIA levels are slightly later than those from Jebel Aruda, Sheikh Hassan and Hassek Höyük so the later levels may date to the period after the abandonment of the Tabqa sites. The next level of Arslantepe, VIB is post-southern contact and shows elements of East Anatolian origin (Palmieri 1985): red-black burnished, handmade pottery; new building techniques and elaborate hearths linked to sites in the Kurban area.

C-14 dates from Arslantepe VII suggest c.3600 BC (Calderoni *et al.* 1994) - the assemblages point to this phase belonging to the end of the pre-contact period. The samples from VIA levels give an average calibrated date of 3263-3030 BC (Alessio *et al.* 1988: 578) and most of the southern style contact period ceramics are in the lower levels of VIA. Post contact levels VIB1 date to 3145-2935 BC and VIB2 to 3054-2827 BC (Alessio *et al.* 1988:579).

At Hassek Höyük, three C-14 samples were taken from House 1 in level 5 and gave calibrated dates of between 3400-3200 BC (Bin-2730 4470 ± 40 BC, Bin-2731 4390 ± 50 BC (charcoal) and Bin-2732 4400 ± 60 BC (carbonized grain) (Behm-Blancke 1985: table opposite Fig. 1). Thermoluninesence dating on a group of burnt flints from the Q20 structure, also from level 5, gave a slightly earlier average date of 3413 ± 181 BC (*ibid.*).

### 4.1.2.iii. Habur

Hammam et-Turkman level VA, is viewed by the excavator as contemporary with Leilan V (Akkermans 1988: 123) based on the similarity of the so-called 'Coba bowls' to the flint-scraped bowls of Leilan V. However, the resemblances are limited and include types that, although recognized in assemblages of the north Jazira and at Grai Resh, are actually not common at Leilan (Lupton 1996).

Leilan level IV shows very little ceramic change from level V except for the appearance of BRBs (1% of the sherds). Wheel made ceramics also appear. One C14 dates from stratum 44 in period IV and two from the succeeding IIIa indicates a mid-fourth millennium date of Leilan IV (Ehrich 1992: 233; see 4.2). The handmade 'chaff-faced' assemblages of V-IV are found at Tell Brak CH9-12. They are similar to Chaff-Faced Simple Ware of Amuq F in paste and temper but with different shapes.

Assemblages at Hammam et-Turkman VB are dated to the early fourth millennium by a series of calibrated C-14 determinations taken on a burnt beam found in the monumental stratum 7 building which represents the last phase of period VB. The dates cluster around 4000 BC (Loon 1988: 704, Table 152). Leilan IIIa dates (UM-1815, UM-1813) cluster around 3400-3500 BC, and Leilan IV at (stratum 44) (UM-1812), ca. 3400-3500 BC.

### 4.1.2.iv. North Jazira

The chronology of north Mesopotamia is dominated by the long stratified sequence recovered at Tepe Gawra (Tobler 1950). Major problems exist however, mainly because the complete Gawra assemblage is not repeated at other sites. Thus we have a picture of regional differences and the occasional connections between them do not allow a fine chronology to be established.

Gawra Stratum XII was violently destroyed. In the next levels XI-A-X, parallels can be drawn with Qalinj Agha levels III and II: flat-based bowls, double-mouthed pots (al-Soof 1969:15). The latter are also known from Eridu and are suggested to be contemporary with Uruk-Eanna XIV-VII (Lloyd 1948:51). Seals are also similar between Gawra and Qalinj Agha and Susa levels 27-23 (Amiet 1980: pl. 6/118).

There is a stratigraphic break between levels IX and VIIIC although the material of VIIIC-A has only a small number of new ceramic forms from levels XI-IX. While Rothman (1988:159) prefers to date level VIII to the Late Uruk, Gut (1995) in her reanalysis of the Gawra ceramics prefers to link the level much closer to the earlier fourth millennium levels with the site being abandoned at the end of the Early Uruk period. There are no bevelled rim bowls reported at Gawra and the correlation of Gawra IX to VIIIC with the Late Uruk and Jemdet Nasr periods in the south is based rather tenuously on seal designs. Level VIII may lay in the

Middle Uruk (pre-contact) period (Lupton 1996:111.84) which is the preferred option here.

The largest area of remains contemporary with Gawra was recovered at Tell Brak. Tell Brak area CH, levels 13-14 (called 'Early Northern Uruk' by the excavator) produced stamped and incised pottery comparable to that of Gawra XI-IX (Oates & Oates 1994). CH 13 does not immediately precede levels 9-12 which had BRBs, flower pots and chaff-faced pottery like Leilan V-IV. Closely comparable pottery to CH 9-12 has been discovered in situ in Middle Uruk contexts in Area TW (Phases 14-16) (Oates & Oates 1993: 170).

TW Phase 13 produced a beaker with pouring lip which is absent in the following phase 12 and also absent at Habuba Kabira. There was also a large soft-stone cylinder seal (4.5 x 3.0 cm) similar to those recovered from Sheikh Hassan level 10 (Boese 1989: Figs 36-39) and Telloh (Parrot 1948, Pl. 2 see also Lenzen 1960: Pl. 25a). In phases 9-12 the use of Riemchen-like bricks continued throughout. From Phase 12 seventeen pots were recovered, all identical with or similar to examples published from Habuba Süd (Sürenhagen 1974/75) - one large storage jar bore a pictographic sign. Phases 10/11 included a fragment of Jemdet Nasr polychrome ware and Phase 10 had an example of a nose-lug jar with hatched or crosshatched triangles on the shoulder which are common at Habuba.

### 4.1.3. Iran

A modern stratigraphic sequence exits at Susa. Susa A/I is defined by Susa Acropole Sounding I: 27-24 (Le Brun 1978:190) The ceramics correlate with Choga Mish Susiana. The chronological relationship with Mesopotamia rests primarily on glyptic evidence. Susa A is possibly contemporary with the Early Uruk. Susa II marks a cultural break (Acropole I:22-17, Acropole II:6-1, Acropole III:10-1). Red-Slipped Ware begins in Acropole I:18 (Le Brun 1978:73-82) comparable to Nippur Inanna XX-XVII (Middle Uruk) and level 17 is related to Inanna XVII-XVI (Late Uruk). A major problem is that Acropole I:22-19 is small and not described in detail so there may be a cultural correlation between Susa II and Early-Late Uruk. Glyptic material is difficult: Acropole I:18-17B is paralleled in Warka IV (Amiet 1972). There are strong ceramic parallels between Acropole I:17 and Habuba Kabira. The numerical tablets of I:17 may parallel those of Eanna IV and the Tabqa examples (Stolper 1984: 6; Weiss and Young 1975: 11, figs 4-5).

Susa III (Acropole I:16-14B) is divided into three by Carter (1978:198, 202, 211) based on internal stratigraphy, ceramic typology and external relationships. Susa IIIA I:16-14B assemblages have links to Post-Uruk levels at Farukhabad and Nippur Inanna XIV-XI (Dittmann 1986: Table 2) though Susa appears to be linked closely to Fars and Proto-Elamite developments.

At Godin Tepe, in the Kangavar Valley to the north of Susa, the Period V ceramics contain features which can be paralleled in lowland Mesopotamia/Susiana. Many vessels such as four-lugged pots and cream slipped varieties with incised shoulders first appear in Susa 17A, Warka Eanna IV and Nippur Inanna level XVI. Four-lugged jars with painted bands above the shoulders are however specific to Susa Acropolis 17 (Weiss and Young 1975: 6). Forty-three tablets or fragments were found. Many of these are similar to those at Habuba Kabira but are closer to those from Susa Acropolis 17 (Weiss and Young 1975: 11).

Based on ceramic parallels, Choga Mish Late Susiana is considered to be contemporary with Susa A settlements such as Susa Acropole I:27-25 (Hole 1978: table 4). In the next phase southern Mesopotamian style ceramics make their appearance along with seals and numerical tablets (Kantor 1976: 24-25). Choga Mish at this time was a major settlement with a city wall and imposing buildings as well as houses (Delougaz & Kantor 1973:189; 1996) and seems to be contemporary with Susa II or Acropole I:18-17. Choga Mish is then abandoned.

Further east at Tepe Yahya, the IVC building may have been laid out to a standard measure close to that used at Habuba Kabira (Beale & Carter 1983). This period has been tied by artefact parallels to sites in the west (Lamberg-Karlovsky and Tosi 1973, Potts 1994: 55). Level IVC2 can be dated to the post-Uruk Jemdet Nasr/Susa III period by artefact parallels: BRBs, proto-Elamite tablets - palaeographic evidence links the tablets with those from Susa Acropole I:16 or Susa IIIA (Lamberg-Karlovsky 1976: 73, fig 3, pl.7) and cylinder seals which have affinities with glyptic of Acropole I:16-14b and Sin Temple I-V. The next level IVC1 has been re-dated recently from the early to late third millennium (Potts 1994: 48).

A calibrated average of 4115-3880 BC exists from ten C-14 samples from Jaffarabad and Susa (Susa A/I) (Table 1 In Ehrich 1992). The late fourth millennium (post-Uruk) is represented in the south east by a series of C-14 determinations from Tepe Malyan, Iran (Voigt & Dyson 1992) which range c.3100-2900 BC.

Based on the relationships established between regions together with a series of absolute dates provided by C-14 samples, the chronology adopted in this work is set out in Table 2.

## 5. SOCIETY AND MATERIAL

Past analysis of typological sequences of artefacts had suggested that they represent the manifestation in material terms of "past historical entities, such as cultures or peoples, and that such entities tend towards homogeneity within a spatial and temporal domain." (Jones 1997:130). It is now recognised, however, that such an equation is invalid (Jones 1997; see chapters **3.2.** and 6.1). However, identical or similar forms of culture at different sites can represent evidence, either in whole or in part, of a shared social system. These shared elements alongside cultural differences can encourage cultural change (chapter **2.1.**). In this sense similar forms of both public and domestic architecture at widely separated sites will suggest, at least when they are first erected, some common connections and concerns. These concerns, however, have generally been viewed as a manifestation of social, political and economic developments, e.g., a form of political control or the development of long distance trade networks. This approach is often extended to the entire urban environment "which effectively relates urban development to the development of society as a whole." (Harloe 1977:5). Social stratification is therefore emphasised and buildings (e.g. factories, palaces) are seen as reflecting this development somewhat incidentally rather than in a central way. What is often ignored is "just why buildings emerge with the particular shape, location and appearance that they have, or what meanings such forms have for their inhabitants" (King 1980:5).

Studies in social and material anthropology have shown how forms of social organisation are expressed in spatial form on the ground, how buildings carry symbolic meaning, and how the religious beliefs and world view of particular social groups are represented in settlement form (King 1980: 3). The pioneering work in this area was undertaken by Rapoport (1969) who showed that buildings and spatial organisation can be related to social variables, including not only how social factors affect the physical and spatial environment, but also how people are affected by their environments. As part of this recognition, Duly (1979), for example, shows how "important social and tribal life are reflected in a community's domestic buildings and usually symbolically expressed in their design and decoration." More recent work (e.g., Hillier & Hanson 1984) has also emphasised the way in which built space will not only reflect social organisation but be very much part of the fabric of society, with social messages, either consciously or subconsciously, built into the shape and form of buildings which can act to encourage socially desirable behaviour. As such, the buildings both constrain and encourage cultural developments. People, therefore, build environments to create a particular world order. Wheatley (1971) demonstrates this on a grand scale in China where the Great City Shang was laid out to reflect cosmological and social organisation. This illustrates that the human mind attempts to impose order on the world and that the environment can be expressed through signs, materials, colours, shapes, and size, in other words a non-verbal message system (see chapter **3.3.**).

To be raised within a cultural group allows one to 'read' and understand this world view as expressed in the non-verbal message system. But while the meaning behind this system can only make full sense for its own cultural group, in order for communities to function social action must interlace with the non-verbal message system which it uses. Inevitably, therefore, there is a close relationship between social forms and built form. Buildings provide "a frame of reference for active behaviour because they carry non-verbal signals about the patterning of space and time" (Fletcher 1995:20) and serve to control the level of interaction between members of a community, i.e., space plays an active role in promoting acceptable conduct. A given social ideology will thus produce a particular form of material expression (in this case buildings) since there is an accord between verbal usage, active behaviour and material form. Although the archaeological record is rarely able to furnish us with knowledge of the verbal interactions and only occasionally of social activities, it is possible to recognise the shape, size and form of a settlement with which they are associated. However, while there is some correspondence between social activity and material patterning, this should not imply some kind of universal predetermination: two culturally discrete communities occupying the same geographical area will arrange their own distinct residential space, and this will not be determined by the environment since particular communities may make differing use of materials depending on their cultural requirements.

Just as the social ideology of a community will influence the spatial arrangement of the settlement, the buildings and their ordering in turn regulate the activity of the community (since the built form acts as a channel for the signals essential to the functioning of the community) and thus actively reinforces the social ideology. Once people begin to move beyond the geographical area where a particular form of social ideology and associated settlement spatial arrangement exists (through colonisation, military conquest, population expansion etc.), only a near duplicate of the existing form would be acceptable for their social system to persist. However, new signals will inevitably be created as the buildings are constructed within a different cultural region, and change may be triggered by external pressures and disturbances (not necessarily in the building form but in the messages the building provides). As the message becomes more complex, change multiplies within the ideological system. This could happen at any time because any new message may create a new relationship with a previous inconsistency in the system. Thus change results in the same fashion as the propagation of memes (see chapter **2.1.**), where the material (building) messages, and both non-verbal and verbal behaviour 'evolves' through internal and external influence and the overall message becomes altered. This 'evolutionary' approach does not imply that large scale social, political and economic transformations (e.g., the emergence of the state) are the result of predictable, or inevitable developments of smaller scale phenomena. Charles Lyell's doctrine of uniformitarianism - "the notion that current and observable causes, acting at characteristically minute and gradual rates, can produce all the grand effects of earth's history by accumulating their tiny increments through the immensity of geological time" (Gould 1996:163) is now generally rejected to explain all events (chapter **2.2.**). Rather change could be brought about rapidly by an apparently unimportant development which kicks "the positive feedback machine of human herding and copying behaviour into its upward spiral" (Gould 1996:224). It is simply the scale at which entities like the state operate that provides their observable characteristics.

For the large time scales dealt with by archaeology it is usual to investigate artefacts and monuments rather than individual human intentions and actions which rely on much finer time scales (generally invisible to the blunt tools of archaeology). Fletcher (1995:18) argues that material remains can act in the same way as behaviour and that the material (built) forms and the information they reflect, the scale at which these signals are transmitted or regulated and the consequences of the building for the community's life, will change through time (see Hassan 1996). Buildings, although created over relatively short periods, in the long term change through disintegration, restoration and alteration and their associated messages will also change. Indeed, they will often endure and have an effect that persists beyond the lives of the people whose intentions created them. They will come to obstruct development and place constraints on social and political change. The larger and more durable the buildings the more they come to obstruct development and the restoration or adaptation of the social ideology and so place constraints on social and political change. For example, Westminster Abbey is associated with coronations and the burial of monarchs. This reinforces a particular order of society through tradition, even at times when that order is being questioned and eroded. In this sense, rather than simply reflecting a social ideology and any new signals which are accommodated within the system, buildings themselves are active participants in the development of a community's world view.

It is clear that any particular building may not be associated solely with one area of social interaction. For example, while a building might seem to be most obviously related to religious belief and practice, it is equally evident that its construction may be related to the economy, to tribe or kinship, or that it is a major symbol of social stratification, and can thus be a means of social control through occupation or ownership. And while it is conventional practice in sociology and social anthropology to approach the study of society through a study of its institutions, different societies will institutionalise different activities. For example, in simple societies institutions may be relatively undifferentiated such that priest, medicine man and political leader may be indistinguishable. As societies grow, differentiation occurs, and with it the growth of institutions (King 1980: 9). A straightforward functionalist interpretation of a particular building is however unnecessary if one accepts that, regardless of whether one identifies a building as a temple or a palace, they are part of a wider social ideology.

By identifying common architectural typologies which appear over a broad area (perhaps beyond the geographical environment in which they first develop) it will be possible to suggest the presence, at least initially, of a common social ideology. Buildings are constructed with the implicit assumption that the ideas, values and social forms they embody are either already present or will develop. The 'proper' use of the buildings will require appropriate behaviour and the adoption of social and cultural rules which are assumed in their design. In other words, when buildings are constructed in a foreign tradition it is not just buildings that are imported but an entirely new way of life and the built environment thus becomes an essential part of the transformation of the culture. In these circumstances, the local physical and social environment is not necessarily understood before the new culture's ideas and beliefs are incorporated into built form. The imported buildings may be influenced and modified over time by the indigenous ideology unless there are internal social rules which prevent this from happening.

## 5.1. Monumental building

The second half of the fourth millennium BC witnessed the emergence in Mesopotamia of new cultural styles and social forms. Methods of recording, cylinder seals, mass-produced plain ceramics and a variety of new items crafted of stone and metal appeared from around 3500 BC. This phenomenon is visible not only at sites in southern Mesopotamia but also in Susiana and Syria and take its most impressive form in a style of monumental architecture and associated decoration.

The basic way that human beings symbolise power is through conspicuous consumption and it is generally assumed that control of this consumption is the fundamental measure of individual or group power. Monumental architecture is perhaps the most obvious example of conspicuous consumption "which supports large numbers of energy consumers, the production of high energy-consuming luxury goods, and an emphasis on non-useful movement (processions, needlessly large rooms etc.)" (Trigger 1990: 120). However, while the scale of monumental architecture may reflect a society's ability to produce and direct surplus labour, the creation of monuments takes predictable forms because of their potential for communication. "As a communication media, monumental architecture is actually relatively efficient. The initial costs of construction may be great, but once built a massive building or plaza can be seen by thousands of people over great lengths of time, broadcasting continuously for even thousands of years" (Blanton 1989: 413). "Monuments serve as unambiguous markers of social relationships, not only because of their scale, but because of their functional unity and visual prominence." (Moore 1996: 97).

The defining evidence for the characteristic style of monumental architecture of the Late Uruk was recovered more than sixty years ago at Warka. The majority of excavated buildings lie close to (and probably under) the focus of major religious buildings of Ur III date (c.2100 BC) known as Eanna 'House of Heaven' (chapter 5.2.1.vb.) While none of the prehistoric buildings has an altar or any other equivocal furnishings of a sanctuary, the niched walls and the plan are generally interpreted as characterising temples. However, one should be wary of pigeon holing buildings simply on the basis of architectural design. As pointed out above, a building will not relate solely to one aspect of society, particularly one of modern manufacture (spiritual and secular). There are, however, a number of buildings which may fall more readily into such a classification. These are: the Late Ubaid structures at Eridu (5.2.1.ii.), the 'Painted Temple' at Tell Uqair (5.2.1.iii.); the 'White Temple' at Warka (5.2.1.va.); the 'Red' and 'Grey temples' at Jebel Aruda (5.2.2.ii.); and, possibly, the level 6 'temple' in squares 2132-2232/33 at Sheikh Hassan (5.2.2.iii.). They all have internal furnishings of a typical religious building, i.e., an emplacement ('altar') at one end of a central hall and, with the exception of the building at Sheikh Hassan, have external buttressing and are isolated from other buildings on a platform. The similarity of plans between these temples and other monumental and domestic buildings may be related to a concept found in the historic period where the temple is simply the god's house (Sumerian é).

## 5.2. Uruk Sites

Excavation of the following sites has revealed monumental architecture of fourth millennium date (see chapter **4**). They are subdivided based on the distinct geographical regions identified above (chapter **3.1.**). By investigating the structural features, associated objects and context within the wider settlement it will be possible to build up a picture of feasible ideological links. Modern maps showing sites of fourth millennium date clearly only reveal the distribution pattern of archaeological survey or excavation work. This has resulted in a bias in favour of the southern alluvium where the first extensive work had been undertaken and thus it is this area that is often viewed as the 'core' from which any developments emerge. More recent work has revealed monumental architecture of fourth millennium date across the whole of Greater Mesopotamia, covering eastern Anatolia and Syria through Mesopotamia to south-west Iran, (Fig. 1.). Uruk sites are distinguished in Fig. 2.

### 5.2.1. Southern Plain
i. Tell Abu Salabikh
ii. Eridu
iii. Tell Uqair
iv. Ur
v. Warka.
   va. 'Anu Ziggurat'
   vb. 'Eanna'

### 5.2.2. Middle Euphrates
i. Habuba Kabira-süd/Tell Qannas.
ii. Jebel Aruda
iii. Tell Sheikh Hassan
iv. Hacinebi Tepe

### 5.2.3. Upper Euphrates
i. Hassek Höyük
ii. Arslantepe

### 5.2.4. Habur
i. Tell Brak

### 5.2.5. Iran
i. Susa
ii. Choga Mish
iii. Godin Tepe

### 5.2.1.i. Tell Abu Salabikh

A solid town wall, 20 meters across in places appears to circle most of the so-called 'Uruk Mound' (surface survey recovered material from Early to Late Uruk); the southeastern portion of the mound was probably a later settlement (Pollock *et al*. 1991: 63, n. 4). The wall was composed of mud bricks ranging from 10 x 20 cm to 13 x 27 cm as well as occasional bricks of up to 10 x 29 cm. and were laid in alternating patterns across the full width of the wall. There is at least one wide buttress on the outer edge of the wall (Fig. 3). The pottery recovered from the level at which the wall was founded was assigned to the Late Uruk (Pollock *et al*. 1991: 63).

Near the northeast edge of the Uruk Mound (which may have been an open area later covered over by debris from clearance of a water channel) a great deal of bitumen was recovered (Pollock *et al*. 1991: 66). It was formed of a stack of bitumen sheets 30 x 45 cm in diameter and 22 cm high. Many pieces showed impressions of reeds, reed matting, string and possibly wood. They are suggested to have been Middle Uruk in date.

On the Main Mound the mortar of walls dating to ED II contained "a surprising frequency of clay wall-cones of the familiar Uruk type" (Postgate 1984: 108). It is suggested by the excavator that the mortar was mixed from destroyed mud-brick walls of an earlier building which had been decorated with the cones.

### 5.2.1.ii. Eridu

Stone was widely used in the architecture and this was taken by the archaeologist as a diagnostic feature of the Late Uruk period (compare the widespread use of stone at Warka, chapter 5.2.1.v): "the whole mound had been surrounded by a retaining wall of undressed white limestone in gypsum mortar, to make an emplacement for a new sacred *temenos*. Above this, the temple-platform rose at a sharp angle, its face constructed of pale pink limestone in small stepped courses in gypsum plaster. At a point some 15m. above the surrounding plain, this stepped face gave way to a vertical facade" (Lloyd 1954: 464). And "the city-walls and bastions are partly built of rough masses of gypsum which is found not far off in the desert" (Hall and Woolley 1927: 66 n. 1). In addition, "a wall two-and-a-half metres thick, standing to an average height of a little under a metre and built entirely of small bricks of white gypsum (sizes 42-45 x 10 x 10; 22 x 10 x 10 cm.)" (Safar *et al*. 1981: 81, fig. 32) which are suggested to be gypsum plaster bricks, rather than stone, because of their standard size (Moorey 1994: 339). In structures below the ziggurat at Eridu, attributed to the period Uruk IV-III, were Riemchen gypsum bricks 45-42 x 10 x 10 cm. (a few half this size) (Safar *et al*. 1981: 64, fig. 14; cf. also 78). Level I had circular columns on the platform with stone mosaic cones - some of the heads were covered in copper plating (Safar 1947:107; Safar *et al*. 1981: 240, fig. 118).

Traces of murals were uncovered on walls dated to the Uruk period (Safar *et al*. 1981: 35) and another example (possibly post-Uruk in date) included "a man holding a bird on the wrist, with a smaller figure near him, in red paint" (Taylor 1855: 410).

A building in square H5, possibly Early Uruk in date, on the southeast edge of the mound, has a tripartite arrangement with a central hall nearly 12m long. Room 8 has a platform occupying 2/3 of the room with a ramp giving access. On the platform was a two storey kiln lined with bitumen and surrounded by pottery and BRBs (Safar *et al* 1981: 70-1). It is possible that the kiln was for processing bitumen. The use of BRBs for transport/storage of bitumen is known later elsewhere, e.g., Hacinebi Tepe (5.2.2.iv.).

In Squares EF/4 an oblong 'Portico' building, ran parallel with the northeastern side of the ziggurat some 10 m from the retaining wall. It is divided into three long chambers (13.8 x 1.9 m) each having three entrances leading to the neighbouring chamber. Like the building on the southeast edge of the mound, this one was also filled in with wind blown sand and possibly dates to the Early Uruk although Lloyd suggests it should be dated a little later than the H5 building (Safar *et al* 1981: 84)

### 5.2.1.iii. Tell Uqair

Excavations revealed a monumental building and series of mud brick platforms dating to the Late Uruk period (Lloyd and Safar 1943). The earliest platform (level VIII) was revealed in the northeast on the tell revealing a buttressed facade. Stage VII saw the construction a platform consisting of two terraces to support a monumental building. The northeastern buttressed facade was extended. At the same time, or perhaps later, an extension to the upper terrace was made on the southeast side with semicircular unplastered buttresses on its southeast side. Two staircases led to the first terrace with steps 27 cm wide and an average rise of 10 cm. They were composed of mud bricks laid on edge and repeatedly plastered. A channel lined with bitumen ran down the outside of the staircases. From the first terrace, another staircase reached the building on top of the second terrace. At about 3m from the NE and SE facades there was a shallow step in the pavement covering.

On the facade of the platform buttresses rose 4.6m to a lower line of a cone mosaic band. The cones were arranged in five rows set into bitumen with their heads projecting about 1 cm. In the centre of the flat end was a circular depression and were dipped into black paint to a depth of about 5-10 cm. Their greatest diameter was 8 cm and the length 20 cm.

Near the north corner of the temple platform a coat of red water-paint seemed to have been added over this pavement. At about 3m from the NE and SE facades there was a shallow step in the pavement covering.

The monumental building was heavily denuded and possibly only about half the plan survived (Fig. 4.). The facade of the building was covered with a layer of mud-plaster 3-5 cm thick and then a coat of white gypsum paint. Small vertical flutes were sunk in the plaster of the buttresses - 3 for each normal buttress and 4 where the spaces at the corners became wider. The building appears to have consisted of a central hall with four smaller rooms on the northeast side. The walls were constructed directly upon the bitumen-coated upper surface of the temple platform. On top of the bitumen there were layers of fine clay and a whitish gypsum layer pavement finish.

The interior was coated in mud plastered and covered in colour washes or painted ornament. The paintings appeared to depict a row of humans and animals: "Unfortunately, none of the human figures was recoverable above the waistline, owing to the proximity of the surface" (Lloyd and Safar 1943: 140). They stood above a dado (about 1m high) and a band of geometrical ornament about 30 cm high (Lloyd and Safar 1943: 143, pls. X, XVIIIA). The latter appears to represent cone mosaic decoration. There were also images of leopards painted either side of the 'altar' - one seated, one recumbent. At the northeast end of the central hall was an 'altar' built of solid brickwork 80-90 cm high, 2.6 m wide and with a projection of 3.6m. On the right side a flight of six shallow steps led up to a side platform whose top was flush with that of the main altar. The fact that wall paintings continued behind the altar suggests that the emplacement was a later addition. The outline of another emplacement was noted in the centre of the hall (Lloyd and Safar 1943: Pl. IXa).

Level VI saw the filling in of the building with large rectangular bricks (40x25x10 cm) rather than Riemchen (Lloyd and Safar 1943: 139). The platform was extended, possibly into an oval shape. In Level V a second filling took place and this included 'gypsum or cement bricks' which the excavators used as a chronological indicator of the Uruk period (Lloyd and Safar 1943: 149, pl. XVIa). The temple then went out of use.

### 5.2.1.iv. Ur

In the west corner of the Ur III ziggurat terrace the retaining wall of a platform built of Riemchen bricks with a covering of limestone rubble may possibly date to the Late Uruk (Woolley 1939: 8, pls. 1-2a). Behind the platform retaining wall stretched a mud-brick floor covered with baked clay cones (Woolley 1939: 5-6, pls.II, 14b; 1956: 28, 188, pl. 15 lower).

### 5.2.1.v. Warka

Covering an area in the Late Uruk of about 250 ha. (Finkbeiner 1991: 194), the site appears to have been once divided by the river Euphrates and, although this was probably no longer the case by the Late Uruk, two distinct areas may have still been visible (Nissen 1998). These areas are referred to today by their historic names of Anu Ziggurat and Eanna. They are located in the centre of the settlement with buildings of various design. Most of these are elevated on platforms.

### 5.2.1.va. 'Anu Ziggurat'

This consists of an irregularly shaped brick platform decorated by buttresses formed of various rebuildings dating back to the 'Ubaid period (Heinrich 1982: 61-3, Abb. 78-90). The so-called White Temple is on platform level B although similar buildings existed in the lower levels C to E (Heinrich 1982: Abb. 81-95). Although the buildings are not constructed directly on each other they retain a similar layout and scale (Fig. 5.). The dating of the temple level B is not clear but it is probably contemporary with Eanna level IVb (see chapter 4). It stands on a socle of asphalt some 30 - 40 cm high. Access was possible through all but the northern wall. The building is 22.30 m long and 17.50 m wide, with a central hall and four doorways leading off each long side into a row of rooms. There is an emplacement in the centre of the long hall with another blocking the northwest corner of the hall.

Long rooms in the south corner may represent stair supports to the roof. In plan, the White Temple appears very similar to the incomplete plan of the monumental building from Uqair. Niches decorated the facade and the ramp leading to the top of the platform was decorated with jars with open mouths. Like at Uqair there was a lower platform and here red paint survived outlining the a plan of a building together with what may have been a temporary building marked out by post holes on a raised socle. Both plans appear to mirror the organization of the rooms in the White Temple. Whether they represent plans for buildings which were never constructed or have a ritual function is unknown.

At ground level on the east side of the Anu Ziggurat at ground level is the *Steingebaude*, the walls of which were preserved to a height of 3.2-3.4 m. The building was set in a pit with three concentric rectangular rooms with an entrance to each on a different side. The walls of the central room were formed of gypsum plaster blocks with one or two courses of limestone on top. The outer walls were of limestone blocks. They were built on a pavement of well-jointed limestone slabs (Schmidt 1972: pl. 7a). In the *Steingebaude*, as appears usual throughout the site, the stonework had been covered with layers of gypsum plaster and sealed with bitumen (Heinrich 1982: 67-8). The building was filled with alternating layers of stone and mud in the central room while in the outer corridors only the lowest stone packing survived. Its use is debated but it was deliberately infilled while the plaster was still damp. In the centre is a raised podium with burning. It is suggested that there was temporary roofing, perhaps a cenotaph building although Forest (1999) interprets it as a temple building. It is thought to be contemporary with the White Temple (i.e., Late Uruk).

### 5.2.1.vb. 'Eanna'

About fifty metres to the east of the White Temple were the walls of the area known as *Eanna* ('House of Heaven') - a focus of major religious buildings dating to the Ur III period (*c*.2100 BC). The following allocation of buildings to Uruk levels largely follows Heinrich (1982: 70-83):

Level VI Very fragmentary possibly with *Steinstifttempel*

Level V The first major phase of building is represented by the *Kalksteintempel* the foundation courses of which were formed of flat, irregular limestone pieces about 10 cm thick mortared with bitumen. It was reconstructed with mud-brick foundations and the stone was possibly reused in foundations elsewhere (Heinrich in Noldeke 1934: 7). Nearby is the *Steinstifttempel* building within its own courtyard area covered with bitumen. Above a level of asphalt, limestone blocks, laid in mud mortar, had been used for the wall foundations and stone blocks set in bitumen were used to line the lower parts of walls. The walls of the structure above the foundations were made from moulded gypsum plaster mixed with crushed mud brick measuring 53 x 10 x 10 cm (Lenzen 1959: 13, 15-16). It is suggested that these blocks had been manufactured in wooden moulds exactly like mud bricks, though some were considerably larger than the conventional mud Riemchen bricks. (Moorey 1994: 338). The building sequence of this structure is very unclear mainly because of subsequent intrusions and stone-robbing (Lenzen 1959: 8 ff.; pls. 36, 40; Heinrich 1982: 70 ff.). The *Steinstifttempel* is stratigraphically connected to *Grosser Hof* by a trench 5m long, and both buildings were rendered watertight, the former with burnt stone cone inlay and the latter by its mud bricks coated in bitumen (Matthews & Wilkinson 1991: 182; Boehmer 1990). Limestone was used to line a water channel (Heinrich 1935: 6ff.).

Level IVb The precinct was rebuilt with a series of buildings focused on 3 platforms: A, B, and a large platform with the *Rundpfeilerhalle* - a sunken court leading by stairs to eight pillars on a platform much of the facade of which was decorated with clay cone mosaics (Noldeke 1932: 12, pl. 8; Moortgat 1969, pl. I). Such decoration appears especially on freestanding columns and walls with buttresses and niches (Finkbeiner: 1986: 126-7).

Level IVa All 3 platforms are enclosed by a large platform with buildings D and C (reconstructed as a combination of tripartite and 'T' shape hall, 2 hearths in each part). Other buildings include a square building with multiple rooms around a large courtyard and elaborately decorated with buttresses, and the *Pfeilerhalle* decorated with clay cone mosaic. The precinct of buildings was approached through a gateway and at least partially surrounded by a wall decorated with buttresses. Possibly at this time the *Reimchengebaude* was dug into the *Steinstifttempel* building - standing on a platform of limestone blocks taken from the *Steinstifttempel*. It has a nested plan, packed with burnt objects, perhaps deliberately fired, replastered and doors blocked. It may represent a ritual burial of goods belonging to the stone-cone-mosaic building when it went out of use or, according to Forest (1999), an early temple building. Traces of murals with figured designs were recovered in the *Reimchengebaude* (Nunn 1985). Dating to the same level, Temple E (Heinrich 1982: 77-8, fig. 115), had at least one room with mud brick walls set on limestone blocks (Lenzen 1968: pl. 9b). Stone foundations were widely used at Uruk (Jordan 1931: 48 ff., pl. 4; 1932: 16 ff., fig. 2). The late prehistoric terrace (*Alte Terrasse*) had foundations formed from a paving of limestone fragments (Heinrich 1939: 22, 30; pl. 30b), possibly robbed from the *Steinstifttempel* (Lenzen 1961: 17). The monumental buildings of level IVa were enclosed with a mud brick precinct wall decorated with buttresses. A monumental gateway gave access into the precinct.

At the end of level IVa the whole platform was leveled and cleared for the construction of a new layout of buildings. While traces of stone in buildings are dated to Uruk III (Lenzen 1961: 14; 1962: 10) after that date at Uruk, as elsewhere, the practice of using stone for architecture ceased.

### 5.2.2.i. Habuba Kabira Süd

Habuba Kabira Süd has the most extensive excavated Late Uruk material from north Mesopotamia (Fig. 6.). The site was founded on virgin soil and built in three stages on the west bank of the Euphrates just above the flood level (Strommenger 1980a; Vallet 1996).

The earliest phase was a small and apparently short-lived occupation (judging from the limited number of replasterings of its walls) in the north of the site. This was replaced by a well-planned urban settlement with the installation of the drainage system and laying down of the main streets (Ludwig 1977). There were three large roads: one parallel to the river, two crossing it from east to west. These were clearly important as a lot of care was taken with their construction. They have a covering of fluvial gravel and at the edges calcite stones form an embankment to protect the lower part of the house walls. All the smaller side dead-end lanes between buildings do not have such a covering (Strommenger 1980: 35; Vallet 1996: 49). The main road system was also provided with a net of drain pipes.

A large number of houses, all made from the type of Riemchen bricks that were associated with Uruk period constructions in the south were erected. Most were variations of the Mittelsaal type (see below). Vallet (1996: 57) argues that the residential area, running parallel to the river where formed from parcels of land of 28 x 15 m, that is 420m$^2$ each. Some buildings along the main central street have external buttressing.

At a slightly later date the whole settlement was surrounded by a wall. This overlay some earlier structures leaving an open space between the houses and the inside of the wall (Vallet 1996: 55, fig. 7). The wall was well constructed of bricks (50 x 50 x 14 cm) with the exception of the external facing, the gateways and certain bastions which are carefully constructed using Riemchen bricks. At its thickest the wall was 3-3.30 m reinforced every 13.5m by bastions of 5.5 m long, projecting between 3.5-4.2 m from the wall and accessible from the interior of the town by a stair shaft. The whole face of the wall was ornamented with niches and two gateways allowed access to the town. A smaller outer wall restricted access to the former. Running south from the southern (Qannas) gateway and four metres to the west of the *avant mur* is the remains of part of a second small wall about 1m wide without bastions but decorated with niches. Between the walls was a filling of pebbles and fluvial gravel. The riverside aspect of the site seems to have remained undefended. The walls, estimated at 840 m long (Vallet 1996: 49), enclosed an inner city of c.8 ha although with the final phase of building the minimum extent of the settlement might have been close to 18 ha (Strommenger 1980a: 33).

### 5.2.2.ia. Tell Qannas

Located in the south of the settlement and occupying a natural elevation, Tell Qannas, was a series of monumental buildings. (Finet 1975; 1979). They must have been visible not just from within the entire inner city but from some distance beyond the walls (Lupton 1996: 62).

Although many of the structures are heavily eroded the plan of a number of buildings could be recovered (Fig. 7.). Like the city of Habuba Kabira Süd, they were built over several stages. Vallet (1998b: 66) reconstructs the development of the complex in direct relation to the enlargement of the settlement.

The buildings are constructed on an artificial terrace formed from Riemchen bricks (the dimensions vary from 20-25 x 10-13 x 9-10). Following Vallet's (1998b) reconstruction of the development of the site, the first phase is represented by the 'central complex'. The central room measures 12m x 5m. Bordering the central room are 5 rooms, 2 in the north, 3 in the south (Finet 1975; 1979). Within the central complex debris was recovered clay cones with pierced ends (Finet 1979:93). As part of part of this extensive range of rooms is the East Temple, oriented west-east and situated in the north of the complex. This has a tripartite arrangement with a staircase room. The plan mirrors many found in Habuba (Strommenger 1979: Fig. 3; chapter **5.5.**) itself and is only distinguished by its larger size - measuring on the exterior 14.1 m east and on the west 15.7 m.

The second phase involves the 'North Temple'. Like the East Temple it too has a stair case room and is tripartite. The central hall measures 16 x 6 m and is decorated with alternate large and small niches (Finet 1979: 88). It is built at an angle to the central complex but follows the alignment of an earlier building on which it sits (Finet 1979: 90). The exterior wall measures 18.6 m (the east is 18.3 m because of erosion of 30 cm) x 16.4 m. The entrance was via a door in the west wall, later bricked up and replaced by an entrance in the south after a violent fire.

The final phase is the 'South Temple' which consists of one large room measuring on the exterior 14.4 x 10.3 m (Finet 1979: 90). The interior is decorated with wide niches separated with three vertical flutes sunk in the buttresses.

With the exception of the 'East Temple' which is oriented east-west, the long rooms all appear to be oriented North-South.

### 5.2.2.ii. Jebel Aruda

Located on a natural ridge 60m above the flood plain of the Euphrates, the site is roughly 2 hectares in extent, although it may relate to a larger unexcavated complex suggested by the excavator to exist on a higher spur (van Driel 1998; Fig. 8.). Like Habuba Kabira Süd, Jebel Aruda was founded on sterile soil and there are three phases of building (van Driel and van Driel-Murray 1983). The site was first levelled and terraced followed by two settlements organized around a monumental building, the 'Red Temple', on an artificial platform delimited by a wall of 2.3 m high decorated with niches. As at Habuba, Vallet (1998a: 83) convincingly posits that the well built houses of the surrounding settlement represent rectangular parcels of land (30 x 15 m each). The houses are mostly Mittelsaal in plan and constructed of Riemchen bricks.

In the second phase another monumental building, the 'Grey Temple' is built alongside the 'Red Temple' on an extended platform. In the final phase the monumental complex was filled in and raised to form an oval shaped platform, presumably for monumental structures. Many of the houses were abandoned in this phase before a major fire. The site was abandoned relatively soon after.

The southern monumental building, built with the first phase of construction, measures about 13m north-south, and 12m east-west, was constructed of red chalky (subsoil) mud bricks. The plan may have been tripartite (the eastern wall was not recovered) with a central hall and parallel rooms. The exterior was decorated with niches. What remained of the walls stood on a platform which was between 2 and 3 bricks higher, i.e., about 25 cms, than the surrounding courtyard. A high block-like 'altar' was built against the north wall of room 4 with steps on both sides and there was a higher threshold in the door to the northeast. The steps and altar, both of soft grey mud brick are secondary additions. Unexplained are shallow semicircular depressions on both sides of the three entrance doors. They were filled in later on, a fate shared by two deeper holes (for poles?) which were noted in the middle of the spaces between the doors.

A second building to the north, not completely recovered due to erosion, was made of grey mud bricks brought up from the river valley (van Driel & van Driel-Murray 1979). What remains are two entrance rooms from the west, a rectangular central hall with a small 'altar' against the south wall with a little room to the west, leading to a long room which occupies the complete length of the south side of the building. To the east there is a door from the central room to a subsidiary room. The pilasters on the outside were decorated with the same vertical grooves found in the southern structure.

The buildings rest upon an artificial platform consisting of an outer rim of bricks which has a greater thickness at the base than at the top though the outside is vertical. The interior is filled with stones. This platform may be a secondary development as the plaster on the temple walls continues below the lowest plaster found on the platform.
The outer wall of the courtyard, 2.3m high and decorated with niches, was about 20m west of the facade of the building. The courtyard and the surrounding enclosure wall was built of the same Riemchen bricks as the temple. Two gate houses have been identified (one has a line of rooms attached which are accessible only from the courtyard).

In the final phase of construction the whole complex was filled in with grey bricks and raised to form an oval shaped platform, presumably to support new monumental buildings. This was highly eroded but clearly heavily destroyed by fire.

### 5.2.2.iii. Sheikh Hassan

On the west of the site a large settlement wall of sun-dried mud brick 3m wide, was discovered in level 13 (Middle Uruk) (Boese 1989: 72). There are buttresses on the wall about 1.9 m broad, the niches are about 1.35 m broad and 60 cm deep. The sounding in area 1832 (I) revealed a wall jutting from the outer facade of the city wall towards the south. This is interpreted as the eastern flank of a tower or gate. Two parallel stone walls running parallel to and in front of the southern facade of the city-wall at a distance of about 1.5m and 2.5m may be an avant-mur or a support for the slope or glacis. One of the projections at the southern facade was coated by a stone facing which was preserved in three layers (Boese 1989: fig. 17).

The wall turns at right angles to the northeast in square 2130/31. Inside the wall at level 7 to 6 there are three monumental buildings (Fig. 9.). There are no drains or water channels. An intriguing structure abuts the city wall in the south corner (squares 2131 and 2132) (Boese 1995: Abb. 5). Built of mud brick, the outer walls are up to 1.5m thick. It consists of nine chambers with no doors. The chambers were plastered but clean of objects. It existed through 3 phases and each time was filled with soil and bricks, sealed and then rebuilt (Fig 10). A similar structure may be represented on a seal impression from Uruk (Fig. 21).

In Level 6 two walls consisting of stone rubble foundations and a mud-brick superstructure more than one metre broad were revealed in squares 1932/33, 1932 (II), 2032IV. These, together with the city wall form a room (Boese 1989:72). To the northwest along the city wall and abutting it in square 1933 was a building identified as a temple with walls some 60-70 cm wide (Fig. 11.). It is reconstructed as tripartite and has a central emplacement and a 'frying pan' hearth as found at Warka, Jebel Aruda and Habuba Kabira. It is thus closer in organization to a domestic structure. The central hall is approximately 7.5m long with a niche (Boese 1995: Abb.6).

A rectilinear building (Fig. 12) in 2132/33 and 2232/33 is built of mud brick walls approximately 0.5m thick with internal buttressing and a podium of bricks (similar to that at Gawra, e.g., level VIIIc), filled with snail shells (like the podium in the Red Temple at Jebel Aruda). Under it, in level 7, was a structure of rough stones.

In area 2132 III, at the western edge of the site, was of a structure built out of unusually large mud- bricks (22/23 x 43/44 cm) and continued far to the east. A minimum width of more than 4 m suggests some sort of terrace. By the next level 5 the terrace had walls annexed to it in the west and east. Another terrace in the northern part of the excavation (area 2033 II/III) was built from yellowish and greenish Riemchen-like mud bricks, some of them bonded with broad joints others packed in an irregular fashion. The clay-plastered facade of this structure had buttresses about 2.2m wide and niches about 70 cm deep and 1.65 m wide (Boese 1991a: 167). It is possible these two platforms form one large installation.

A tripartite building appears late in the Uruk period but a common three roomed building appears throughout which has close parallels with the domestic architecture of Jebel Aruda and Habuba Kabira Süd. The brick sizes were 6-9 x 12-13 x 26-30 cm, that is not Riemchen. However, level 5 revealed a wall built out of Riemchen-like mud bricks and more than 1 m broad.

### 5.2.2.iv. Hacinebi Tepe

The north east slope of mound saw construction of three substantial platforms. Each abutted its predecessor to form a series of terraces down the slope. Buildings on the highest (and earliest) level were removed by later construction. Six superimposed building levels were discovered on the middle platform. Mostly only stone foundations, lower massive structures gave way to smaller domestic ones. There was a mixture of southern and local ceramics. Few southern ceramics were found away from this area. Two dumps from the early building levels contain nearly all southern style ceramics. Wall cone fragments were also found in the area.

Operation 11 exposed a massive stone wall (wall 68) with a series of wide niches and buttresses on its east face. The wall is 3m wide at the base and is preserved to a height of over 3.3 meters. The wall is constructed of large rounded cobbles and angular pieces of limestone, thought by the excavator to have been quarried from the bedrock outcrop at the southern edge of the mound (Stein *et al*. 1996a: 90). The exposed portions of the east face were decorated with three buttresses and niches - two m. wide and 1 m. deep - which began 2 m. above the base of the wall. Ceramics associated with the earliest deposits at the base of the wall suggest it was built in the pre-contact (Early Uruk) phase A. There is little evidence that the wall served a defensive purpose since it is not oriented parallel to the southern edge of the mound; instead, it runs north-northwest for 10.5 meters before continuing into the north profile of ops. 11 and 12. No evidence for turns or intersecting walls was found along the east face of the wall. Nor were any parallel walls found contemporaneous with the early phases of construction. It is suggested that it may have formed part of an open air enclosure. Only the uppermost 50 cm of the west face of the wall has been exposed in Operation 12. The wall continued in use with substantial repairs additions and modifications up through the contact period. During phase A, east-west oriented stone wall 120 was built to the southeast forming an open area (possibly a gateway) with wall 68. This was later sealed off by an additional wall. The area to the northeast of walls 68 and 120 seems to have remained open for a long period, before the construction of massive mud brick and stone platform 111/121. The platform was constructed of mud brick on stone foundations and was preserved to a height of over 1.5m. Platform 111/121 fills the entire northeast quarter of the trench and extends 4.5 m. N-S and 5.5. m E-W, continuing into the north and east profiles. The platform was designed to run parallel to the east face of wall 68, forming a street 1.8 m. wide. The dating of the platform is uncertain. It is constructed on top of precontact ceramics phase A. The earliest deposit in the street running up against the base of the platform contains only Local Late Chalcolithic forms, with no evidence of Uruk types (it is suggested to have been built in early phase B before the beginning of intensive southern contact. BRBs and clay cones were associated with the abandonment of the platform in the later part of phase B. A series of poorly built single course stone and mud brick walls were constructed over the platform and ran up against niches and buttresses of wall 68. Uruk ceramics occur in association with Local Late Chalcolithic wares in this late building level. The platform is similar to the upper stone platform known in area A at the north end of the site which is also thought to date to early in phase B

Spatial distribution showed both Uruk and local ceramics are present over almost the entire area of Hacinebi but the vast majority of Uruk ceramics were restricted to the northeastern corner of the site where the appearance of the Uruk wares coincides with a major architectural reorganization. A massive 2.8 m high stone terrace wall was constructed and the area behind filled in with alternating layers of mud and pieces of angular limestone. A mud brick wall was built around the top of this raised platform. Uruk ceramics appear in the earliest deposits resting against the terrace wall and are absent from the deposits underlying the wall. A series of non-monumental rooms were built up against the base of the terrace platform. Both local and Uruk wares were present in the rooms and associated trash deposits on top of the platform terrace. Mortuary practices of child burials in jars in the rooms continue the earlier pre-contact (phase A) tradition. 9 phases were revealed on top of the platform. In all cases the buildings are oriented north-west/south-east parallel to the line of the terrace wall. The latest building levels are mostly mud brick. The earlier level buildings are well-planned, large stone structures. The earliest preserved architectural evidence on top of the platform is wall 71; a well-built stone wall with a rounded buttress in the SE corner and apparently part of a public building. The earliest refuse contain large amounts of Uruk pottery, and clay wall cone and a carved limestone eye idol. On the western side of operation 1, wall 10 (which is the same as wall 45 in operation 6) ceramics consisted almost exclusively of local Chalcolithic types. On the eastern side ceramics were almost entirely Uruk (4300 fragments of BRBs, from a single deposit 3 x 3 m wide). This concentration of Uruk materials in the northeastern corner is also reflected in evidence recovered from surface finds - a bulla filled with tokens and covered with impressions of two Uruk style cylinder seals.

BRBs and clay cones were associated with the abandonment of the platform in the later part of phase B. A series of poorly built single course stone and mud brick walls were constructed over the platform and ran up against niches and buttresses of wall 68. Uruk ceramics occur in association with local Chalcolithic wares in this late building level. Clay cones were associated with the abandonment of the platform in the Late Uruk. The plain , 'dimpled' and bitumen dipped wall cones (Stein *et al*. 1996a: fig. 8: B-D) find close parallels in the wall cones from the Uruk deposits at sites like Sadi Tepe 15 km to the south (Algaze 1989:281), and with those of Hassek Höyük and Samsat to the northeast (Stein *et al*. 1996b: 217).

### 5.2.3.i. Hassek Höyük

A small site, about 1.5 hectares in extent, built directly on virgin soil (Behm-Blancke 1991-2). It is roughly oval in shape with a complex of buildings surrounded by a wall 2.5 to 3 metre thick (Fig. 13.). A narrow gateway provided access to the settlement. In the south of the site was a thick walled building with external buttressing which has been interpreted as a temple. It has a tripartite arrangement of rooms with the central hall approximately 18m long (however, much of the structure was identified by tracing rather than excavation).

House 1 shows clear parallels with the Mittelsaal houses of Jebel Aruda and Habuba Kabira Süd although the associated fireplace is not the 'frying pan' or 'keyhole' type as seen at both of these sites but is rather a local Anatolian-style ocak.

Wall cones and stamped plaques for making cone impressions were associated with the destruction debris of level 5.

### 5.2.3.ii. Arslantepe

On the southwestern part of the mound were exposed period VII (Middle Uruk) levels built of large mud-bricks which could not be excavated over a wide area owing to later disturbance (Fig. 14). The remains suggest that the VIA (Late Uruk) monumental public building area could overlay a pre-contact period forerunner. This is supported by recent period VII discoveries in grid squares D6-E6 which have revealed a succession of thick-walled buildings, directly underneath similar-sized structures from period VIA (Frangipane 1993b). The building has walls up to 1.20 metres thick, a number of rooms, most decorated with red and black geometric designs on white plaster backgrounds (Frangipane 1991: Fig 6-7). All but one room which contained an oven, had mud brick columns built against one or other of the walls - these do not appear to have been structural. They may be similar to those found in the partially exposed structure in CH level 14 at Tell Brak (Oates, D. 1982a).

In level VIA a series of four public buildings were revealed. The earliest period of VIA saw the construction of a monumental gateway and associated storeroom complex known as building IV (*cf.* Frangipane and Palmieri 1989: Fig. 1; Fig. 15). An elaborate wall painting depicting a human figure positioned on some kind of rectangular seat with raised side parts was discovered on the end wall of the central room of this complex (A364 - Palmieri and Frangipane 1990: Fig. 5). Building I called a temple (A) because of the presence of a mud- brick basin, A84, built against the end wall of the long room A42. It was positioned between two niches and was flanked by a subsidiary bench (Frangipane and Palmieri 1988a; Palmieri 1978). A mud brick 'offering table' was also found in the middle of room A42. The complex includes a second 'temple' to the east 'Temple B (Frangipane 1997). This building is bipartite with a large cella almost 12 m long . Collapsed walls suggest an original height of 5-6 m. The cella like temple A had two simple niches on the long side facing the entry and contained two platforms. One had a slightly concave surface, flanked by a low bench, forming an altar. The other was larger and lower and backed onto the long wall in front of the windows and contained a large hole with wood inside. In the centre were two podiums with a slightly concave top arranged on the edge of a low rectangular hearth, slightly sunken in the floor. The walls of the buildings are about 1 m wide.

Southern style ceramics and southern influenced sealings exists in level IVA (chapter 4.1.2.iii.) but are far outnumbered by local Chalcolithic material. There are no tablets or cylinder seals carved in southern style and Arslantepe is clearly on the periphery of the Uruk world.

### 5.2.4.i. Tell Brak

The site was clearly important in prehistory with Ubaid and Uruk material recovered as much as 12 meters above the plain level (Oates, D. 1982b: 62). There is good evidence for contact with the south as early as the Ubaid (Oates and Oates 1994: 170). By the Middle Uruk southern-style pottery is present at the site (Matthews 1994: 178) and Late Uruk ceramics have been recovered over some 65 hectares of the mound along with local Chalcolithic material (Oates 1993: Fig. 39). The site was surrounded by eleven smaller settlements with Uruk ceramics, either representing the lower town or dependent settlements and representing an additional 45 hectares.

The best known building at Brak is the Eye Temple, excavated by Mallowan (1947) (Fig. 16). This building went through a series of reconstructions, the last two or three dating to the third millennium BC (Oates and Oates 1994: 170). However, the ancillary rooms to the east of the Eye Temple are considered to be contemporary with the Uruk shrine. They possibly represent the earliest example of ritual storage (Oates and Oates 1994: 170). This is not an obvious feature of public buildings in the Uruk world and may belong to a local Chalcolithic tradition (*cf.* associated temple buildings at Arslantepe 5.2.3.ii). Cone mosaic was found in the Eye Temple prehistoric levels (Mallowan 1947: 96, pl. VI.3).

Some 100 metres to the east of the Eye Temple, area CH revealed a part of the mound which had been continuously terraced and rebuilt on and left few genuinely in situ deposits. Better stratified sequences in TW are providing a guide to dating CH material. A numerical tablet and an earlier bulla with cylinder seal impression may possibly be Middle Uruk in date.

In area TW Phase 12 (Late Uruk) a small square (10 x 10m) revealed part of a large building built of Riemchen-like bricks, industrial debris of flint and obsidian and seventeen complete pots identical or similar to examples at Habuba Kabira Süd (Oates and Oates 1993: 171). However, the house lacked the frying pan hearths typical of Habuba, Jebel Aruda and Warka.

The extent of overburden, limited excavation and the problems of infill make the Uruk presence at Brak difficult to define. The Late Uruk levels have deposits of 2 meters. Riemchen-like bricks were found through the Uruk and post-Uruk levels (phases 9-12). In area TW no Chalcolithic material was found with Uruk material which may suggest a localised occupation of the site by Urukians (Lupton 1996: 59).

### 5.2.5.i. Susa

A 9 ha upper town was established during the Middle Uruk period on the remains of the buildings of Susa I. The lower town extended several hundred meters to the north and covered at least 25 ha. Evidence of larger buildings (Stéve and Gasche 1971) and administrative activities comes from the upper town (chapter *6.1.1.*). However, there may have been larger buildings in the lower town as well (Stéve and Gasche 1990). There is little evidence that the lower town was occupied during the Late Uruk period.

Both loose examples of *Tonstifte* and *Grubenkopfnagel* clay cones (see chapter 5.4.5.ii) were discovered on the Acropolis (Steve & Gasche 1971: 148 ff., Pl. 33) although the form of decoration may have its origins in the earlier (Susa A) non-Uruk platform which was faced with brick into which were set four rows of ceramic cylinders with flared, pierced heads 'clous' (Pollock 1989: 284).

### 5.2.5.ii. Choga Mish

The site was refounded in the late Middle Uruk period, when its upper town occupied the remains of the small fifth-millennium citadel of little more than a hectare, and its lower town spread over the low ruins of the early fifth millennium. During the Late Uruk, the lower town grew to cover at least 17 ha. On the southwestern slopes of the High Mound (M-N9) a chamber about 2.4 x 4.6m with walls over 3m thick was revealed (Delougaz & Kantor 1996: 27). It is presumed to be the lower courses of foundations. In the West Area (J-K14) a platform of very hard mud bricks extended over at least $350m^2$. It was a polygon of irregular shape. Two large projections to the east might be the remains of buttresses or towers (Delougaz & Kantor 1996:33). Any structures on the surface of the mound had been eroded.

Clay cones were scattered 'abundantly' over the surface of the site and in the Late Uruk strata. Some still retained red or black paint on their heads (Delougaz & Kantor 1996: pl. 31 S-T). Others were light buff or dark grey; many of the latter are large in size and have a central hollow for inlay (Delougaz & Kantor 1996: pl. 31 KK-LL). So far none have been found in situ.

### 5.2.5.iii. Godin Tepe

A Chalcolithic site (VI) has at its highest point a small Uruk settlement (V) behind a sun-dried mud-brick oval wall up to 1.5m thick surrounding approximately $550m^2$ (Weiss and Young 1975: 3). The clay for the oval was brought up from the lower level and constructed in a non-Uruk style. It was built on an abandoned area of the wider settlement although there is an early period V structure beneath the oval. Of the buildings recovered 4 rectilinear rooms of apparently independent structures were decorated with internal niches (or, more properly, *tokhches* which do not extend down to the floor, but end in a shelf) (Weiss and Young 1975; Young 1986; Fig. 17.).

### 5.3. Settlement layout

The most obvious feature of the Uruk sites is the enormous effort in organisation and labour that was required to create them. For example, Falkenstein (1939: 24 n.2) has calculated that the Anu ziggurat could not have been constructed by less than fifteen hundred people working ten hours a day for five years. The extensive excavations at Habuba Kabira Süd revealed a settlement that appears to have been planned in advance with a regular network of roads and well constructed buildings enclosed behind a well built city wall. The site is divided between a raised area for monumental buildings and a lower town. This organisation is also reflected in settlements on the Susiana plain. While the internal spatial arrangements of Susa and Choga Mish is far from understood, by the Late Uruk they seem to be organisationally similar in their overall spatial structure. The sites show a distinct separation between a smaller, upper town situated on the mounded remains of an earlier settlement and a larger newly founded or re-founded lower town. This arrangement is also present at Abu Fanduweh where a 4 ha. upper town was established on the remains of an earlier abandoned platform and a lower town extended to the north during Middle and Late Uruk times to cover an additional 6 ha or more (Johnson 1987; Wright 1998).

The process of urbanization, accelerated by the Uruk social ideology (chapter **6.3.**), resulted in numerous new Uruk settlements. Many like Habuba Kabira, Jebel Aruda, and Jerablus-Tahtani (Peltenburg 1999) were built on virgin soil. Even at Warka a deep sounding sunk down to the virgin soil in the main area of the Eanna district failed to produce anything earlier than material from the latest phase of the Ubaid and only from the Middle Uruk are there remains of monumental architecture. The first Eanna structures are built directly on the ground with the elevated area represented by the neighbouring Anu Ziggurat. During the Late Uruk, however, this situation was reversed when Eanna was increasingly extended on a series of platforms towards and above the terrace of the Anu Ziggurat (Nissen 1972). Within local Chalcolithic sites Uruk occupation favours abandoned tells (as in the Susiana Plain) or the highest point which clearly has significance (Godin Tepe, Hacinebi, possibly Tell Brak). Whether this was for strategic reasons and was settled through an aggressive takeover is problematic. There is limited evidence for conflict during the Uruk period and sites like Godin Tepe show direct continuity between local Chalcolithic and Uruk occupation (chapter 5.2.5.iii.).

The enclosure of the settlement is a feature of the Uruk world with settlement walls, often of enormous size (Abu Salabikh, Sheikh Hassan, Habuba Kabira Süd, Godin Tepe and Hassek Höyük). A fortification wall was also identified at Samsat in level XXIV of Late Uruk date (Mellink 1989: 114). Although settlement walls are known much earlier in the archaeological record of Greater Mesopotamia, e.g., Tell Maghzaliyeh (Bader 1993: 66), and Tell-es-Sawwan (Breniquet 1991), as well as a 'guard' tower, e.g., Choga Mami (Oates 1982), the scale of the Uruk constructions, such as the 20m thick wall at Abu Salabikh, suggests that they have something greater than mere defensive use and may have a strong symbolic value (Pollock *et al*. 1991: 64). The walls pursue predetermined alignments over a considerable distance, ignoring topography emphasizing urban planning. They isolate the site from the surrounding countryside. This isolationism is emphasized by walls surrounding the monumental architecture, setting them apart from the lower town such as at Warka (the Steinstifttempel and later precinct wall), Jebel Aruda and possibly also Tell Shmid on the southern plain (Adams 1981: 211). Eanna's precinct wall has a gateway surviving which parallels those of the settlement wall at Habuba Kabira. This close ideological association between the settlement wall and the enclosure of the monumental buildings is reflected in the buttress decoration on both, otherwise restricted to some, presumably important, domestic buildings (chapter **5.5.**). The fortifications may therefore have been primarily symbolic although the dangers from raids, real or imagined, meant that the walls were built on a scale with real defensive possibilities. City walls were thus symbols of civilization - props to a system of beliefs about how society should be properly ordered.

Within the settlement there are also groupings of houses with a specific organization. It is possible that these represent the allocation of parcels of land within which a formalized layout of space was constructed (Vallet 1998a; 1998b; Forest 1998; see chapter **5.5.**).

This high level of organization involved in the layout of sites like Habuba Kabira has been appreciated since the site was excavated (Strommenger 1980a), but the implications provide an important insight into the assumptions that the Uruk people made about their world which has not previously been considered. The emphasis is on planned order. The administration required to accomplish this, reflected in such objects as the Blau Monuments, will be discussed below (chapters 6.1-2).

## 5.4. Organisation of monumental architecture

### 5.4.1. Platforms

A feature of Uruk period settlements is the provision of a raised area for monumental architecture. This tradition has its origins in the Ubaid period which, on the limited evidence available, appears to be a tradition of the south. The best known example of platform architecture is probably at Eridu where levels XI-VI represents the continual elaboration of a mud brick platform (the earlier levels XVII-XVI represent domestic structures or levels XV-XII simple occupation levels). Resting on each of these is a monumental mud brick temple building. Of these, levels VII-VI are the best preserved and date to the end of the Ubaid period (Lloyd 1984; Safar *et al* 1983; Heinrich 1982: 28-9, Abb. 60-68).

Dating from the same period, the so-called 'Anu Ziggurat' at Warka (5.2.1.va) is formed from an irregularly shaped brick platform and consists of at least 12 rebuildings or refurbishings (Heinrich 1982: Abb. 78). Like at Eridu, these levels, together with associated temple buildings, continue to be constructed through the Uruk period. With the latest of the preserved prehistoric levels the facade of the platform is buttressed.

From the late Middle Uruk the Eanna precinct at Warka was provided with a series of platforms to support monumental structures. The process of enlargement and elaboration resulted at the end of the Late Uruk in a huge platform which abutted and overshadowed the neighbouring Anu ziggurat (Nissen 1972).

Other examples of southern platform architecture, decorated with wide buttresses are found at Tell Uqair (5.2.1.iii) and are possibly represented within the later platforms at Ur (5.2.1.iv) and Tell al 'Ubaid where under the Early Dynastic platform was a line of foundations in red sandstone, running at an angle of 45 degrees to the platform itself (Hall and Woolley 1927: 66). All appear to date to the Late Uruk.

Further to the east, Susa was possibly founded as a religious centre at the end of the Ubaid (Susa A Phase 4200-4000 BC) (Pollock 1989). A monumental platform (the *terrasse haute*), which was partially destroyed in the earlier excavation work of Morgan, is some 10 to 11 meters high and roughly 80 meters long and 65 metres wide (Pollock 1989: 284). As the interior has not been penetrated, it is not clear whether the platform is the result of one or of many periods of construction. This platform was built upon thin debris of the first settlement of Susa. Pollock (1989:284) suggests a surface area of about 5000 m2. The platform was faced with brick into which were set four rows of ceramic cylinders with flared, pierced heads ('clous') (also found at Jaffarabad and Bendebal). It was probably also recessed. At some time in its use the platform was destroyed by fire, its facade crumbling and covering over the adjacent cemetery area. After its burning it was left temporarily in disrepair, then rebuilt (Canal 1978). It was then destroyed again in the Terminal Susa A period (see chapter 4; Table 2).

Beyond the alluvial plain there is less evidence for platform construction before the late Early Uruk. At Tepe Gawra, for example, none of the large buildings, which are interpreted by some as temples, are associated with platforms. If, as seems likely, Gawra was abandoned during the early Middle Uruk (chapter **4**), the influence of platform architecture had yet to develop in a major form in the north east.

Along the line of the Euphrates, however, from the Early Uruk, a number of non-Uruk sites began to develop platform architecture. At Hacinebi Tepe a massive mud brick and stone platform in area 111/121 was constructed of mud brick on stone foundations and was preserved to a height of over 1.5m. In the Middle Uruk period the north east slope of mound saw the construction of three substantial platforms. Each abutted its predecessor to form a series of terraces down the slope associated with Uruk ceramics and wall cone fragments (Stein et al. 1996b).

In level II Tell Qalinj Agha a huge platform of mud bricks was constructed over earlier level III (Early Uruk) buildings (al Soof 1969) but the dating of this is very unclear and may be considerably later in date. However in the Early Uruk at Hammam et Turkman level VB stratum 7, debris from stratum 6b was leveled before the construction of a massive 1 metre thick mud brick terrace or podium that served as a foundation for a monumental building (Meijer 1988).

The creation of platforms to support monumental buildings appears to have its origins on the southern alluvial plains associated with religious architecture. During the Early Uruk a number of northern sites adopted this form which is probably due. at least in part, to the increasing economic contact and growth throughout the region. Such platforms would prevent buildings on the top from being seen except at a distance. The line of view would be restricted and help emphasize the isolation of the structure. This approach, developed for religious architecture, is adopted for buildings associated with the urban administration (chapter 7).

### 5.4.2. Orientation

There is a general orientation of the exterior corners of the monumental buildings and precincts to the cardinal points although the internal arrangement of rooms is not consistent and direction of access varies between buildings (this is consistent with buildings with different roles or different cults). The buildings listed in Table 3 represent those where sufficient evidence survives to reconstruct their internal arrangement. Nonetheless, some of these buildings are also extremely fragmentary and are dependent on reconstructions which cannot be confirmed. As a result, the buildings marked as 'fragmentary' may have had entrances facing directions in addition to those identifiable.

Interestingly the buildings at Jebel Aruda and Tell Qannas do not have their corners directed to the cardinal points but this may give a clue to the actual source of orientation. Both sites overlook the River Euphrates and are aligned to the river flow. Although major changes in the river flow pattern make precise evaluation difficult, buildings at many sites appear to lie with their axis parallel to the Euphrates.

Before the construction of the Tabqa Dam the Euphrates formed various channels in the region of Sheikh Hassan. This was probably the case also in antiquity and may account for the different orientation to Jebel Aruda and Habuba Kabira on the opposite side of the river. Further south the Uqair temple lies parallel to the river. At Warka the buildings may have overlooked the channel of the Euphrates that once cut through the centre of the settlement (Nissen 1972) separating the Anu Ziggurat from Eanna. Such orientation may have had symbolic meaning but equally represented a natural focus for the architectural plan. It is worth noting however, that in later literature, the Sumerians and Babylonians oriented themselves in relation to the 'four winds' of north, south, east and west (Geller 1999, personal communication).

At the edge of the Uruk world, the temples of Arslantepe show no specific orientation. Temple B long room lies on a NNE-SSW axis while Temple A bears no relationship, oriented NNW-ESE (see fig 5.14)

### 5.4.3. Standard Units of measurement

It has been long recognized that from the Ubaid Period there was a standard unit of measurement for monumental architecture (Frank 1975; Beale and Carter 1983, Kubba 1990, 1998, Forest 1991).

Frank (1975) analyzed a number of structures at Habuba Kabira and concluded that the ground plans were laid out using a linear unit of 49 cm. This was close to that used in later third millennium BC Sumerian, the kuš, a unit of *ca.* 50 cm. However, not all the interior dimensions of the rooms could be divided into complete units, many measurements were fractions of a kuš. Nonetheless, more than half the rooms exposed in Habuba Kabira's complex do measure out as non-fractional multiples of a 49 cm kuš. Beale and Carter's (1983) analysis of Tepe Yahya (level IVC) suggested a more reliable length of 72 cm. It is possible that this is related to the Sumerian kuš-gal or large cubit of 75 cm (Beale & Carter 1983: 84). Working on these findings Kubba analyzed the Ubaid architecture at Eridu and argued that the design and laying out of their important buildings were also based on a standard unit measurement of 72 cm. He also argues that the Ubaidians were familiar with numerous geometric principles such as the 3 : 4 : 5 and 5 : 12 : 13 triangles (Kubba 1990; 1998). The basic convention was that important buildings were planned and laid out from the outside in, from the faces of external walls to the centre lines of interior walls. This explains the apparent inconsistencies in the interior dimensions and proportions of some of the rooms. It is possible that by the Late Uruk both the 49 cm and 72 cm kuš measurement were in use, comparable to the dual lengths used in the later third millennium. The various methods of accounting developed by the bureaucrats of Uruk (see chapter **6.1.**) demonstrates that different systems were used for counting different objects. It is possible that the two lengths of kuš may reflect different building uses.

Applying the kuš measurements to the Arslantepe temples resulted in no clear evidence that either length was used in

| Site and Building | Orientation of central hall | Entrance(s) to central hall |
|---|---|---|
| *Eridu (_Ubaid temple sequence) | NE-SW | level 8   SE (fragmentary) <br> level 7   NW, SE, NE <br> level 6   SE |
| *Uqair | NW-SE | NE (fragmentary) |
| *Warka - White Temple (level D) | NW-SE | all sides |
| *Warka - White Temple (level B) | NW-SE | NW, SW, SE |
| Warka - *Kalksteintemel* | NE-SW | NW, SE (fragmentary) |
| Warka - Temple C | NW-SE | NW, SW, NE |
| Warka - Temple A | NW-SE | SW, NE (fragmentary) |
| Warka - *Pfeilerhaller* | NE-SW | all sides |
| Eanna precinct | | SW |
| Tell Qannas (north building) | N-S | W (fragmentary) |
| *Jebel Aruda (Red Temple) | N-S | W |
| *Sheikh Hassan (level 6, 2132-2232) | NE-SW | NW |

*Identified as temple buildings (chapter 5.1).

Table 3. Orientation of Uruk monumental buildings

the layout. This would therefore argue against a scheme adopted generally by architects and make it culture specific.

Tepe Yahya level IVC probably dates to the proto-Elamite period (Potts 1994: 72), that is post-Uruk, but the continuity in traditions following the end of the Uruk phenomenon demonstrates the strength of certain Mesopotamian traditions (see chapter 7).

### 5.4.4. Building Materials

#### 5.4.4.i. Stone and gypsum

Stone is an important element in the monumental architecture of Uruk sites in the south. At Warka, Eridu and probably Tell al 'Ubaid where, under the Early Dynastic platform, was a line of foundations in red sandstone, running at an angle of 45 degrees to the platform itself (Hall and Woolley 1927: 66) possibly relating to a late prehistoric structure (Delougaz 1940: 42), stone forms an important element. Much of the stone is locally available sandstones and limestones (Moorey 1994: 336). In the centre of the alluvial plain stone work was also found beneath plano-convex (Early Dynastic) bricks at Tell Adab (Bismaya) suggesting that materials were transported, presumably along the rivers. It may be an expensive version of the plaster that covers many building. It does not appear to be an essential element of monumental structures but provides waterproofing alongside bitumen and generally is found in foundations. It does however imply the ability to organize its acquisition and use in construction. After the fourth millennium the use of stone disappears in monumental buildings. Such elaborate use of stone is not found in the north associated with the excavated Uruk structures although stone is used for foundations (e.g., Sheikh Hassan level 6) and settlement walls, e.g., Sheikh Hassan (chapter 5.2.2.iii) and Samsat in level XXIV (Mellink 1989:114).

#### 5.4.4.ii. Mud Brick

In the Uruk period brick sizes with smaller proportions emerged. These were mass produced in standardized moulds producing a regular square cross section and known as Riemchen. However, the actual dimensions varied, perhaps to suite particular parts of a building. It is possible that the smaller size allowed two bricks to be handled together (Moorey 1994:307). Bricks were also baked in kilns for the first time when required for special purposes. The impression is of efficiency of construction and standardization of techniques.

Finkbeiner (1993: 166-68, § 3) provides a survey of the brick-shapes used at Warka through the later Uruk levels. Riemchen bricks of square section are the commonest in level IV. Riemchen vary in size from 16 x 6 x 6 cm up to 26 x 10 x10, the length to width ratio is never consistent although the cross section is always square. Rectangular bricks appear more rarely and for specific purposes, as in the use of large-sized mud bricks in terraces or small baked bricks in the water channels and basins and measure 80 x 40 x 14-16 cm to 40 x 20 x 8. Large-size Riemchen bricks persist through level III, but rectangular sectioned bricks were increasingly used.

At other Uruk sites Riemchen bricks are regularly used in construction of both monumental and domestic structures. Where local building practices (and perhaps by association, local workers) were used however, e.g., at Godin Tepe, Riemchen bricks do not occur (Badler 1998). This would indicate their cultural significance within the Uruk world. Interestingly, it is not until level 5 at Sheikh Hassan (Late Uruk) that Riemchen-like bricks appear (chapter 5.3.2.iii) suggesting that their use is a late development and could be used as a chronological marker.

### 5.4.4.iii. Bitumen

Bitumen is widely reported from Uruk sites, both as an element of the architecture (presumably generally for waterproofing) and as an item of processing/trade. This is not a surprise since it is a natural waterproofing for buildings and boats and is used extensively throughout Mesopotamian history (Moorey 1994: 332-5). There are numerous sources in southern Mesopotamia and the adjacent region of Khuzistan in southwest Iran. The most frequently cited source in secondary sources was that at Hit on the Euphrates but this may be a false assumption (Moorey 1994: 334). Associated products like asphalt were also available in the Zagros Mountains (Connan & Deschesne 1996: figure 4). The processing of bitumen is known in south Mesopotamia from the Ubaid period. For example, at Ur bitumen packed into baskets is suggested by Woolley (1956: 8). This tradition continued into the Uruk period when there is evidence of massive amounts of bitumen incorporated into the monumental buildings at Warka. At Abu Salabikh there is good evidence for the storage and processing of bitumen (see 5.3.1.ii). In the north bitumen is rarely ever reported from Local Chalcolithic sites. However, at Uruk sites in the region there is frequent references. Much bitumen is reported at Jerablus-Tahtani (Peltenburg 1999). At Hacinebi, bitumen was found in deposits with exclusively Uruk pottery (Stein *et al.* 1996b: 216-7). Some pieces were shaped and bore reed impressions on one side and the shape of the bowl container on the other. Another piece had the impressions of parallel wooden beams, perhaps from the waterproofing of a roof or raft. It was also used for lining large storage jars and at least one small juglet as found as residues in nine BRBs. It seems to have been brought in to site as blocks and then melted down. Bitumen is also known from Habuba Kabira (Connan and Deschene 1991 : 156) and Sheikh Hassan (Boese quoted in Stein *et al.* 1996b: 217).

### *5.4.5. Decoration*

#### 5.4.5.i. Buttresses and Niches

Sievertsen (1998) has provided a detailed analysis of buttress-niched buildings throughout Mesopotamia down to the Early Dynastic. During the Ubaid period external decorative buttresses appear at Eridu, Warka and Gawra (levels IX, VIII A-C) and both external and internal at Gawra (level XIII). In the Ubaid and Uruk residential as well as official buildings can be provided with both forms of decoration and appear as symbols indicating status. Whereas the public buildings were visually emphasized against the settlement by their size, some, but not all, were also marked out by the facade ornamentation. Many, but again not all, also possessed ample decoration in their courtyards and interior rooms.

It has been generally assumed that buttressing represents religious architecture (chapter **5.1.**). However, the fragmentary nature of many of the buildings means it is often difficult to determine whether particular walls (internal or external) have buttress/niches. There is little consistency in the internal organization of the monumental buildings and use of mud brick decoration. The *Steinstifttempel* does not have external buttressing, although it is surrounded by a buttressed precinct wall (5.2.1.vb). The later 'White Temple' at Warka (5.2.1.va), the Uqair building (5.2.1.iii) and Jebel Aruda's 'Red and Grey temples' (5.2.2.ii) all have external buttressing. This could therefore be an indication of religious architecture. Nonetheless, other buildings with external buttressing do not correspond in design to the temples, e.g., the *Kalksteintempel* and buildings D, F, G, and H, the *Bau mit den vier Salen* and the *Pfeilerhalle* at Warka (5.2.1.vb). The various designs could however be explained by suggesting these buildings were the focus for a variety of different cultic practices. Nonetheless, there is little to suggest that they were temples and would be better described simply as public architecture. There is also public architecture with only internal niching such as Tell Qannas (very fragmentary), and Sheikh Hassan (level 6). Vallet (1998a) argues that the Tell Qannas buildings fulfill the role of 'town hall', a meeting place for the élite. This is a convincing theory and could be applied equally to other Uruk sites where internal buttressing and cone mosaic (chapter 5.4.5.ii.) may rather reflect assembly areas rather than religious architecture.

In contrast the residential buildings at these sites show nothing more than simple interior room decoration which have been taken to indicate that these served a specific role in the reception of visitors (Forest 1998; see chapter **5.5.**). At Habuba Kabira a number of domestic units are distinguished by buttressing on the walls facing the central road. The niche arrangements may assign the individual buildings their position in a social hierarchy or highlight an important part of the roadway.

Buttressing is also a feature of late Chalcolithic monumental building: multiple buttressing occurs at Tell Hammam, level 5 (Early Uruk period). However, at Arslantepe (Late Uruk period VIA) there is no niching or buttressing associated with the temple buildings (chapter 5.2.3.ii.).

#### 5.4.5.ii. Cone mosaic

Closely associated with public architecture of the Late Uruk period is the use of thousands of baked solid clay cones, the sharp end embedded into thick plaster covering the mud-brick walls with the blunt end, usually flush with the surface of the wall and decorated with paint, inlay or impression. It is possible that the stone-cone mosaics decorating mud brick walls of monumental buildings at Warka and Eridu (Noldeke 1938: 28, pl. 34; Safar *et al.* 1981: 66, 81, 240, figs. 118- 19) were the forerunners of terracotta cones. Similarly, the use of 'clous' in Susa A platform may be related form of display (5.3.4.i). An alternative to cone decoration, though clearly related, was the use roundels of stone, pierced for suspension with copper wire, as at Merejib near Ur (Woolley 1939: 83). The main evidence for cone mosaic decoration comes from excavations at Warka where three main types of terracotta cone were recognized (Lenzen 1974; Finkbeiner 1993): those with blunt coloured ends (*Tonstifte*); various sized cones (many very large) with hollowed-out blunt ends (*Grubenkopfnagel*); and hollow, coarse-ware cones of clay, much like pottery vessels (*Tonflaschen*). It is argued that mosaic may have first appeared in the Late Ubaid period (Schmidt 1978:12) and survived in some form into ED I (Schmidt 1978: 12; Adams 1981: 211) but the majority fall into the late fourth millennium and are thus good archaeological 'fossils'.

It is possible that the patterns formed by the blunt ends of the terracotta cones (dipped in black, white or red, less often yellow or dark blue), derived from patterned rugs or mats hung as decoration on the walls of the earliest shrines (Moortgat 1969: 3). Moorey (1994: 310) suggests that there was a close connection between the use of the cones for decoration and protection of walls from erosion by wind and water. At Uruk and elsewhere terracotta fragments, particularly for corners, imitate patterns made by hollow-ended cones (Noldeke 1932: 32, fig. 19), whilst models illustrate facades with cone mosaic decoration (Noldeke 1937, pl. 48).

An Uruk building is suggested to have existed at Tell al 'Ubaid by the presence of baked clay cones and very small rectangular bricks, with circular holes. (Hall and Woolley 1927: 48-9, 51 ff., 153, pls. XIII. 6-7, XV.2). Indeed terracotta cones appear quite regularly in the surface surveys of southern Iraq and Khuzistan (Adams 1981:77). They have been found, for example, at sites like Larsa (Parrot 1968: 219-20, fig. 12), Telloh (Parrot 1948, 35-7, pl. 7b, p), and Mishmar, where clay cones were mixed with Uruk/Ubaid pottery and "part of a wall with clay cones in situ still stood above the surface" (Adams 1981: 211). In the survey of the southern plain, cones were found on the surface of eighteen sites, including the larger sites of Tell Shmidt (5 hectares); and Umm al-Aqarib (5 hectares) and WS 181 (5.8 hectares), where smaller cones lay on the area assumed to be the site of the public buildings of this settlement. The cones were found in heaps along the outer face of what may have been an enclosure wall. Cones also occurred on much smaller sites. "All possible variations in length and appearance were found, from cones 15 cm long with a hole in the head to cones only 5 cm long" (Adams 1981: 211).

Beyond the southern plain and Iran there is less evidence of coloured ends other than black bitumen (an important material within the Uruk world - see above). Of the 14 Uruk sites covered by this analysis cones were found at 10. But they are also known from sites that have been surveyed or have limited excavation where there is a clear presence of Uruk pottery, such as at Samsat (Mellink 1989: 114).

The widespread use of the cones has been taken as an indication of the presence of monumental religious buildings. Indeed Johnson (1973:105;1975: 319) connects the presence of cones on small village sites in Khuzistan to the presence of shrines. However, a survey of the monuments where cones are found in situ show that this connection is unsound. The buildings that may be identified as temples, (chapter **5.1.**) do not have cone decoration, although the Uqair temple had paint decoration possibly imitating cone mosaic and at Warka open mouth jars decorated the ramp leading to the White Temple and cone mosaic decorated the last casing of the Anu ziggurat (A3-A2) (Finkbeiner 1993: 4-6). However, many of the buildings with cone mosaic are open courtyards and hallways with multiple access. The fact however that they have been recovered at many Uruk sites suggest they represent an important part of the Uruk decorative scheme but are not *per se* indicators of religious architecture but rather are associated with particular parts of administrative complexes such as open assembly areas where the walls required a certain amount of protection. The Steinstifttempel may be the exception but the burnt stone cones were here used for waterproofing a building thought to be linked to the cult of a water deity (Matthews & Wilkinson 1991: 182; Boehmer 1990).

Possibly related to the wider spread of the Uruk culture are cones, made in local clay, discovered at Buto in the Egyptian Delta (von der Way 1992; Moorey 1994: 64-5), though there is no current evidence from these excavations for any associated Uruk material.

Perhaps associated with cone mosaic decoration are stamped plaques. They have been interpreted as protective devices for the courners of niche decorated buildings (Behm-Blancke 1989: Figs 3 and 4) or as templates for stamping cone impressions onto plastered wall. These have been recovered in south Mesopotamia at Warka (Jordan 1931: Pl. 19), Jemdet Nasr (Matthews 1992: Fig. 12: 8) and Uqair (Lloyd and Safar 1943: 155) and in the north at Tell Brak (Mallowan 1947: 12) and Hassek Höyük (Behm-Blancke 1989) found in destruction debris with clay cones.

Forms of mosaic inlay continue to be popular in southern Mesopotamia into the third millennium, e.g., at Tell al-'Ubaid set into bitumen with copper attachments (Hall and Woolley 1927). Cone mosaic, however, disappears with the end of the Uruk period and is thus a good archeological fossil for the period. The stone rosettes with stalks, probably for mounting on the walls of temples as found at Tell al-'Ubaid and Brak (Reade 1991: 27) are not related to the cone decoration and date to the Early Dynastic period.

### 5.4.5.iii. Paint decoration

There is limited evidence but wall painting in the Uruk world. Those from Eridu (5.3.1.ii) and Uqair (5.3.1.iii) suggests that the figured designs correspond closely with those on contemporary cylinder seals and carved stone vases (see chapter *5.6.2.*). The emphasis is on processions of humans and animals. At the local Chalcolithic site of Arslantepe, an elaborate wall painting depicts a human figure positioned on some kind of rectangular seat with raised side parts was discovered on the end wall of a central room A364 (Palmieri and Frangipane 1990: Fig. 5). According to Frangipane (1997: 64-66) this painting can be related to "the iconographic elements of an Uruk seal interpreted as a ritual threshing scene" (Frangipane 1997: Fig. 16: 2). It was thus a "re-elaboration of a number of elements of southern origin, particularly those with the greatest symbolic significance referring to power, used by a local élite with its own forms of expression. . . .they probably needed to refer to a number of values that were specific to powerful élites with which they strengthened their links and which clearly reinforced the legitimation of their power." A similar argument applies to the well known elements of Uruk iconography found in Egypt (chapter **7.7.**).

## 5.5. Domestic architecture

It is generally agreed that the classic layout of Uruk domestic buildings has its origins in the Ubaid period when a tripartite division emerges (with a 'T'-shaped or modified rectilinear central hall), the so-called Mittelsaal house (Roaf 1984).

Forest (1983b) has interpreted such buildings in terms of a division between the sexes, though other divisions are of course possible and valid, e.g. taboo activity/non-taboo activity, etc.. Whatever the correct interpretation of the social ideology embedded in the architectural plan of these buildings, it is clear that those traditions persist into the Uruk period where they are found in both monumental buildings and non-public structures.

Our understanding of Uruk period domestic architecture in southern Mesopotamia is limited to the H5 building at Eridu (chapter 5.2.1.ii). Further north, the most extensive remains come from Habuba Kabira and Jebel Aruda. At Habuba most houses have an average area of 300m$^2$ consisting of a middle hall house and a courtyard complex apparently divided into two parts: a more public one around the courtyard and a more private one (Sürenhagen 1986: 18). Frying-pan style fire places were found in most house, mirroring those found in buildings at Sheikh Hassan (5.2.2.iii) and Warka (5.2.1.vb).

Examining the variety of structures, Vallet (1998b) has proposed a basic three roomed building with one long hall from which basic theme there are a number of variations (Fig. 18). The same basic design is found at Sheikh Hassan where tripartite units only appear late in the sequence (Fig. 19).

Vallet (1996; 1998b) argues that Habuba Kabira was divided into regular parcels of land on which were constructed a tripartite building (or a variation) which he suggests is a reception area alongside a domestic unit and an open space (Vallet 1996: Fig. 6). Forest (1998) comes to similar conclusions in his study of the non-public buildings at Jebel Aruda where he argues that the layout represents the emergence of new ideas developed from the Ubaid architectural predecessors. He suggests that the organization of Ubaid house was focused on the occupants but claims that in contrast the Uruk houses provide a new complex of rooms as a reception area for visitors. The domestic part of the house is therefore isolated. These arrangements are expressed by the perspectives of openings into the building, the provision of many doorways into the reception room, and the placing of wall niches in the reception area. Forest concludes that the Urukians were interested in non-family members and social appearances.

The major difficulty with Forest's interpretation is the identification of the niched rooms as a specifically reception area (Tunca 1998). In addition niches do not occur in all buildings. Nonetheless, houses do follow a pattern of design which suggests common concerns about accessibility and internal organization (albeit with variations) as well as a common size and structure of families and dependents. There were thus mechanisms of ideological integration in the architecture. While there is certainly individualism in many of the structures a certain order was maintained. Returning to Vallet's (1998a; 1998b) arguments that the planning of both Habuba Kabira and Jebel Aruda involved the allocation of parcels of land, together with the erection within it of a particular arrangement of buildings, this may relate to the self contained enclosures at Abu Salabikh which are suggested to have housed co-resident extended families (Postgate 1983; 1992:91). Society may therefore have been based on kin-based residential groupings organized either from above or from within through the power of social convention.

A number of houses are distinguished by external buttressing at Habuba Kabira (Vallet 1996: 57). The walls face into the main road and so either mark a significant point in the road or distinguish the building, perhaps highlighting a high status owner. If this is an indication that the society was hierarchical, the house owners nonetheless maintained the same internal organization of their homes as elsewhere at the site.

## 5.6. Associated indicators of a common ideology

### 5.6.1. Pottery and food

The Uruk period witnessed the emergence of new forms of pottery. With a few exceptions, there was a disappearance of decoration together with the introduction of many new shapes (chapter **4**). Ceramic production is generally conservative, the disappearance of old forms and the introduction of new ones may imply the introduction of new foods and drinks, techniques of food and drink preparation and approaches to storage. It may also be related to changes in technology and social developments. Pottery was less subject to political and cultural manipulation than objects like seals, so sudden changes between phases are not likely.

Early Uruk was typically red or grey burnished although a northern variety was painted. During the Late Uruk period there were changes in ceramic production. Updraught kilns were typical but shallow clamps were also used. Hand-painted decoration was dropped in favour of rapidly incised designs or simple plainware. Many vessels were grit-tempered and thrown on a wheel although others were handmade. New types included conical beakers, tall jars with short spouts, droopy-spouted jars and globular storage jars with perforated vertical lugs, sometimes with burnished red slip or incised decoration.

This new technology produced new ceramic shapes and created additional techniques of manufacture such as ceramic ring scrapers possibly used to thin down vessel walls after throwing (Alden 1988, but for alternative views see Barrelet 1968). It is argued by Alden (ibid.) that the widespread adoption of this innovation is related to the development of centralized workshop production and regional distribution. Indeed, Sürenhagen (19784/75: 89-90, 95) concludes that most of the ceramic production at Habuba Kabira was the work of professional potters. Wright and Johnson (1975) argue that fourth millennium economies were characterized by a high degree of specialization and certainly potters are listed among other specialists in the Late Uruk Standard Professions List from Warka (Nissen 1986: 329). Potts (1997: 153) thinks that "the sophistication of most of the Late Uruk pottery repertoire and the difficulty of achieving many of the forms by which it is characterized, such as composite vessels with high, carinated shoulders, nose lugs, spouts and strap handles, not to mention the use of the wheel argue strongly against the possibility of large scale household production". However, the concept of household could include the extended units with specialists serving a number of these (see chapter *3.2.1.*) - a survey of pottery production on the Uruk Mound at Abu Salabikh shows it was distributed throughout the settlement but with concentrations in certain places (Pollock *et al.* 1991).

But why the need for standardization? Production costs and streamlining of efficiency are modern concerns but an increased population focused within an urban environment (chapter **6.3.**) would have required a more concentrated supply of resources. This would, however, have not necessarily encouraged standardization of form visible across the Uruk world (regional variation between regions would probably have been likely as is evident in the local Chalcolithic ceramic tradition - chapter *4.1.2.*). However, the widespread use of similar forms suggests that pottery played a significant role in the Uruk approach to life.

Eating and drinking vessels are used to categorize people, their contents and the events at which they appear. "The matching dinner service shows our wealth and the formality of the occasion, the status of the host and guest - as do the different types of glasses on the table" (Barley 1994: 71). Appropriate pottery is assigned according to the qualities of food, user and event, and so transmit messages about participants and the relationship between them.

The distribution of Uruk pottery suggests it was part of the Uruk social ideology, where foreign, i.e., non-Uruk forms were rejected in favour of locally produced Uruk style vessels. This is especially clear within the local Chalcolithic regions of north Mesopotamia. At Habuba Kabira there *is* pottery of non-Uruk type, mainly containers of Amuq F chaff-faced ware which in some cases contained remains of grain and, probably, dried out oil (Sürenhagen 1986a: 21) but this represents a tiny percentage of the vessels recovered, all of good Uruk typology. At Middle Uruk Tell Brak surveys show that local Chalcolithic and southern style ceramics are found across the entire site as well as over a number of outlying mounds (Oates and Oates 1993: 183, fig. 39), although by the Late Uruk (Phase 12) southern vessels are found only over the main mound. In area TW (Phase 12) of the main mound no local Chalcolithic material was found together with Uruk ceramics. This was a limited investigation in a square 10 by 10m but might suggest that Urukians were living in a specific part of the site (Lupton 1996: 59). A similar pattern of occupation is proposed at Hacinebi (5.2.2.iv) where on the western side of operation 1, wall 10, ceramics consisted almost exclusively of Chalcolithic types while on the eastern side ceramics were almost entirely Uruk.

At Godin Tepe however there was an incomplete Uruk assemblage. This has been explained by the utilization of local village potters to reproduce selected Uruk pottery types, and the lack of demand for certain Uruk domestic vessels due to the possible absence of Uruk women at Godin (Badler 1998). The attempts by Local Chalcolithic potters to produce specific forms here suggests their importance in the life of the Urukians at Godin (surely using local wares would have been easier and more convenient!). Thus the pottery distribution suggests that at sites in the north Urukians lived very differently to the local Chalcolithic people around them. Their demand for specific ceramic forms is also reflected, or conditioned, by differences between themselves and the locals in food preferences.

Human food selection is always associated with, and partly shapes, complex systems of norms, rules and representations which cannot be necessarily related to anything biologically functional (Fischler 1981). The human mind shapes, categorizes and tends to force reality into them. Notions of purity and pollution - and consequently the borderline between edible and non edible - are rooted in a culture's specific social ideology. With urbanization (chapter **6.4.**) it is possible that an increasing number of people had become mere consumers, that is they consume food they have not helped produce, or even seen produced. As a consequence their perception of food was modified.

Studies of fourth millennium faunal remains is limited but it is possible to see an emphasis on specific animals. During the Uruk period in southern Mesopotamia as well as southwestern Iran and the Hamrin there was a heavy use of caprids (Pollock 1999: tables 4.6 and 4.7). This emphasis on sheep and goat may be a sign of a growing importance of secondary products, such as milk, wool, and hair which is also reflected in the Uruk ceramic repertoire and iconography (chapter 5.6.2.i.).

At Hacinebi local Chalcolithic faunal remains indicate a fairly diversified herding system (caprines 45%, pig 32% and cattle 20%). In contrast caprines form 83% of the sample in the Uruk deposit, with only small amounts of pig and cattle present (Stein *et al*. 1996b: 258-60). This pattern fits closely with the evidence from Tell Brak where sheep represent 75% of the animal remains analyzed from area TW (with 10% cattle and 5% pig) (Oates 1998). At Habuba Kabira the percentage of cattle is more substantial (37%) but sheep still represent the most numerous animal (62%) (Pollock 1999: table 4.7). These figures do not necessarily reflect eating preferences as much as the basis for the Uruk economy and geographical conditions favouring particular species.

Crops form another important part of the diet. Archaeobotanical data on plant use is very limited and, as pointed out in chapter *3.1.1.*, there is little evidence for a difference in plant cultivation between the late fourth and third millennium BC. One of the chief crops was probably barley which appears to be confirmed in the archaic texts from Warka where quantities of up to 135,000 litres of barley beer are mentioned (Nissen *et al*. 1993: 36). Analysis of beer residue on ceramics from Godin Tepe suggest that it may have been produced there or was brought in (Michel *et al*. 1992).

The cultivation of grapes is also suggested from the remains found in Late Uruk period levels at Kurban Höyük (Miller in Marfoe 1986: 88) and grape seeds have also been recovered from archaeobotanical remains at Hacinebi Tepe (Miller 1994: Table 1) but it was not possible to tell if the seeds were domesticated or wild. Recent discoveries of grape residues have also been made on southern ceramics from Godin Tepe and Warka (Badler et al 1990; Michel, *et al* 1993).

Many of these products were new developments and their storage and transport is reflected in the shapes of Uruk vessels. Using the archaic texts from Warka, Potts (1997:139-150) has suggested possible correlations between vessel shape and contents. Delougaz (1954) first suggested that the depictions of vessels on the texts stood for particular liquids and were graphic representations of the containers which held them. In many cases these had spouts so that the liquid could be decanted, flat bases so that the vessel could sit securely and high shoulders tapering to a slender base, perhaps so that the vessel could easily be held while pouring.

No doubt the most important liquid in the Uruk world was water (see 5.4.5.ii.) and this may have been stored in the tall bitumen lined vessels or in a type of 'water bottle' still in use today in parts of the Near East (Strommenger 1980: Abb 25 and 26). The second most important liquid was probably beer. The sign for beer (kaš) in the archaic texts is a straight-spouted vessel, and variations in the vessel form in the texts as well as cylinder seals may well reflect different varieties (Szarzynska 1969:16-24; Baudot 1978-79:5-67).

Milkfat is generally represented in the Archaic texts by a straight-necked vessel without a spout, although one of the signs used for it may include either a spout or a strap handle (Potts 1997: 143). Milk production began around 4000 BC (perhaps earlier, see Renfrew and Bahn 1991: 264). It is marked by a new range of closed pottery vessels, including butter churns. Thus the cattle scenes with milk vessels in Late Uruk glyptic (chapter 5.6.2.i. and 5.6.2.ii), along with signs for milk and its by-products in the Archaic texts is part of the emergence of new food types, distribution and associated messages. Among the Archaic texts from Uruk is a small group of approximately eight documents which, with one exception, "seem to record exclusively measures of liquid goods, in all likelihood animal fats and milk products" (Englund 1991: 101-4). One of the Archaic signs which has been identified with Sumerian *ga*, 'milk' (Green and Nissen 1987) occurs on Late Uruk glyptic as well (Sherratt 1981: 281)

Oil is another product represented archaeologically, e.g., as residue at Habuba Kabira and Jebel Aruda and also appears in the Archaic texts where the Sumerian term *dug šagan* is represented by a pointed vessel (Potts, D. 1997: 147-8).

The standardization of ceramic types is perhaps best demonstrated by the hand made bevelled rim bowl (BRB). Much ink has been devoted to interpreting the role of this vessel. Nissen has pointed out the similarity between bevelled rim bowls and the sign for 'cereal ration' (*ninda*) in the Archaic texts and the presence of the same sign as part of the pictogram $GU_7$ meaning 'ration/distribution' (Nissen *et al*. 1993: 15). They would have been employed for the allocation of food rations, "and was frequently discarded immediately after use, like the aluminum foil containing a modern take-away meal" (Reade 1991: 24).

Less widely accepted ideas include their use in the separation of curds and whey (Delougaz 1952), created as bread moulds (Millard 1988; Chazon & Lehner 1990), as salt containers (Buccellati 1990), or used as food bowls at large banquets held by the Uruk aristocracy and discarded after each meal (Forest 1987). Generally rejected in favour of the ration bowl theory is Beale's (1978) idea that they served as presentation bowls - "a means of presenting, on special occasions, a token amount of some commodity, probably most often grain, to the gods or a priest-king". This suggestion, however, might be demonstrated by the relief on the famous Warka Vase where a procession of naked men (priests?) apparently bring offerings, perhaps in BRBs to the temple of Inanna (Fig. 29). In the top register, one of the figures standing on the back of a bull, perhaps within the temple, appears to be holding a stack of BRBs as so often found crammed by their hundreds into pits, e.g., at Choga Mish (Delougaz and Kantor 1975: 97).

Archaeologically it is also known that BRBs were used to store and transport bitumen (chapter 5.4.4.iii.). This might suggest multiple uses within the Uruk world. The standardization of their shape and form (Johnson 1973, but see criticisms by Beale 1978) and the mass production mirroring that of wheel-made pottery suggests that they formed an integral part of the social ideology of the Uruk world and their distribution is solid evidence for long-distance similarities. Beale (1978) suggests that they were produced in households but this is rejected by Potts on the ground that they are too uniform in appearance (Potts 1997: 153). As with the production of more specialized ceramics, this could have been achieved with augmented families (chapter *5.6.1.*). Whether for presentations, allocations or transportation the BRBs' varied use and cheap and easy form of manufacture ensured their adoption beyond the Uruk world (e.g., at Hama) and their possible survival (at Tell Brak) following the collapse of the Uruk phenomenon (Oates 1993: 405; chapter **7.7.**).

### 5.6.2. Images of ideology

In their representations on seals and ceramics, both pre-Uruk and Uruk peoples chose to focus on certain natural features. Jacobsen (1976) argued that the attributes of Mesopotamian deities, at least as far back as the fourth millennium, related to these forces and features of nature. This overwhelming concern, especially where they concerned agricultural fertility, stemmed from the society's fundamental dependence on agricultural production (chapter **2**). He considered that each Mesopotamian perceived the cosmos as a state in which "he is caught in the interplay of giant forces", but that "he saw the cosmos as order, not anarchy" (Jacobsen 1946: 127). It was the duty of humans, and particularly the communities' leaders, as the god's representative, to maintain that order. The world was thus "a battle-ground of opposing powers" (Frankfort 1970: 29). It perhaps comes as no surprise that the forces of chaos are represented by the Mesopotamians as elements of the natural world and, much less frequently, the mythical world of strange animals, which threatened the agricultural urban society - wild animals and the wilderness in which the creatures lived.

The earliest texts from the beginning of the third millennium BC suggest that the polytheistic religion of the historic period was already formulated (chapter **3**). It is also clear that throughout the three thousand years of Mesopotamian history these ideas were constantly being reformulated to account for political, economic and social developments (Jacobsen 1976; Leick 1991; 1994; Livingston 1986). However, many stories survive in the cuneiform texts which present a mythology where the facets of civilization were believed to be divinely inspired and to have been gradually introduced by various deities or, in another tradition, the task of teaching mankind the achievements of culture was ascribed to Seven Sages (Leick 1991: 151)

Thus in the Sumerian myth of Lahar and Ašnan/Cattle and Grain, the Annunaki (senior gods) had to eat grass like sheep and drink water from a ditch before the grain and cattle goddesses were created and the gods were able to drink milk. Humans are then introduced to agriculture and animal husbandry to feed the gods (Leick 1991:109). A similar idea of the primordial world is envisioned in 'Ninazu and Ninmadu' where people eat grass like sheep before the gods bring grain to Sumer from the *kur* (here representing the countryside) (Leick 1991: 129). Alongside the control of nature for agriculture, the Sumerian texts emphasize civilization as literally life in a city and this is often most strongly expressed when the city was contrasted with the uncivilized world - the steppe land, desert and mountains; the homes of nomads (Brüschweiler 1983; Mieroop 1997: 42-61). Thus the great city of Agade falls prey to the mountain dwelling Guti (Kuhrt 1995: 56) and the Ur III empire collapses due to the uncivilized Amorites 'who know no house, nor town.... who does not bend his knees (to cultivate the land), who eats raw meat, who has no house in his lifetime, who is not buried after his death' (Roux 1980: 166).

In the Sumerian tales of Enmerkar and Lugalbanda the heroes confront a foreign power called Aratta but this is conceived in the same terms as Sumer itself and is not seen as fundamentally different; a ruler living in a city worshipping the same goddess, Inanna. Yet the threat to this way of life was always present and the antithesis between the city and desert is found in the stories of Gilgamesh, hero of the ancient city of Uruk. In a Sumerian tale Gilgamesh and his servant Enkidu confront and defeat the demon Huwawa who lives beyond the city in the forests of the Zagros (George 1999: 149-166). In the later Epic of Gilgamesh, the role of Enkidu has changed and he now represents the wilderness, an equal opponent to Gilgamesh, who has to be 'civilized' through sexual intercourse by a representative of Inanna, the city's patron goddess, anointed with oil, and dressed like a man before fighting the predatory lion (Leick 254-256).

Thus Enkidu faces the most hostile of threats to a civilized man and woman, the lion. The theme of hero battling lions reappears again and again through Mesopotamian history represented most famously in the first millennium BC lion hunt reliefs of the Neo-Assyrian king Ashurbanipal from Nineveh (Reade 1998). The association between monarch and lion was even adopted and revised during the Crusades when the lion became not the opponent but the symbol of kingship of western monarchs (Dalley 1984: 168). This confrontation with the wild during the third millennium onwards takes its most obvious form in the so-called combat scenes carved on cylinder seals. They developed from the late fourth millennium examples (see below) but now involve humans and increasingly bull-men in the struggle with wild beasts (Collon 1987: 197).

Although the dangers of retrojection have already been highlighted, an analysis of Uruk imagery confirms that this antagonism between the city and the wilderness outside the walls is a central aspect of the late fourth millennium social ideology.

### 5.6.2.i. Seals and sealings

The functional role of seals and the implications for understanding the role of Uruk ideology will be discussed in chapter **6.1**. However, regardless of whether their use and imagery reflects a strongly centralized and administered economy or a more decentralized, household-based organization, the images that appear in the Uruk glyptic and sculptural art provide an important insight into the assumptions that the Uruk people made about their world. The fact that the message remains not only consistent across a wide geographical area but apparently unaffected by foreign traditions indicates that they were more than just a representation of reality, if at all, but rather a representation of an ideal (Matthews 1997: 191-2; chapter **7**).

### a. Animals

The stamp seals of the pre-Uruk period emphasized sheep and goats though whether these were viewed as wild or domesticated is unclear. Dogs appear frequently suggesting a control mechanism for the animals being farmed. More infrequently wild animals in the form of gazelle, deer, onager and pig are depicted (Amiet 1980).

In the Middle and Late Uruk periods there are changes in the emphasis and structure of animal representations. Sheep and cattle are now presented as clearly domesticates associated with humans and structures (pens, houses). Wild lions, pigs, deer and fish, also appear regularly, often in banks and rows (Amiet 1972: pls. 56-77). The whole of nature was thus shown as more domesticated and ordered and this order could be represented repeatedly by rolling the cylinder seals. Some of the larger seals are also decorated with knobs dowelled into the top which are in the shape of animals cast in copper (chapter 3.4.1.iii.).

There are a number of common images and, although the details vary, the overall message appears to be the same.

### b. Animals, temples and divine symbols

Processions of animals to a temple (Amiet 1980: pl. 23, nos. 385-395). The rectangular structures on these seals are generally interpreted as representing the niching and buttressing of monumental buildings (chapter 5.4.5.i.). Their association with the divine is indicated by the symbols of the gods (ring pole and ring-pole with streamer) the latter associated with the goddess Inanna of the historic period (Collins 1994). Animals move towards or away from the building (depending where the one starts to 'read' the seal). These may represent the temple flocks or animals brought to the temple as part of offering/tribute or the animal attribute of the deity. Other seals emphasize the association between animals and specific deities/temples where they are shown with the divine symbols (Fig. 22; Amiet 1980: nos. 618-335). The animals appear to be domesticated varieties.

### c. Wild animals

Wild animals are shown together or attacking domesticates (Amiet 1980: nos. 412-416). More rarely, a wild animal, such as a lion, is attacked by a cow (e.g. Amiet 1980: no. 1612). Only in the early third millennium does the lion attack frontally and man intervenes. (Collon 1987: 185-6, no. 885).

### d. Humans

Pre-Uruk seals depict composite human animal figures often grasping animals. In Susa these are particularly elaborate, grasping snakes or lions (Amiet 1980: nos. 117-120). They are often apparently engaged in various activities with other similar figures (Amiet 1980: nos. 121-123). These creatures have been interpreted as priests or deities. Seals from Gawra have humans with horns on their heads (e.g. Amiet 1980: no. 40) or figures surrounded by caprids.

In the Uruk world the so-called 'priest king' appears to replace this figure (Amiet 1986: 60; 1993: 24). He is depicted fully human and identified by his beard and specific outfit of broad head band or cap and net-like skirt which reaches either to his knees or his ankles. He is naked from the waist up although he can be depicted completely naked in sculpture (see below). When he appears it is normally on finely cut seals but there are exceptions (e.g., Amiet 1980: pl. 45, nos. 645-51). The 'priest-king' undertakes a variety of activities which suggests his importance (Schmandt-Besserat 1992: 176-7) often within a ritual context - leading processions to temples with offerings by land and boat (Fig. 23; Amiet 1980: pl. 46, no. 655). He feeds a variety of plants to animals, often on seals from Warka in association with the standards of Inanna (Amiet 1980: nos. 636-641)

The 'priest-king' is also shown involved in conflict. On two sealings from Warka he appears in front of a number of bound humans who are apparently being beaten or driven forward by other figures wielding sticks or whips. The 'priest-king' holds a staff or spear (with point down) (Fig. 31.). Two sealings from Susa depict him holding a composite bow in two instances aiming arrows at opponents some of whom he has shot and some are shown falling off the roof of a two-tiered 'temple' building. (Fig. 30)

Humans, not distinguished by a particular costume, are also shown engaged in procession towards temples (Figs. 5.19 and 5.20; Amiet 1980: pl. 46, nos. 656-658). Interestingly, the grid-like structure in Fig. 21 parallels the building found at Sheikh Hassan level 6 (chapter 5.2.2.iii.). Similar rows of figures are depicted on the smaller 'Jemdet Nasr' seals (chapter *6.1.1*.). They are shown moving in procession holding 'standards' including that of the goddess Inanna (Fig. 27. far right). The pig tailed figures on these seals, often interpreted as females appear to be undertaking various activities such as weaving or pot making (e.g. Fig. 24). They squat down and many of them parallel votive figurines suggesting these activities are part of a symbolic, religious, role. Such figurines have been found at Brak, Uruk, and Susa (Figs. 5.24 and 5.25).

There are a few seals/sealings where humans interact with wild animals (e.g., Amiet 1980: nos. 239-40, 602-609). In these the humans grapple with mythical animals or hunt wild animals in the marshes.

5.6.2.ii. Sculpture

In historic times "all Mesopotamian statuary was intended for temples; the human form was translated into stone for the express purpose of confronting the god" (Frankfort 1970:45). Most of the images have been recovered from public architecture. This is therefore not popular art. Even relatively common stones in Mesopotamia, like gypsum and limestone, were overwhelmingly employed just for statuary for use within the temple or court. It is a significant phenomenon at Uruk, not again paralleled until the first millennium BC in the north

The 'priest king' who appears on cylinder seals also appears on relief sculptures and works in the round. A large basalt boulder was utilized at Warka to depict two 'priest kings' (or the same man with different weapons) killing lions with a spear and arrows (Noldeke 1934: 11-12, pls. 12-13; Borker-Klahn 1982: nos. 1-3). This relief is similar to another of the same date (Curtis 1986). The stone possibly came from the Syrian Jezirah (Moorey 1994: 24), perhaps having been carried to the south by the Euphrates rather than brought or traded.

A number of other images of the 'priest-king' sculptured in the round have been recovered. The provenance of Fig. 28 in the Louvre Museum (25 cm high) and a very similar example in Zurich (Orthman 1975: fig. 11b) is uncertain. However, his nakedness, unlike on seals, suggests purity and perhaps a priestly role since nudity distinguished some priests in the historic period (Black and Green 1992: 150; Reade 1991: 30, fig. 34., 28, fig. 32). It is equally possible that the sculptures decorated a religious area which required nakedness rather than indicated a specific role (see Warka vase below). A finely made alabaster head and upper torso of the 'priest-king' (18 cm high) wearing the head-band and beard was discovered at Warka (Lenzen 1960: 37f.; Orthman 1975: fig. 10). A similar figure is shown on the Blau Monuments, two tablets, made of a slate schist, named after a previous owner which seem to form a pair. Their provenance is unknown and their use and meaning is not fully understood. They may record a transaction in which land was exchanged for various goods with the carved figures representing the individuals involved (British Museum WA8620-1; Gelb *et al* 1991: 39-43, pl. 11, 12; Collon 1995: 51, fig. 34). As on seals, the 'priest king' appears to holds a vase and an animal as if making an offering.

Female figures have also been interpreted in the sculpture of the Late Uruk period. A large head from Warka made of limestone (Ht. 21.2 cm) may have been part of a composite statue (Collon 1995: 50, fog. 32). Dated by style, a statuette from Khafajeh depicts a woman with bare torso and hair hanging down her back (Frankfort 1970: 32, fig. 21). Women also feature as small, possibly votive figurines, such as Figs. 5.24 and 5.25 from Susa, and as tiny amulets, often found in deposits within the public architecture. The amulets are shown in a similar posture to the small figurines, that is kneeling, perhaps engaged in ritual activity or praying (Collon 1995: 52, fig. 35c).

The majority of amulets, however, represent animals (Behm-Blancke 1979; Spycket 1981: 39 ff.). They are made of variously coloured limestones and calcites, as well as sandstone and darker soft stones like steatite, serpentine, and chlorite as well as shell. They come from numerous unidentified sites as well as Warka, Susa (Harper *et al.* 1991992: 58-67), Tell Brak (Weiss 1985: nos. 44-47; Reade 1991: 25, fig. 26) and Habuba Kabira (Weiss 1985: 110, no. 28). Some appear to have functioned as stamp seals since they have simple drilled designs on the base, also representing animals but impressions have not been found. Shallow holes on the surfaces of many were inlaid with colour. The animals represented are generally wild varieties, for example, bears, fish, lions, frogs and hedgehogs.

Images of animals, especially domesticates are common in sculpture, for example, a stone bull, with inlaid flowers (Orthmann 1975: taf. 18) and head of ewes from Warka, one made of sandstone (Frankfort 1970: 28), the other of terracotta (Reade 1991: 14, fig. 13). A gypsum trough from Warka (British Museum WA120000) is carved in low relief with processions of ewes and rams towards a reed building decorated with the symbols of the goddess Inanna. This is clearly a ceremonial object as to view the scene the trough would be too high for practical use (Collon 1995: 50, fig. 33; Delougaz 1968: 186-7). This emphasis on animals is continued in prestige vessels also from the context of public architecture.

### 5.6.2.iii. Prestige vessels

The vessels found at Uruk reveal many exotic features, perhaps not a surprise considering their context. The vessel shapes are part of the established tradition of bowls and jars, with a tendency to imitate more elaborate contemporary ceramic shapes, but the use of unusual materials and methods of decoration are not conventional. "Never again, it appears, were stone vessels to be quite so varied and, at times, so spectacular as in the final centuries of the fourth millennium BC." (Moorey 1994: 36)

The so-called Warka vase is the best known vessel with friezes in low relief. Made of calcite, it is very large (1.05 m high) with a hollow foot (cf. Heinrich 1936: pls. 2-3; Amiet et al 1980: pl. 27). Like cylinder seals, it portrays an ordered world but whether the registers reflect a hierarchy of order from the narrower band to the top is unknown (Fig. 29). It was discovered in the *Sammelfund* in Eanna (Heinrich, 1936: pls. 2-3; Lindemeyer and Martin 1993: Tf. 25) which belongs to Archaic level III but stylistically the vase dates to the earlier level IV (Basmachi 1947: 119; Frankfort 1970: 27). The it was broken into fifteen pieces with a large section of the rim and much of the base missing. Following restoration, the upper frieze is interpreted as the presentation of goods to a priestess (Basmachi 1947: 119) rather than the goddess (Ashur-Greve 1985) of the Inanna temple. The interior is possibly shown behind her, including vessels of various kinds and shapes (animals of lions and horned animal) figures on stands supported by bulls hold objects up including what looks like a stack of bowls (BRBs?). A procession of animals and then naked men (priests?) holding a variety of vessels (BRBs?) appear to move towards the upper register. The missing figure from the break at the top is interpreted as the 'priest-king' wearing a net skirt.

Images of animals again feature on vessels. Amiet suggests that such vessels may have been brought as offerings to the temple where they substituted for living animals. While vessels shaped like animals are not unique to this period (e.g., Hassuna period examples in Bonatz *et al* 1998: 23-24) elaborate varieties make an appearance, such as a bird-shaped vessel and a cosmetic jar set on the back of an animal (Behm-Blancke 1979: no. 86, pl. 27: 149). Like the low relief work, the style and motifs appear to suggest Mesopotamian production.

There are also vessels usually in limestone though sometimes of more exotic stones, consisting of open bowls with animal friezes and men in boats carved on the exterior (e.g., Basmachi 1950; Woolley 1956: pls. 31; Amiet 1977; Lindemeyer and Martin 1993). Similar relief decoration is found on vessels from the Diyala, made of limestone and of green 'lavas' (Perkins 1949: 138; cf. Frankfort *et al.* 1936: fig. 54). Dark stones are rarely used to produce this style of vessel; one example, in 'dark steatite', and decorated with a frieze of bulls, was found in a house of the Achaemenid period at Ur (Woolley 1956: 32, 52, pl. 35; *cf.* van Buren 1939: fig. 71).

A vessel support, carved in relief with figures of hero(es) and animals, in steatite or soapstone was discovered in the Archaic Ishtar Temple at Assur (Andrae 1922: 81, fig. 60, pl. 50a-e). It has been dated by Moortgat (1939) to the later prehistoric period. A number of vessels were cut from blocks of limestone with elaborately carved supporting groups of heroes, animals, or birds in such high relief as to be almost free standing sculptures. One such spouted vessel was found in association with the Warka vase (Heinrich 1936: pls. 22-23a; Amiet 1977: 1224), together with a fragment of another (Heinrich 1936: pl. 23b, c). They are also known at Ur (Woolley 1956: 173-4, pl. 42: U.7560) and the figure of a man grasping lions as a vessel support was found at Tell Agrab in the Diyala Valley (Amiet 1980: 616; Frankfort 1970: figs. 17-19). The hero figure, naked except for a wide belt, is a common image in the third millennium on seals and sculpture (Collon 1987: 193; Frankfort 1939: 78-9). Why he should appear only on vessels and their supports of the fourth millennium is unclear since these are the only obvious representations of direct human domination of animals in this period.

Other types of prestige vessels have inlaid polychrome designs. Vessels with dark stone bodies but with necks and spouts of lighter colour were found in the *Sammelfund* at Uruk (*cf.* Heinrich 1936: fig. 4). Coloured limestones and lapis lazuli were also used to form inlays. Cavities cut in the body of the vessel were filled with the coloured stone and secured with bitumen. They were generally arranged in horizontal or vertical bands, but also appear in the form of rosettes or geometrical shapes (Noldeke 1936: pl. 24g; Heinrich 1936: pl. 25). Animal statuettes were also decorated in a similar fashion (Blehm-Blancke 1979: no. 5).

There were only a few stone vessels reported outside of Warka. A few were recorded at Tell Brak although stone was widely used for amulets. A few miniature jars are described as made of "steatite, white alabaster and white limestone" (Mallowan 1947: 210, pl. LII). Fragments of stone vessels in 'alabaster' were discovered in the East Temple at Tell Qannas (Finet 1977: 78 ff.; Weiss 1985: nos. 30-1). A miniature blue-green stone jar from Habuba Kabira imitates a typical lugged jar (Weiss 1985: no. 29); but there is no exotic material to match that found at Warka so far published.

# 6. FACTORS EFFECTING AND AFFECTING THE SPREAD OF A SOCIAL IDEOLOGY

## 6.1. Management, administration and economy

For Weber (1978) ideas and values have as much impact as economic conditions on social change. He stressed the meaningful, purposive nature of human action and within this management and administration play a central role. Clearly bureaucratic control involves the use of recognizable systems and methods which those involved must learn and, for the information to mean something to later generations, pass on that knowledge to others.

At the very end of the fourth millennium BC textual evidence from south Mesopotamia demonstrates that the management and recording of a system for the redistribution of subsistence products in the form of rations was a central economic activity and concern for large institutions. It is clear that these sophisticated methods of bureaucracy included the development of some of the first writing and notation systems (e.g., seals, tokens, pictograms) used to store information on commodities and quantities (Nissen *et al* 1993). It is a common feature in literature dealing with the Uruk period to see these systems, together with seals and seal impressions, as part of economic and political developments that are related to the emergence of state authority. An information-processing metaphor for the state is therefore emphasised and the routine elements of a bureaucratic administration are viewed as a grand political system (Wright 1977; Brades 1979; Dittmann 1986; Algaze 1993; Pittman 1994; Matthews 1997).

### 6.1.1. Seals and sealings

A precursor of the system is assumed to be reflected in the use of seals. It is clear that sealing had long been a feature of the prehistoric Near East though the purpose of the earliest seals and seal-pendants is far from obvious. Prototypes of stamp-seals have been found at a number of sites in north Mesopotamia dating to the Hassuna period, for example at Bouqras. By the Halaf period (e.g. levels 5-6 at Arpachiyah) clay tags with impressions are evident and extensive sealing practices have been reconstructed at Sabi Abyad (Akkermans and Duistermaat 1996) while isolated seal-pendants had penetrated to the south by early in the Ubaid period, for example at Telloh (von Wickede 1990). By the end of the Ubaid (late fifth millennium BC) evidence suggests an expansion in the use of stamp seals: there was an increase in their recovery at Tepe Gawra from level XIII, peaking late in the Ubaid in level XII (Tobler 1950:176). Comparable to those from Gawra XI-IX are contemporaneous examples from Norsuntepe and Qalinj Agha where round, oval and rectangular stamp seals were designed with an ibex and branch and geometric patterns and simple figures (Lupton 1996:28). By the Late Uruk period the scale of seal use is demonstrated at Arslantepe VIA where over 5000 sealings were recovered in 18 dump horizons from room 206 (Palmieri and Frangipane 1990).

Though stamp seals are known from southern Mesopotamia they were superseded, though not completely, by the cylinder seal from the Middle Uruk period. It is usual to see the cylinder seal developing first in SW Iran or southern Mesopotamia. The evidence from Warka for the earliest cylinder seals is clouded by stratigraphic uncertainty and the majority of the seals (found in the *Sammelfund* dating to the late fourth millennium) were not in their original context. However, a cylinder seal with a fish design has been found in Middle Uruk contexts at Susa Acropolis I, levels 21-20 (Amiet 1980:200). This has been compared with material from Tepe Sharafabad (Wright, et al 1980: Fig. 6, 7-9) although the connection has been doubted by Dittmann (1986: 333, n.5). A bulla with multiple seal-impressions from Tepe Farukhabad in Iran is also considered to be Middle Uruk in date (Wright 1981: 172). The cylinders are large with rows of animals or geometric designs in a heavy coarse style. A baked clay geometric design cylinder seal from Middle Uruk level 7 (Lupton 1996: 59) and three spherical bullae with cylinder seal impressions from earlier level 10 (Boese 1989: Figs. 36-39) of Tell Sheikh Hassan suggests an equally early date for a northern development. However, it is important to note that the seal appears along with southern style ceramics. An example of a drill bored cylinder seal was recovered from Middle Uruk level TW 13 at Tell Brak (Oates & Oates 1993: 176). In addition, fragments of probable cylinder seal impressions (alongside stamp impressions) come from levels 14-16 and examples have also been found in trench HS1 (Matthews *et al.* 1994: Fig. 4, 2-4). However, the chronological uncertainties at Tell Brak (see chapter 4) do not resolve the issue in favour of a northern origin for the cylinder seal.

Certainly by the Late Uruk, cylinder seals are found throughout greater Mesopotamia though closely associated with Uruk sites. These Late Uruk seals consist of two main types. The first are large cylinders where the engraving is often of an extremely high standard although there are also coarsely cut examples. The designs carved on the cylinders fall into three broad categories: animal files, mythical or heraldic beasts and, what Frankfort termed 'action scenes' (1939:16) depicting ritual and hunting (chapter 5.6.2.i.). There are apparent differences in the use of these seals as impressions of the action scene seals are relatively rare while, in contrast, some designs with more mythological or abstract motifs like the high quality images of snakes or birds within braid patterns survive only as impressions with no actual seals of this type having survived (Collon 1987: 15).

The second type of Late Uruk cylinder seal are the so-called Jemdet Nasr seals which are contemporary with the first variety (Collon 1987:15). These are small, squat cylinders worked to a large extent with the drill. The designs consist of schematic rows of animals, humans, often apparently with pig-tails engaged in various activities (e.g., Fig. 24), and geometric designs. The cylinders are more widely distributed than the larger form although there are few surviving impressions.

The designs engraved on Late Uruk cylinder seals have been accepted by many scholars as reflecting a system of both site and administrative hierarchies. Brandes (1979) argues that each type of seal represents a branch of the centralised administration. Nissen (1977: 19-20) suggests that the fine seals were used by individuals and that the schematic seals were used by institutions, while Collon (1987: 16), developing Brandes theory, distinguishes between seals used by predominately male temple institutions and the smaller, drilled (Jemdet Nasr) seals which she suggests were used by female institutions (represented by the lines of pig-tailed figures) connected with the production of manufactured goods. Two very different interpretations have been made of the role of seals within economic system at Susa. The excavators suggested the sealings record transactions between individual entrepreneurs (Le Bun and Vallet 1978). Others argue that various economic sectors were administered through a centralized organisation as suggested for Warka, consisting of higher ranking individuals and lower ranking institutions, the hierarchy of which is reflected in the seal imagery. Chief among the proponents of this idea is Dittmann (1986) who followed Brandes' ideas, proposing an elaborated hierarchy of administrative departments on the basis of multiple sealings of fine seals with different subjects on small bullae or tablets.

Thus it has been argued that the schematic seals were badges of identity rather than for making seal impressions (Matthews 1997: 193). The fine seals were used by the central bureaucracy to communicate with each other and control goods entering or leaving the centre, while the schematic seals were used by persons who were intermediary between the bureaucracy and the administered population. Matthews (1997) emphasizes the consistency of seal design and suggests this expresses identity or adherence to a system with an 'official seal style'. This system he interprets a strongly centralised state (a monarchy) which exercised control, through military power, over the geographical spread of the Late Uruk culture. "It difficult to see how such widespread cultural uniformity could otherwise have been achieved" (Matthews 1997: 192). While Matthews is right to emphasize the role of the seals in representing a common ideology the details of his reconstruction will be challenged in chapters 6.4 and 7.

Nonetheless, there are some variations between Uruk sites in the detail of the designs. It is usual to see these modifications as reflecting different economic conditions such as between Warka and Susa. Whereas action scene seals from Habuba Kabira mirror scenes from Warka, where animal husbandry is prominent, Collon (1987: 15) has contrasted a number of seals from Susa which instead depict grain-storage. At Habuba Kabira only schematic seals were excavated though there are impressions of fine seals while many of the Jebel Aruda seal impressions are of drill-bored types with figurative and geometric designs, rather than the fine sealings with large human and animal figures (van Driel 1983: 57-58). Baked clay tokens (see below), common at Habuba, are also rare at Aruda (van Driel 1979:26; Sürenhagen 1986). On the basis of this evidence the sites have been viewed as part of an administrative system with Aruda as the centre (Strommenger 1980).

Several features of seals found within the Uruk 'colony' sites also appear to emphasise east-west connections across north Mesopotamia (Levant, Syria, Susa). Indeed, it is this route that is associated with the development of the cylinder seal. A striking feature is the frequent appearance of the griffin like those of Susiana and Egypt (Teissier 1987: esp. 31 and n. 2). Some of the variations in seal design are more difficult to relate to aspects of the economy. For example spiders are very popular on seals from Iran, perhaps related to textile production through weaving. But the meaning behind scorpions that are popular on seals from Syria alludes us.

Indeed, the theory of administrative departments works well for many of the seal designs but "those with mythical or heraldic beasts or monsters, cannot be so easily categorised" (Collon 1987: 15). To suggest that the different types of schematic seal represent different sectors of the administered economy would be to speculate since there are no known differences between their distributions and the arguments that various administrative departments can be recognised on the basis of multiple sealings of fine seals with different subjects on small bullae or tablets is questionable since such direct correspondences do not exist in later times when symbolism tends to be more complex. Nonetheless, the work of Brandes and others presents a powerful argument for some kind of administrative scheme reflected in the seal designs.

The long lived northern stamp seal tradition did not disappear with the wide spread use of cylinder seals in the Late Uruk period. Even in the colonies the two traditions exist side-by-side, e.g., three cylinders and one stamp were recovered from Jebel Aruda (van Driel 1983). Schemes of decoration on both cylinders and stamp seals follow broad conventions, but it is clear that Uruk glyptic influenced stamp seal design. For example, at Arslantepe VIA clay sealings included impressions from both stamp and cylinder seals (Palmieri and Frangipane 1990: Fig. 3, a-c). 10 cylinder seal designs reconstructed from the 798 analysed pieces were locally produced as nine of the designs are identical to contemporaneous stamp seals (Ferioli and Fiandra 1988). The other design shows a man riding a covered ox-drawn sledge and has been compared to a small stone plaque thought to have originated in Mesopotamia (Surenhagen 1985: 230-232) and is similar to a wall painting at the site (see chapter 5.4.5.iii.). Similarly at Hacinebi Tepe phase B southern style cylinder seal impressions are present but one or two may have been local designs (Lupton 1996:65). There were powerful messages in the Uruk glyptic which were adopted by local Chalcolithic seal cutters but it appears to have been a one way process.

Nonetheless, a similar variety of functions for seals and sealings is evident in both north and south Mesopotamia, from door-locks and jar seals to seals on cloth or leather bags. Ferioli and Fiandra's (1988) study of the Arslantepe sealings suggested that the VIA administrative system was a localised regional phenomenon, as had been suggested for those operating in the pre-contact period. They conclude that the system was comparable with the evidence from Jebel Aruda in the degree of centralization involved (Frangipane and Palmieri 1988-89:549). Both systems were concerned with storage and distribution. A similar use of stamp seals is reconstructed for Early Uruk Tepe Gawra (Rothman 1988). He argues that Tepe Gawra, from the Late Ubaid (level XIII) to at least the Middle Uruk (level VIIIA my dating, chapter **4.2.**), was the centre of a small economic and social sphere and that religion was as important as economics. Even were that not the case, the economic system he convincingly reconstructs primarily utilized locally available resources such as wool or flax, stone and wood. Imported prestigious resources like lapis lazuli and silver (3.2.2.ii.) link Gawra directly to the hilly country of Iran and southeastern Turkey.

On this basis, there is no need to postulate such a strongly centralized administration for the Uruk world as that proposed by Brandes and others. A more decentralized, localized household based economy is possible with the seal designs reflecting aspects of production as well as an indication of a wider social ideology (below and chapter 5.6.2.ii). Seals in later Mesopotamia have more than functional roles - as amulets, ornaments, and votives, they were important for influencing and communicating ideas, in other words, seal impressions concern transactions that transcend the purely economic sphere (Gibson and Biggs 1977). For example, seals found in the cemetery at Ur were, according to Woolley (1982: 94) owned by 'soldiers' as badges of office or medals. In addition Moorey (1977) has argued that designs of seals can be used to distinguish between male and female occupants of the Royal Graves. The spread of the Uruk cylinder seal might therefore imply something greater than the adoption of a more efficient administrative tool.

### 6.1.2. Tags, tablets and bullae

Interpreted as part of the administrative-recording tools developed towards the end of the fourth millennium were solid oblong or biconical clay tags bearing sealings, hollow balls, often sealed, containing tokens (counters) and square or oblong tablets of clay bearing numerical impressions which correspond with numerical markings on later cuneiform tablets. The tags are considered by many to have been tied to bales or merchandise (Amiet 1971: 70). They are called bullae by Schmandt-Besserat (1992:109) and she proposes they were used to join the ends of a string of clay numerical tokens. They have seal impressions and some have impressed markings as on the hollow balls and impressed tablets. The hollow balls, either spherical, ovoid or oblong in shape are confusingly called envelopes by Schmandt-Besserat but known as bullae to other scholars (e.g., Nissen *et al* 1993). Here I adopt the terms tags for the solid clay pieces and bullae for the hollow clay balls.

Schmandt-Besserat's (1992) controversial but highly influential theory of the development of writing from a long lived token system, sees the tags and bullae as part of an evolution in the technology of record keeping towards cuneiform writing. There are however major chronological problems to overcome in positing a sequence of progression from one type of object to the next. The sealed bullae are said to be a functional link between tokens and numerical tablets. From the mid fourth millennium tokens increase in number and variety although whether these are related to the earlier tokens is debated (Michalowski 1993). The oldest numerical tablets and sealed bullae also date to this period. Schmandt-Besserat argues that the earliest bullae come from the Eanna district of Warka because they show particularly archaic seal impressions (both stamp and cylinder) and bear no numerical markings. They were, however, not found *in situ* but nonetheless may date back to level VI. However, bullae like those of Warka, holding identical tokens and also bearing similar seal impressions, have been recovered at several sites, e.g., 25 plus at Choga Mish (Delougaz and Kantor 1996: 120) and two from Habuba Kabira (Finet 1979: Fig. 22), which may be more evolved than those of Warka since they bore signs depicting the tokens inside (Schmandt-Besserat 1992: 69). Bullae from Susa were recovered in level 18 and the example from Farukhabad also dates from the Middle Uruk period (Wright 1981:156).

Most of the bullae contain clay tokens of abstract and geometrical shapes and many of these tokens are virtually the same as those that occur in older levels. Some bullae have impression marks though only a few are known and generally the tokens presumed to have been within the ball are missing. While numerical impressions on bullae are similar to those on the numerical tablets there is no obvious connection with the pictographic forms which develop into cuneiform writing in the south (Nissen et al 1993: 127). Both bullae and numerical tablets are widely dispersed and many date into after the post-Uruk period, for example, some numerical tablets and bullae come from Proto-Elamite levels in Iran (marked § in Table 4).

Despite the chronological difficulties in seeing a technological evolution between tags, bullae, impressed and pictographic tablets there is clearly some relationship as recording devices. It is not yet possible to know if they belong to one recording system. Like the seals, there are differences in style and technique across their wide distribution.

"A comparison of various sites demonstrates that neither the signs' shape nor the way or even the sequence in which they were written followed a common, interregional convention" (Nissen *et al* 1993:128). It might be argued that this is a result of chronological problems where we are unable to recognize the fine distinctions in the development of the system at different sites. However, it seems as though notations on bullae and tablets originating from a single find context often exhibit internal differences so there may not have been even local conventions for sign forms during that period. For example, clay bullae from Susa bear impressions made by a stylus, fingers, impressed with counters or scratch marks (Nissen et al 1993: figs. 8, 109, 112). It is, of course, possible that many originate outside the site *if* they accompanied incoming goods.

| Site | Tags | Bullae | Impressed Tablets |
|---|---|---|---|
| Warka | | 25 (*UVB* 21:31) | 65 |
| Khafaje | | | 1 (Frankfort *et al*. 1936: 25, fig. 19) |
| Mari | | | 1 (Parrot, Syria 42:12) |
| Chagar Bazar | * (Curtis 1982: 81) | | |
| Nineveh | * (Wiseman 1962: pl. 32) | | fragment (Collon & Reade 1983:33) |
| Tell Brak | * (Oates 1982: 66) | | 1 (Curtis 1982:64-65) |
| Sheikh Hassan | | 3 (Boese 1989: Figs 36-39) | |
| Habuba Kabira | * (Strommenger 1980: 63) | 2 (Finet 1979; Fig 22; Strommenger 1980: Fig. 58) | 10 (e.g. Strommenger 1980a: Fig. 56) |
| Jebel Aruda | | | 13 (van Driel 1982; 1983) |
| Hacinebi Tepe B. | | 1 (operation 1) | 1? (Stein *et al*. 1996) |
| Tepe Farukhabad | | 1 (Green & Nissen 1987:39-40) | |
| Susa | * (Amiet 1972) | 23 (Amiet 1972: 69) | 90 (Schmandt-Besserat 1992:130; Amiet 1972: 68) |
| Choga Mish | (Delougaz, & Kantor 1996) | 25+ (Delougaz, & Kantor 1996:120) | 5+ (Delougaz, & Kantor 1996:120) |
| Godin Tepe | | | 42 (Weiss & Young 1975: 8-11) |
| Tall-i Ghazir | | | 1 (Carter & Stolper 1984: fig. 7/15) |
| § Tepe Sialk | | | 14 (Ghirshman, :65-68, pls. XCII-XCIII) |
| § Tal-i Malyan | | 6 | 4 (Potts 1994: table 2.3) |
| § Shahdad | | 1 | |
| § Tepe Yahya | | 1 | |
| §? Dharan | | 1 (Schmandt-Besserat (1980:363, n.24) | |
| §? Dumah | | 1 (Schmandt-Besserat (1992:112) | |

Table 4. Distribution of late fourth millennium accounting tools
(details of tokens may be found in the comprehensive work of Schmandt-Besserat 1992)

There are similar differences with numerical tablets. For example, a tablet from Warka, (Nissen *et al.* 1993: fig 113) which is similar to those from Habuba Kabira and Choga Mish has numerical impressions which do not parallel notations from later texts. The same lack of rules is evident on a tablet from Jebel Aruda (Nissen *et al.* 1993: fig. 114) where signs were organized in a way different from all known later numerical and metrological systems. Even materials for the tablets vary between sites. For example, a number of tablets from Warka were made from gypsum, widely used in the Late Uruk architecture at the site (Nissen *et al.* 1993: fig. 110). These may have had a different function than the clay examples.

13 notational systems have been identified from the Warka tablets (Nissen *et al.* 1990), yet only three have been found in the earliest period II examples at Susa. This may indicate that fewer things needed to be counted at Susa than at Warka. As Potts (1999: 63) points out, the arrangement of the Susian numerical signs on the tablets is very different from those which developed on the proto-cuneiform economic texts at Warka. This therefore argues against a political force from Warka moving into Susiana during the Late Uruk period as one might expect the full administrative techniques of the conqueror to be introduced, or even if only part were required, that it should appear in the same form (chapter **6.4**).

Numerical tablets are found widely across the Uruk world but Englund (quoted in Potts 1999: 60) has suggested that those from Godin Tepe are more like tablets from north Mesopotamia (Nineveh, Khafajeh) and Syria (Jebel Aruda, Tell Brak, Mari), whereas those from Susiana (Susa, Choga Mish) are most like examples from Warka suggesting two traditions: a northern and southern Uruk world.

This lack of apparent convention in the use of numerical notations stands in contrast to the relatively strict rules already obeyed at the time of the Eanna IVa texts. Before this time there was clearly a very flexible use of recording devices rather than a symbolic system with binding conventions. With the last phases of the Late Uruk period it is possible that a centralized schooling system emerged, reflecting an ever increasing emphasis on order.

By far the largest body of early writing comes from Warka, written on clay tablets in the pictographic signs which later developed into the cuneiform script. An early phase of writing development may be represented by two tablets with simple pictographs from Tell Brak (Finkel 1985:189) but their poor archaeological context makes this uncertain. The date of the tablets at Warka is also a problem; the layers from which they were recovered is currently taken to be around 3200-3000 BC. The tablets appear to have been part of a rubbish dump used as fill for the large terrace below the buildings of level III. It can be assumed that they are no older than Archaic IV since no tablets were found in the layers below them. Tablets were probably thrown away at regular intervals. The distribution and concentration of tablets in various areas unconnected to major buildings suggests that no contextual relationship existed between certain buildings and groups of texts (Nissen et al 1993:6). Through palaeographic comparisons between the scripts of Uruk IV and III it has been possible to establish differences between the two phases as changes in the techniques of writing had significantly altered the shapes of the signs.

The organizational structures of society and economy were already well established when literacy came into being as, although the great majority of texts deal with administration, lists of cities, professions, vessels, metal objects, trees etc. also exist and may be part of scribal education (Nissen *et al.* 1993: 110-115) The professions list exists back to the oldest phase of script development, Uruk IV, and as a popular lexical text was copied for over a thousand years. (Nissen 1986). Whether the list reflects some kind of hierarchy is unclear. It starts with a poorly understood term, translated in the later copies of the list as *šarrum* (king), followed by 'leaders' of justice, city, plow, barley and various other high officials including a possible leader of the 'assembly' - though according to Englund the sign for 'assembly' is simply a representation of a pot (quoted in Baines and Yoffee 1998: 221).

The association between the tablets and the monumental structures at Warka has led to the assumption that administration was focused within these buildings. In fact tablets have been found across the site of Warka (Nissen 1998), at Choga Mish tablets were found in domestic contexts (Delougaz, & Kantor 1996: 120) and at Habuba Kabira the numerical tablets were found in the Building 2 in the northern sector of the city (Strommenger 1980a: Fig. 56). This limited evidence would suggest a decentralized administration.

Administrative devises are, therefore, not necessarily characteristic of large public controlling institutions, since they played a role in household management in the third millennium BC Mesopotamia (Martin 1988). It is likely that the three modes of exchange - reciprocal, redistributive and commercial - coexisted and were not mutually exclusive (chapter *6.2.1.*) and the complexity of their interaction means the neat divisions for the use of sealing and accounting devices is not possible.

As Adams (1981: 77) has noted,
> "Nothing we know of the historic records of any society (wherever there are such records), however would allow even the full battery of administrative routines (assuming optimistically that they could ever be known archaeologically!) to stand as surrogate for its political system as a whole. The routines not only constitute a gross over-simplification of politics but also provide a misleading picture - one lacking in the pervasive but volatile and usually

unexpressed elements of contingency, calculation, and coercion."

## 6.2. Trade and economy

### *6.2.1 Trade*

The study of trade and exchange has dominated the archaeology of late fourth millennium in recent years. The emphasis on the relative lack of stone and wood, and absence of metals on the southern plain has resulted in theories where trade for these commodities has been interpreted as playing the dominate role in the transformation of society (e.g., Wright and Johnson 1975; Algaze 1993). Indeed, it is clear that by the mid-third millennium the city states of the southern Mesopotamian plain were dependent on imported raw materials (Crawford 1973; 1992). These materials came from Anatolia, from the Gulf, Iran and even Afghanistan and the Indus valley. The presence of this material has increasingly been viewed as the successor to trading links established in a widely organised form during the mid to late fourth millennium (which themselves almost certainly reflect earlier lines of communication and exchange, e.g., Renfrew & Dixon 1976).

The pattern of Uruk settlements along the Great Bend of the Euphrates and in Susiana has suggested to many researchers that they represent the establishment of colonies by southern polities. The scale of the settlements, however, both in terms of size and distance, has raised the question of long-distance trade and the sites are often interpreted as collection points for coveted peripheral resources acquired in exchange for core manufactures. Thus it is suggested, "highly integrated lowland centres succeeded in establishing a variety of isolated far-flung outposts in areas at the periphery of the Mesopotamian lowlands. In an alien hinterland characterised by less complex societies, the outposts were commonly established at the apex of pre-existing regional settlement hierarchies and invariably at focal nodes astride important trade routes." (Algaze 1993).

Although trade across very wide area of the Near East is known from as early as the Upper Palaeolithic (e.g., the presence of Red Sea dentalium shells at widely dispersed sites throughout the region), Algaze reconstructs the Uruk presence as the creation of an informal economic empire by city states based on the import of raw materials to southern centres. This is taken to indicate a source for some of the exotic materials found at Warka such as found in the *Kleinfunde* (Lindemeyer and Martin 1992 and 1993). The Uruk phenomenon has therefore been discussed in terms of "centre and periphery". City states or other independent units (early state models) traded both at local level and through their centres. Such a flow of goods lay the basis for a larger economic unification. This idea is related to Wallerstein's (1974 & 1980) 'world system'. But there are dangers of exaggerating the effects of what may be quite modest trading links and presenting a picture of dominance (by the supposed core area) and dependency (of the supposed periphery). This in turn leads to an explanation of change by 'dominance' (i.e., diffusion) alone.

The evidence, however, is simply not sufficient to demonstrate 'high trade', as opposed to a rather more episodic movement of luxury goods. As Schwartz (1989: 309) has questioned, if the northern resources "were much more easily and cheaply obtained by allowing the indigenous communities already exploiting them to continue, provided they could be persuaded or coerced into trade at terms favourable to communities of the alluvium," why did the southern Mesopotamians find it necessary to establish a set of urban enclaves along the Euphrates? Indeed Steinkeller (1993) argues that there simply was not the organisational abilities and resources required to launch a program of colonisation on the scale that Algaze proposes.

More recent archaeological work in Syria and Anatolia and northern Iraq has revealed a series of local Chalcolithic settlements exhibiting many of the characteristics found in the south: monumental architecture, sophisticated recording systems, high status goods, storage and distribution of commodities (e.g., Tell Brak, Hammam-et-Turkman, Hacinebi Tepe, Qalinj Agha, Tepe Gawra). It is possible that the abandonment of some of these sites in the Late/Middle Uruk (chapter *4.1.2.*) could have 'forced' southerners to move north in order to maintain their supply lines, but they were clearly moving into a region with a well developed political and economic structure and there is no evidence for southern domination of that system or systems. Uruk 'colony' sites are constructed in regions with little evidence of previous occupation, e.g., Tabqa sites (chapter *5.2.2.*) or are represented by enclaves within existing late Chalcolithic settlements. The limited adoption of the cylinder seal in the north along with designs in the local stamp seal tradition suggests that the northern economy was not dominated by an Uruk presence.

Butterlin (1995) redefines Algaze's thesis by suggesting the Uruk expansion reflects the development of a 'world economy' like that which developed in Europe between the fifteenth and eighteenth century AD. A much more fluid arrangement of interaction between equal trading partners. The problems with accounting for the scale of Uruk presence and the lack of evidence for any major interaction with the local Chalcolithic society argues against this reconstruction. Other scholars have interpreted the evidence in terms of political expansion and domination (Lamberg-Karlovsky 1996) with Warka acting as the 'capital' for an Uruk empire (Matthews 1997). There is, however, limited evidence for the kind of military activity that would presumably have been necessary to 'take over' the northern economic systems (chapter **6.4**).

It is clear from the pictographic tablets recovered from Warka and the few numerical tablets found elsewhere in the Uruk world (though whether they functioned in the same way is unclear) that some bureaucratic structures were already in place (chapter *6.1.2*); what is less clear is what is being organised beyond the distribution of rations to personnel. It has been suggested from certain pictographs of the Uruk III tablets that slaves and prisoners of war were part of the exchange system (Zagarell 1986) but this has been disputed (Nissen *et al* 1993) and certainly in the historic period formed a limited component of southern Mesopotamian productive labour. Texts record the receipt and distribution of commodities such as grain, beer, milk products, cattle, pigs, birds, fish, wooden objects, metals and metal objects (Nissen 1986; Englund and Nissen 1993). With the exception of metal there is little in the list that suggests the distribution of the kind of exotic materials that many theories assume account for the Uruk expansion.

Indeed many of the stones found at Uruk sites in Babylonia were available locally. Gypsum used at Warka, Ur, and Eridu was extracted from the nearby formations at Eridu. Basalt and other conglomerate substances were available in outcrops along the desert margins, the western flanks of the Zagros, and the Jebel Sinjar. Other stones appear as river boulders brought down in the floods. Copper certainly arrived through long distance trade, perhaps with Anatolia and Iran and the Gulf; references in the Uruk III tablets to copper from Dilmun appear to confirm this and there is some very limited evidence for an Uruk presence in the Gulf, e.g. a bulla and pot from Dhahlan, though this may date to the post-Uruk period (Schmandt-Besserat 1980: 363, n. 24). Copper was inevitably expensive along side other more exotic metals but baked-clay sickles and flint were the main agricultural tools in use until the introduction of utilitarian iron in the first millennium. A major problem lies in the lack of any southern cemetery sites where evidence for conspicuous consumption in death may exist. Such an absence of graves, however, may not be an accident of archaeological discovery. Pollock (1999:204-5) suggests that adult corpses "seem to have been completely removed - physically and symbolically - from the context of both family and community." This may be part of the uniformity of the Uruk world - with the creation of an urban life for a substantial part of the population resulted in alterations in the ideological expressions of both life and death.

If there is little evidence for the major movement of exotic materials to southern Mesopotamia, it is equally unclear what was moving from the alluvium to the north if one accepts that trade was the main factor explaining the presence of the 'colonies'. Prior to the Third Dynasty of Ur, large-scale southern Mesopotamian exports of grain, leather goods, dried fish, dates, and textiles remain essentially invisible archaeologically and undocumented epigraphically (Crawford 1973; Weiss 1989). Indeed, the alluvium may not have been alone in trading invisible exports - timber and the wealth of Syrian steppe flocks and herds were quite possibly being exploited. Indeed "surpluses generated by early agriculturists in northern Mesopotamia have been consistently underestimated" (Moorey 1994: 3) and based on current estimates areas like the northern Jazira is capable of yielding over 700 kg/ha. of wheat (Lupton 1996: 7). Transport of large jars in carrying devices have been identified on some Late Uruk cylinder seals scenes, but their purpose is unknown (Amiet 1980: pl. 16, nos. 264; Baudot 1979: 57, no. 18). It is likely that it was the very exploitation of these local agricultural resources which was the main reason for the Uruk expansion. The economy of southern Mesopotamia was dominated by agriculture and textile production (chapter *6.2.2*). The economic reasons for the establishment of large numbers of Urukians in the north and east, as reconstructed below, was a wider utilisation of sheep, cattle, and production of their products along with wine and beer, largely independent of the local communities. This process was accelerated in the fourth millennium with the domestication of the donkey which allowed larger amounts to be carried over longer distances.

However, a limited exchange in more unusual materials did involve Urukians, e.g., lapis lazuli was found at Jebel Aruda and obsidian was recovered from the Uruk area of Tell Brak (TW phase 12). It is possible that trade was the primary basis for the establishment of small Uruk settlements within local sites in Iran and north Syria/SE Anatolia, e.g., level 5 at Godin Tepe (Young 1986), level 5 at Hassek Höyük (Behm-Blancke 1991). In addition, as has been suggested above, many of the large settlement sites already in existence in the north, such as Carchemish, Tell Brak and Nineveh, are likely to have had a localised occupation by Urukians (Algaze 1993: 36-37; Lupton 1996: 68). It may be speculated that the occupation of these sites can only have taken place with the consent of the local authorities. These developments appear to be similar to a pattern of trade which is apparent for the Early Dynastic period (Crawford 1992) where a variety of trading mechanisms are identified including permanent settlement by merchants in a different cultural area or contact via merchant caravans. None of these mechanisms, however, require us to view their origins as part of a political or economic strategy by southern polities. Indeed, if trade is the main factor here, its complex nature, involving a mix of reciprocity, redistribution and market exchange, inevitably means the picture will be far more complicated then simply the imposition by southern political centres of trading centres in the resource rich north as suggested by Algaze (1989; 1993).

### *6.2.2. Economy*

Johnson (1987) has argued that by the Middle Uruk period the increased number of people living in towns on the Susiana plain would have meant that they could no longer have been supported by resident food producers alone. Towns must therefore have received additional food from village communities. This was brought as tribute to the central authorities of the town and redistributed. He concludes that such increasing tribute demands were responsible for the dramatic decline of settled population on the Susiana Plain in the Late Uruk period. (Johnson 1987: 124-5).

Pollock (1999: 94-96) takes this further to suggest that tribute demands by cities and towns formed the basis of the Uruk economy. These demands were not confined to products but also included labour (corvée) which was required for large construction projects as well as periodic agricultural activities such as harvesting. Bevelled rim bowls were used for tribute and rations (Nissen 1970; Johnson 1973; chapter *5.6.1.*). Texts record the receipt and distribution of these commodities (Nissen 1986; Englund and Nissen 1993; chapter *6.1.2.*).

She argues that demands for tribute continued to grow throughout the Uruk period and resulted in significant repercussions. As village communities found it increasingly difficult to provide for both their own needs and produce enough surplus to meet tribute demands they abandoned a sedentary lifestyle in favor of a more mobile one, emigrating to another region, or moving into towns. Rural emigration would only have increased the burden of tribute on those people who remained, precipitating such crises as the Late Uruk breakdown on the Susiana Plain and presumably the collapse of the northern Uruk colonies. This may have led to a fundamental change in economic organization, resulting in the urban-based economy of the third millennium BC.

This is an interesting and persuasive theory. The textual evidence from Warka certainly refers to large quantities of material being stored or distributed. This however could represent a more diverse system of offerings and tribute. There is nothing to suggest that tribute represented the dominant part of the economy.

As discussed in chapters *3.4.1.* and *5.6.1*, the fourth millennium witnessed the emergence of industrial production across Mesopotamia (e.g., Pollock 1999: Tables 4.6-7, 4.13-15). There was an increasing emphasis on sheep and goats in the southern lowlands and this may reflect the growing importance of secondary products, such as milk, dung, wool, and hair. Indeed, texts bear out the critical importance of textile production in the Mesopotamian economy and glyptic representations of women employed in textile production mirror the third millennium large production units (chapter *5.6.*). As the economy grew so did the demands for new supply sources. This resulted in the establishment of Uruk settlements in new regions where sheep as well as other resources could be exploited. This appears to have been organized around family units, possibly tribal or clan based (chapter *3.2.1*). There is no evidence for the extraction of tribute by these communities from local communities. They are much more internalized in organization with any surplus invested in the community order.

The late fourth millennium was characterized by a complex economy. Many people lived in households that supplied most of their own material needs as well as generating surpluses to meet the community's central demands in labor and products. In addition, some larger units controlled hierarchically ordered and specialized work forces producing luxury goods. There is nothing to clearly demonstrate that any one institution had the monopoly on redistribution or that the administrative devices was restricted to one level of society. It is possible that the many faceted pattern of agriculture encouraged an equally diverse number of redistributive centres from the family or clan to the ceremonial centres (chapter **3**).

## 6.3. Urbanisation

Surely the most significant and lasting characteristic of the Uruk period was the focusing of large populations within an urban way of life. Indeed, for Childe (1936), the beginning of urban life was the signal for the beginning of civilisation. Simply defined, urbanisation relates to the growth of towns or cities from rural conditions. It is, however, more generally associated in the literature with the growth of a city identified as having "typically a large population (often of more than 5000 inhabitants) with major public buildings, including temples and work places for the administrative bureaucracy. Often, there is a pronounced settlement hierarchy, with the capital city as the major centre, and with subsidiary or regional centres as well as local villages." (Renfrew and Bahn 1991: 157). It is the differences in settlement hierarchy which reflect changes in the wider urban environment as increasing emphasis is placed on the servicing central place. In the past it has been common to view the southern Mesopotamian plain as distinctive because of its cities. However, recent survey work and analysis has demonstrated an urban development in the north had reached a scale during the early Uruk period equivalent to areas in the south (Frangipane 1993; Lupton 1996; Wilkinson 1990; chapter *3.4*). A three tier settlement pattern in identifiable in both northern Mesopotamia and in Babylonia with a four tier pattern developing in the latter by the end of the fourth millennium (Adams 1981). The differences in scale between north and south could be a matter of the geography of irrigation versus rainfall agriculture, as Weiss (1986) asserts, causing kinds of agglomeration not necessarily reflecting different underlying organisation (but see chapter *3.1.*).

City-states were an irreducibly essential quality of Mesopotamian civilization. They remained the main political organization until the second millennium BC and even during periods of empire, the city remained an important, often independent element, e.g., the cities of Babylonia alongside the Chaldean tribal groupings during the first millennium BC (Kuhrt 1995: 616). The city had a powerful symbolic meaning "transforming power and productivity into culture and translating culture itself into detachable symbolic forms that can be stored and transmitted" (Mumford 1960:338). Kemp too stresses the psychological factor of permanent occupation of the same tract of land "which came to be expressed in mythic, symbolic terms which in turn creates a peculiar sense of self confidence within the community concerned." (Kemp 1989:32). While the human attachment to an area of land is unlikely by itself to be of sufficient importance to cause the emergence of an urban environment, recognition of land ownership by a community is closely associated with the fundamental development of a unifying ideology, for instance Hoffman, (1980: 146) conjectures that the architectural or human-spatial dynamics of southern Egypt tended toward a more compact or 'agglutinated' settlement and that this pattern was an important element in the development of a distinctive social, political, and economic ethic for the region.

Contact between urban centres may take different forms: communication established between élite groups (gifts, ideas), international trade, employment of workers, sharing of skills, e.g., writing. The form of this communication is essential for understanding the development of a common ideology. However, urbanisation does not necessarily increase communication within the city. In larger concentrations of people, the individual will find it increasingly impossible to know every member of the community. In addition the focusing of social stratification and specialism within an urban environment will also help to encourage a decline in general communication.

However, in a world that was ordered through a strong social ideology, a loss of immediate communication was of little consequence when the rules were written within the ordered architecture, iconography and organization of the settlement. In the Uruk world this was based on the contrast between the systematised urban environment and the wilderness beyond (Chapter 5). The ideology thus actually encouraged urbanisation, and family units, together with their dependants, focused themselves around ceremonial centres and high status groups. As the urban centres expended in size and/or politico-economic strength, the ties between older allegiances, e.g., to kin groups, may have been weakened. Increasingly, the urban form came to be viewed not only as desirable and natural, but with the concentration of the major economic and political players within, it came to be a permanent feature. Urban centres continued to dominate Mesopotamia (both north and south) despite the major economic and social disturbances that seem to characterise the late fourth millennium BC; they was self perpetuating. In the politically divided world of the third millennium the overarching Sumerian culture was maintained and reinforced through the institutions of the city. Identity was with the city (chapter 3.2.3.ii.) and formed the basis for all future developments in the region (Yoffee 1993b; Baines & Yoffee 1998).

### 6.4. Warfare

Although definitions of war are numerous (Ferguson 1984: 3), here it is defined as "armed conflict between governments in pursuit of resources, status, power, and values which has very little to do with individual aggression" (Jacobs 1975: 298). Along with the actual conflict, warfare clearly also involves mobilising people, marshalling resources and diplomatic activity. A number of theories investigating the formation of complex society and the state have emphasised conflict between groups as an important factor in social change. For example, Service (1975) emphasised the emergence of a 'big-man', possibly through bravery in feud and war, as a faction leader which encouraged society to develop from tribal to chiefdom organisation. The inevitability implied by this model has been rejected above (chapter *3.2.2.*). In contrast Diakonoff (1969) followed a traditional Marxist class-stratification model where conflict arose between economically powerful groups and those without access to or control of social resources. However, an emphasis on trade and economics alone ignores the importance of traditional social customs and, like Service's approach, implies that the rise of an élite whose initial basis of power (trade or bravery) allows them to attract other sources of influence. As argued above, the emphasis on one source of authority as the basis of society is not reflected in the evidence for Mesopotamia.

Carniero's work in particular stresses the importance of organised warfare as a result of population growth leading to circumscribed agricultural resources. Through "the conquest of village by village, chiefdoms, the first supra-community political units, came to arise" (Carneiro 1978:210). While in Mesopotamia such forms of complex social organisation arose not in the uplands where demographic pressure would have been greatest but on broad agricultural plains where access to potentially very fertile soil was not restricted by geography, access to other resources like water may have produced similar effects. Ferguson (1984; 1990) maintains that war, at least pre-state war, is carried out for material resources such as land, water, food, and trade goods. Chagnon (1990) adds to this the possibility of mating opportunities and kin welfare and, like Carneiro, envisages that conflict occurs when populations reach the carrying capacity of an ecology and resources become scarce. He suggests, however, that this becomes blurred in state organisations, when organisation and technology can help remove limits on resources. As a result material resources may be the primary issue for conflict between bands, villages, and tribes, war between chiefdoms or states is a mechanism for, but also reflecting, increased social identity. However, while ecological and material factors influence cultural change, these conditions will be interpreted very differently by different groups, depending on the culture through which they are understood. Therefore disputes over access to social positions or materials may or may not lead to war, depending on the history of the group and the way in which that history is expressed by the group. Certainly the issue at stake in the third millennium BC Lagash-Umma conflict (Cooper 1986: 34) appears to demonstrate the concerns of a state, that is the problem of sovereignty rather than the need for agricultural resources of the disputed field. Indeed, having reasserted its claim over the land through victory in battle, Lagash actually rented the field to Umma. The war is therefore fought in terms of an ideology based on identity. Unfortunately it is unknown which sections of the population, apart from the ruler, are represented by the army, (though, if not hyperbole by the scribe, the twenty burial mounds of Umma's defeated suggests the involvement of a substantial number of soldiers).

It has been postulated that elements of the expansion of Uruk culture in the Late Uruk period may rest on aggressive acts by political groupings of the alluvium and particularly for an incursion into the Susiana plain (Algaze 1989). This has not met with universal acceptance. Johnson (1987; 1988/89), for example, argues that there are no the breaks or dramatic changes on the Susiana Plain from the Susa A through to the Late Uruk Period as might be expected if there had been an incursion from Mesopotamia but rather it was a result of long term interaction between societies in Susiana and the Mesopotamian alluvium (as does Amiet 1979; 1994). Rather than invasion by force it is suggested here that the emergence of the Uruk phenomenon in the Susiana plain follows the same pattern as in north Mesopotamia (pages 145 and 147). That is "an infiltration of southern Mesopotamians, probably agriculturalists and their families, potters and other craftsmen who moved into the available agricultural land in Khuzistan and founded new settlements" (Potts 1999: 65). Such a reconstruction is also suggested by a comparison of the Uruk administrative tools in Susa and Warka (page 139). The shape this 'colonisation' took was determined by a strong social ideology.

Despite the rejection of Algaze's thesis of Susa being conquered by invading Urukians, possible conflict is depicted on cylinder seals and impressions from Late Uruk Susa and Warka. These depict the 'priest-king' figure holding a spear (Fig. 31.; Collon 1987: 163, No. 746.) or firing arrows using a composite bow (Fig. 30) while depictions of shields and swords are also known (Collon 1987: 163, Nos. 742, 743). Naked humans appear to have their hands bound behind their backs and are being beaten or stabbed by other naked figures bearing weapons. These scenes are often interpreted as portraying either warfare or 'capital punishment'. However, the 'priest-king' is often depicted elsewhere in a ritual context (chapter *5.6.2.*) while naked figures generally have priestly roles (compare the naked figures behind the 'priest-king' on the Warka Vase, Fig. 28). This suggests that the seals and sealings represent ritual activity.

These images may, however, relate to conflict between independent communities in the Late Uruk world. Johnson (1987: 124) argues that in the Susiana Plain, the site of Choga Mish came to rival that of Susa as a major centre, effectively dividing the region into two (Johnson 1987: Fig. 23). He accounts for the abandonment of villages between the two centres by suggesting that both Susa and Choga Mish came to require agricultural produce from those communities. The pressure on these settlements resulted in their desertion. Whether this led to warfare, however, is a matter of speculation since the evidence (e.g., Fig. 30.) is open to various interpretations.

Often associated with warfare are city walls but, while they may have served a defensive purpose, they were closely associated with the Uruk social ideology (chapter **5.3.**). The importance of the city-wall as a symbol continued into the third millennium BC. It was the duty of the central authority to provide walls for the city as exemplified by the stories of Gilgamesh and later royal inscriptions commemorating the building works of rulers. "If the city's religious identity is expressed in the temple, its fortification walls represent its political identity" (Postgate 1992: 75). Walled cities served as centres of administration and during periods of turmoil they remained as sanctuaries of tradition and when stable condition returned acted to tame and 'Mesopotamize' any conquerors.

City-walls do, however, have a clear defensive role in the northern post-Uruk world. There is evidence for settlement walls at local Chalcolithic sites, for example, Early Bronze Age levels at Norsuntepe revealed superimposed defensive walls (Hauptmann 1972: Pl.66, 1) and large stone foundations indicate the early third millennium site of Tepecik was protected by a defensive wall (Esin 1979: Pl. 53, 5). An EB1 wall also known at Tulintepe (Esin 1982: Pl. 90) and Lidar Hoyuk (Hauptmann 1987). Further south at Tell Habuba on the Euphrates, a fortification wall existed through levels 2-6, including a later additional wall (Heusch 1979). Halawa B was also fortified (Luth 1989). These developments reflect a changing political situation which had a direct impact on contact with the south as communication and ideological systems were disrupted.

While raiding (family or tribal) may have been a feature of group dynamics from the earliest periods, warfare, as defined here, developed with the emergence of a concept of identity focused on the city. For war to take place it needed the identification of an enemy, the 'other' which could be the focus of aggression. Warfare may therefore be regarded as a development of the reformulation of the Uruk social ideology and the emergence of distinct city-states. It is therefore necessary to reject reconstructions of the Uruk phenomenon based purely on aggression. The spread of Uruk culture was not the result of the formation of an empire like that established by Sargon of Agade at the end of the third millennium BC, nor can it be compared with Nineteenth Century AD imperialism, where Western powers acquired territorial settlements, colonies, leases and concessions through military strength.

# 7. SUMMARY AND CONCLUSIONS

'Myths, dogmas, rituals, beliefs and activities . . . endow the social system with mystical values which evoke acceptance of the social order that goes far beyond the obedience exacted by the secular sanction of force'

(Fortes and Evans-Pritchard 1940: 19)

'Every social order is one of the possible solutions to a problem that is not scientific but human, the problem of community life'

(Aron 1954: 325)

The material record of Mesopotamia's past can be interpreted not as a mere passive reflection of a past society but as an active process which served to constitute as well as to reflect social relations. Thus whatever the immediate uses made of artefacts such as buildings and seals, all artefacts are also forms through which a society creates representations of itself and thereby makes itself. They provide an important element in the everyday world in which humans operate whether as individuals and/or as social groups and thus help to create history. The Uruk material culture, including the settlements themselves, are to be considered as artefacts, that is, 'artificial' creations of the Uruk civilization. The kinds of relations they represent would have been instrumental in the organisation of society.

## 7.1. The background to a social ideology

In north Mesopotamia, archaeologists have revealed a sequence suggesting settled occupation with agriculture from at least the seventh millennium gradually developing more sophisticated material culture, trade, and complexity of structures. By the fifth millennium there is evidence for larger buildings representing some form of communal activities and there are regional sequences showing signs of growing complexity from Anatolia to Susa. During the Ubaid period, a number of such regions developed more complex settlement hierarchies, specialized crafts, possibilities for the production and control over goods and new social hierarchies. There were thus highly developed incipient states with towns and monumental architecture from Anatolia and north Syria across to the Tigris (Tepe Gawra) and south to Susa and Eridu. These represented new levels of social differentiation, control over production, and exchange. It seems clear that these developments may be associated with strong widespread social ideologies (e.g., Akkermans 1989; Wright 1987; Wengrow 1998) and acculturation between regions (e.g., Breniquet 1996; Stein 1994).

The southern alluvial plain of Mesopotamia was a relatively homogeneous region. Local variations in the landscape resulted in specialism in agricultural production and interaction between local groupings (chapter *3.1.2.*). Interpretations of Ubaid house structures have suggested that society was based on family groupings which represented independent economic units. Such households included dependents who were non-kin, that is an augmented household structured around a dominant family. One can suggest that members of the more important groups played leading roles in the organization of the community including ritual activity within temple complexes.

In the Early Uruk period there is evidence from north Mesopotamia for a continued growth in the exploitation of resources and elaboration of communities, expressed in monumental architecture and elaborate accounting systems. There is limited evidence from Babylonia for this period but there are good indications that a similar development was taking place across the region, including population growth. Industrial production of ceramics in both north and south Mesopotamia probably reflects not just the development of new techniques of manufacture, but the exploitation of new products (dairy products, wine) and an expansion in the production and distribution of important parts of the existing economy (copper, beer, textiles) aided by the ability to transport more of it and further (domestication of donkeys and the development of the wheel). Although in the first half of the fourth millennium BC, the region's societies remained relatively closed (as demonstrated by ceramics) a continued expansion in the exploitation of resources probably led to a closer interaction between all regions.

At the end of the Early Uruk period there is an abandonment of many local Chalcolithic sites (Gut 1996). The causes of this settlement change is unclear but may be related to the growing political and economic strength of a number of places (e.g., Brak and Nineveh). These developments seem to have coincided with, or were soon followed by, the first Uruk presence in the area (e.g., Sheikh Hassan, Tell Brak). There is no evidence that this Uruk cultural expansion was the cause rather than an effect of the local Chalcolithic abandonment. It is also at this period that developments in administrative technology appear: cylinder seals are found at a number of sites suggesting connections along a route east of the Tigris through north Syria.

This is the first of two phases of expansion from the south and may be linked with a rise in population in that region during the Early Uruk (chapter 3.4). Supplementing vigorous indigenous growth of the settled agriculturalists, there was also either an extensive immigration into the area (from the north?) or a conversion of the semi-sedentary population into settled agriculturalists, or more probably, a combination of the two.

A restructuring of the population throughout Mesopotamia resulted in a dramatic elaboration of forms of social interaction and control on the southern plain. This social ideology (a development of an idea already rooted in the society) produced the distinctive material culture and settlements of the Uruk world.

## 7.2. The Uruk social ideology

The most important feature of the new Uruk settlements is that they were very ordered: the layout appears almost opposed to the natural environment in their planning and regularity. Many sites were established on virgin soil or, when within local settlements, Uruk structures occupy the highest area which may have strategic implications but also a symbolic role (see below). Whereas local Chalcolithic villages and towns developed in relation to the local conditions and betray in that form the developments of the society and inhabitants (a pattern of contraction and expansion of housing units reflecting the growth and decline of families, relations etc.), the Uruk sites were imposed on the landscape. Settlement patterns of Uruk sites like Habuba Kabira and Jebel Aruda were laid out within geometric forms with ordered streets. There are no major differences in the quality of the houses throughout the sites.

This form of planning is also visible in the more widely excavated Uruk non-residential monumental structures. There is the creation at great effort of massive brick platforms using standardised bricks to create the base for these large buildings and all sites seem to include the construction of such a 'tell' or, beyond the flat alluvial plain, the exploitation of natural elevations (e.g., Qannas, Jebel Aruda, Godin Tepe) The plan of buildings on this elevated area often appears as a larger reproduction of that which is found in the lower town. The similarity in design at Habuba Kabira where this design of buildings between the 'tell' and town is only distinguished by scale, might suggest that the larger structures are specific areas for a separate élite class. In the absence of associated élite material in these buildings it may indicate that they simply represent administrative and religious buildings used in the political and ritual control suggested by the creation and maintenance of such homogenous standards throughout Uruk sites. Monumental buildings are separated from the rest of the settlement by platforms, walls, and confined spaces. Where the buildings can be identified as temples (chapter 5.1.) the limited space within and around the structures suggests that there was no congregational approach to the divine which was rather part of the formalized ordering of society. Other areas within the monumental complex, however, consist of courtyards and open buildings decorated with cone mosaic. These may have served as assembly areas. Size again indicates that these could not have accommodated the entire population of a settlement but perhaps the important members of the community (family leaders) gathered there.

Such organisation and planning is also evident in the settlement enclosure walls. Although usually interpreted in terms of defensive structures, there is little evidence for conflict at any Uruk site, except in the Susiana plain where Choga Mish and Susa may have vied for (political/economic?) domination. Without denying the possibility of conflict over such a long duration as the Middle to Late Uruk Period, it is clear that many Uruk sites existed peacefully alongside local Chalcolithic cultures for centuries, (e.g., Hacinebi Tepe, Tell Brak). Although protection from raids by pastoralist groups or wild animals are possibilities, the scale of the walls suggest different concerns, perhaps a symbolic barrier against the outside world or nature.

While the local Chalcolithic cultures developed regional styles of mass produced pottery, the Uruk ceramic styles represent a standardisation that matches that found in architecture and settlement layout. The shapes of the vessels may well reflect their original contents (Potts 1997: 138-154) but they are found over the entire Uruk region and increasing evidence suggests local manufacture rather than trade (Peltenburg & Stephen 1998). The vessels are not markedly influenced by local Chalcolithic types (although limited numbers of Uruk pots or related wares are found in local Chalcolithic settlements) suggesting they were part of an ideological system reflecting food preferences, styles of serving and messages of conformity.

Besides ceramic shapes, Uruk decoration is restricted to a range of standardised forms whether clay cone mosaic on mud brick walls, glyptic art or wall painting. The depictions emphasise architecture, processions to buildings, mythological and domesticated animals and industrial production. The surviving sculpture, although often of very high artistic quality, maintains this conformity in the ideas expressed. There is the elimination of anything which might challenge the order that this standardisation represents. They lose their possibilities of specific reference, and tend towards formalism, referring not to groups of people, regions, or other external factors, but only to the order within which they were created.

The formalism of the Uruk as a set of ordered categories without external references aids in the interpretation of the evidence for ritual. There is no clear representation of a deity unless the figure on the Warka Vase depicts a goddess (Roaf 1990: 61) though this is contested by Ashur-Greve (1985). The most persistent character related to ritual activity is the so-called priest king. He may depict a single individual or a picture of a generic, 'model community representative'. Beyond ritual activities his role is unknown (even when he appears on cylinder seals as a warrior, e.g., Figs. 6.1-2, it is in relation to the temple). By the Late Uruk period a social ideology had developed which emphasised a contrast between the extreme order of urban agricultural life and the chaos of the natural world. To maintain the order against the forces of chaos it was necessary to focus life within an enclosed environment.

## 7.3. Uruk organisation

The penetration of this Uruk formal order was not absolute. An attempt to homogenise subsistence activities over this vast area would have been a disaster, and indeed there is regional variation. Differences in the economies between Uruk and Susa may be demonstrated for example by seal designs and variations in the administrative tools being used (chapter **6.1.**). The survival of the Uruk ideology over such a long period may have depended upon this pragmatic approach. Some settlers probably made use of local builders and building traditions (e.g. Godin Tepe, 'Riemchen-like' bricks at Tell Brak and non-Riemchen bricks at Sheikh Hassan) but, nonetheless, more important elements of the way of life were maintained in the form of ceramics and iconography. Bitumen, which is not widely found in local Chalcolithic sites, also appears as an important component of the Uruk world and so is brought in and processed locally.

Central to the order within settlements was the augmented family. The evidence from Habuba Kabira Süd and Jebel Aruda suggests that the sites were divided into parcels of land for such families. The domestic units reflected the social organisation with each structure divided between domestic and reception areas. These families were probably economically independent but provided offerings and tribute in the form of labour and materials to the temples and central organizational institutions. The leading members of the most important families represented the community, undertaking the necessary ritual activity to maintain the status quo within the natural/supernatural world. It is possible that they represented a form of 'council' or 'assembly' as represented in its most elaborate form by the professions list from Warka (Nissen et al 1993; Green and Nissen 1987; but see chapter **6.1.2.**). In this reconstruction, therefore, each Uruk settlement or, more likely, regional settlement was an independent entity. There was no Uruk political or economic empire organised and controlled from Babylonia (chapter **6.2.1.**).

The economy, therefore, consisted of multiple, interrelated component parts. Many people continued to live in households that worked to supply most of their own material needs as well as generating surpluses. These augmented family production centres, of various sizes, supplied larger institutions (temple, town council, élite family units) with offerings and tribute in the form of finished products and labour (the latter were paid in rations). The perceived natural order was reinforced by an iconography showing the major players in society as imposing or maintaining that system while the industrial centres are presented by ordered images of production and delivery (ritual processions). The wider exploitation of new resources across Mesopotamia encouraged the movement of people into new regions in what may have been a period of 'economic boom'.

## 7.4. The nature of power within the Uruk world

So what was the nature of power and interest in the Uruk world? This is the most difficult question to answer simply because the archaeological evidence is so limited. The failure to locate any Uruk cemeteries means the evidence for social inequalities and for possible traded or prestigious material reflecting the basis of power may be missing. There is evidence for exotic materials from Warka (Moorey 1994, Lindemeyer and Martin 1992 and 1993) but it is limited because of the continual rebuilding at the site and the fact that it comes from a specialised context (ceremonial centre). The apparent deliberate abandonment and clearance of northern Uruk sites at the end of the Uruk period also prevent any survey of distribution patterns of materials within sites (it is of course possible that there was little material to clear). It is therefore difficult to know whether individual Urukians who may be said to have had power enjoyed privileged wealth or conspicuous consumption. The surviving evidence suggests that it was rather the central institutions that received the material benefits of the system (as expressed most obviously in the extraordinary art of Warka). The representations of specific roles are all within a ritualised context.

In the Uruk, therefore, power resided in those organisational forms which ensured the reproduction of order, and which were as productive as they were constraining of social formations. While particular groups may at different times and places have been able to highlight their interests in some practices, this is not obvious in the available material representations which are devoted to this more profound and stable power. Uruk society valued an extreme normative order combined with control over the world. The formal structures, both monumental and domestic, isolated by barriers suggests a rigid, autocratic organisation with influences prevented from leaving or entering the system - there is no obvious acculturation in the Uruk world during the Late Uruk period. This does not mean that there was stagnation but rather a positive assertion of tradition. Nonetheless, it was a highly conservative culture and it was this conservatism that was a force of social reproduction.

There is, however, evidence for borrowing from the Uruk traditions both in local Chalcolithic societies within greater Mesopotamia (e.g. the iconography adopted for seals and paintings) and further afield such as the well known material from predynastic Egypt (Moorey 1987; 1990). It is quite likely that the majority of these images were being adopted by local élites and adapted to be incorporated into their own social ideologies. It is, however, possible to speculate that Urukians may have established centres in these distant regions, e.g. Buto, (von der Way 1992). The possibility also exists both within and outside the Uruk world for some 'conversions' to the social ideology.

## 7.5. The Uruk expansion

In chapter **3** a clear distinction between the organisational pattern of north and south Mesopotamia emerges. These configurations, which developed during the Ubaid period, resulted in distinct regional social ideologies; largely closed systems with interregional connections. By the middle of the fourth millennium BC, however, the culture of Babylonia began to penetrate the surrounding regions.

Various explanations have been suggested to account for the spread of the Uruk culture, many based on models of southern Mesopotamian economic and political domination (pages 145, 147, 151). These reconstructions are, therefore, based on a 'core-periphery' paradigm. What is now clear, however, is that many northern sites have a long history of complexity before the arrival of the Urukians in the region and cannot be described as 'peripheral', e.g., Qalinj Agha (al-Soof 1969); Tell Brak where, in level 18 (Early Uruk), was a monumental mud brick wall up to 2 metres wide (Oates 1998), while another wall (area CH, Early Uruk) had buttresses and niches (Oates 1987: 177, pl. XXXIa) comparable to those at contemporary Tepe Gawra (3.2.2.ii. and 4.1.2.iv.); and Hammam et Turkman, where a 1.25 metre wide wall with decorative recessed buttresses against its western side was built on top of a platform during the Early Uruk (Meijer 1988). With no evidence that these sophisticated societies became dominated by southern polities, an emphasis on core-periphery has been rejected in this book in favour of a model which, while emphasising the importance of economic expansion, views it as a development that occurs right across Greater Mesopotamia: industrial production in textiles, ceramics, metalwork and agricultural produce. It was the exploitation of these various resources, but particularly those already exploited on the southern alluvium, which led the inhabitants of Babylonia to explore new regions in response to the demands generated by population increases and reorganisation, and developments in technology.

Initially, in the Middle Uruk period, Uruk settlements formed a pattern similar to that established by trading mechanisms of the third millennium (Crawford 1992). There was a second phase of expansion, however, in the Late Uruk which resulted from the infiltration of southern Mesopotamians, agriculturalists and their families, potters and other craftsmen into available agricultural land. Whether or not these were refugees fleeing growing political oppression at Warka, as suggested by Johnson (1988-89), can only be left as speculation based of the available evidence. It is significant that the collapse of many of the northern local Chalcolithic sites in the Early-Middle Uruk may have permitted the increasingly rich economic units of Babylonia to penetrate into the north. This argues against the creation of an early empire based on military aggression: comparisons with the Agade expansion of the late third millennium are therefore unnecessary.

The resulting pattern that this expansion took, however, can only be understood by recognising the importance of the developed social ideology. A possible historical analogy, as suggested by Zagarell (1989), is the Greek colonisation of the eighth to sixth century BC. The political and economic background of the Uruk and Greek colonial experience may have been very different - the evidence is simply not sufficient to establish whether Uruk sites were founded by a 'mother-city' or a rather lie in a less formal tribal/kin based structure. However, in both cases of colonialism the social ideology was an essential component of its creation. In the Greek case the founder was an aristocratic leader, always remembered in religious ritual at the core of the community: he organised and commanded the settlers, planned the layout of the settlement, supervised the distribution of land: 'he drew a wall round the city and built houses, and made temples of the gods and divided the fields' (Homer, *Odyssey* 6.9f.). As with the Uruk colonial sites, there were only a small number of initial settlers, perhaps 200 or less (Murray 1980: 110). However, in some of the outer Uruk settlements (e.g. Godin Tepe, Hassak Höyük) the mechanisms proposed by Algaze may indeed be appropriate.

Adams (1981:309) has suggested that the spread of Uruk culture across Mesopotamia was being legitimated in terms of a southern Mesopotamian religious ideology where "the land belonged to the temple gods and humans were merely its stewards, then one may ask whether the Uruk expansion was simply expressing its 'manifest destiny' and claiming those lands in the name of their divinity" (Adams 1981: 309). While religious proselytizing is not a feature of the ancient world, if one substitutes 'religion' with 'social' and 'the gods' for 'urban order', the statement remains valid.

## 7.6. The end of the Uruk phenomenon

It is against this background that we can best understand the particular nature of the evidence for the end of the Uruk. Although the impression is of a strong coherent system considerable changes were occurring in the production, distribution, and consumption of food, along with modifications in social organization and ways of life. It was probably such developments which led to increasing competition between neighbouring centres as tribal-kin identity became focused within a specific urban environment. This is reflected in the conflict reconstructed between Choga Mish and Susa (chapter **6.4.**). Thus the Uruk social ideology, which emphasised and so accelerated the rise of the city, ultimately created one of the factors in its own demise.

Towards the end of the Uruk period there is evidence for a major expansion in the symbols of order. For example, massive platforms were constructed at Jebel Aruda and Warka (level III). In the case of Warka, what ever buildings were intended to surmount this mountain of mud brick they were never constructed. The creation of these major structures may reflect an attempt to shore up the system. This would be consistent with contradictions emerging in the ideological basis of the culture that unified the various elements and justified its continuance.

The end of the Uruk period witnessed changes in settlement patterns in the north as new groups of people, ultimately from east Anatolia/Transcaucasia, had moved into the area (chapter **6.4.**; Lupton 1996: 94-97; Frangipane and Palmieri 1988). Fortifications now encircled many sites, suggesting troubled times. Communications and supply lines may well have been disrupted and access to local resources (e.g. pasture lands) would have been restricted. The rigidly structured Uruk world may have lacked the flexibility to respond to such major changes beyond its home lands in Babylonia. From a practical point of view it may have been increasingly difficult to maintain alien communities at such a time but such events would also have put pressure on the social ideology as it attempted to cope with the increasing pressure from the chaotic world beyond the city walls.

The best evidence for charting the decline of the Uruk world comes from Jebel Aruda (5.2.2.ii.). Already by the time of the fire which virtually brought the settlement to an end, many of the houses were closed up, and their goods packed into a single store room. The decline of the settlement had clearly been going on for some time, as there are signs of changing functions in many of the rooms. Former reception rooms were being subdivided or used for storage or craft activities, and former living quarters were being used for storage (van Driel 1998). The organisational principals embodied in the architecture were clearly breaking down.

The majority of Uruk sites show no evidence of destruction. Habuba Kabira Süd and Godin Tepe, for example, are apparently deliberately cleared and abandoned. There is evidence of some Uruk continuity in north Mesopotamia at Tell Brak (see below), but this is an exception. In the south, the material from the Susiana Plain also shows a change. There is a break in the stratigraphic sequence in the Susa Acropole sounding and a new material culture emerges. This seems to reflect either a the collapse of Uruk influence in favour of communities living on the plateau of Iran, or the entire site was abandoned before being resettled by highland people (Proto-Elamite/Susa III Period). In Babylonia itself, survey data suggests that there was also widespread disruption with many sites abandoned. It is only at the end of the post-Uruk period (Jemdet Nasr) that rural settlement increases at the fringes of Babylonia and at the centre where the population moved from villages to towns (Postgate 1986). Such extended rural settlement is probably a reflection of a return to more peaceful times (Adams 1981: 88).

With both internal and external pressure put on the ordered structure of the Uruk urban social ideology there was a general crisis in the framework of social life and in the way individuals related to each other and to society. Traditional institutions, sociocultural patterns, and scales of values were subject to processes of disintegration.

## 7.7. The legacy of the Uruk phenomenon

If these suggestions about the nature of the Late Uruk culture are true, that it was strongly organized around an ideology which expressed itself in a highly structured system of life, then it is possible that aspects of the ideology might have survived the collapse of the Uruk world. Many ideas may not have just disappeared, but have been a vital source of inspiration in Early Bronze I, with different effects in three distinct regions: southern Mesopotamia, Elam and Syria.

It is only after the Uruk contact period that the use of cylinders became almost universal in Greater Mesopotamia (Matthews 1997: 61). It is possible that this followed from a change in how the use of seals was understood in society. It should, however, be noted that stamp seals continue to be used throughout the same region.

Beyond the Uruk world there is evidence for the adaptation of Uruk cylinder seals or their designs for local use. The so-called Aleppo series of seals (Matthews 1997:58) are defined by special attachments on the seal stones, a handle or a loop-bore. A difficulty is posed by this series in that almost all the seals come from an area of north Syria were most of the material is unstratified, from bad contexts or later provenances. 'Byre-shaped' seals belong in this group and Amiet (1980: 199) has noted that with this type, domestic scenes and animals can appear together on the same seal unlike in the drilled Late Uruk glyptic of Mesopotamia. Since there are no examples of byre seals from any Late Uruk sites, it is possible that these are part of a local tradition which emerged after the Uruk presence had disappeared from the region (Matthews 1997:59).

In the Diyala region a style developed related to fine Uruk glyptic showing animals approaching a 'temple' building (Collon 1987: 16). In addition, seals with rows of fish, birds and scorpions which were made in the Uruk period from Iran to western Syria continued into the post-Uruk early Ninevite V period. Many of these are not clearly related to the main Uruk traditions and may represent independent applications of stamp seal style onto cylinders (Matthews 1997: 57).

Teissier (1987) has demonstrated the close links which exist between stamp seals and early Levantine cylinders, especially in the glyptic of Byblos, in features such as tête-bêche, animal protomes, the griffin and the detail in tails, feet and hands. Her argument is that the inspiration comes from Elam to Egypt. The designs however could be equally at home in the western stamp tradition (Matthews 1997:60). Designs related to Uruk style are also found in Palestine and Egypt certainly demonstrating the extensive network of communication at the end of the fourth millennium (Teissier 1987).

Real continuity in glyptic design after the Uruk period is reflected outside southern Mesopotamia with geometric seals. These may even be connected to the fine Proto-Elamite and the schematic fired steatite cylinders (Pittman 1994). Matthews sees these as Elam attempting to reconstruct the Uruk administration on stronger lines (1997: 194). Indeed, Damerow and Englund (1989) have demonstrated that the numerical systems (with the exception of a decimal and bisexagesimal system) used at Susa during the Susa III period were either identical to or else derived from the systems already in use during the Late Uruk. A Proto-Elamite writing system is found at Tal-i Malyan/Anshan, Susa and across the Iranian Plateau (one tablet found at Tal-i Ghazir, Tepe Sialk, Shahr-i Sokhta and twenty-seven from Tepe Yahya). Nonetheless, the Proto-Elamite script cannot be read and the graphic parallels that exist between the Mesopotamian and Susa III texts that do exist "are of a type which have been observed in widely separated cultures on more than one occasion and therefore should not be accorded much, if any significance" (*ibid.* 1989: 6 and 7, n. 23).

However, the developments of the post-Uruk world would be expected to be reflected in seal designs within the homeland of the Uruk culture if they were part of a supposed Uruk system which had completely disappeared. Yet little difference can be detected between the seal impressions on the Uruk IV and Uruk III tablets which is surprising as seal styles usually change quickly. Matthews (1997:17) suggests that the Uruk III (Jemdet Nasr Period) impressions are in fact Uruk IV but this sounds like special pleading. He argues that the Uruk world was a politically unified region and questions how it would have been possible that a style which originated in such a context could have survived the collapse of the system without showing any stylistic changes. However, the lack of rapid change may be the result of a conservative ideology able to ensure social stability and continuity in changing conditions (but clearly only in a region where the ideology had its origin and was deeply rooted in society). The archaic impressions therefore preserve an essentially Uruk view of the world.

The Babylonian post-Uruk (Jemdet Nasr) period also saw developments of Uruk administrative tools other than seals. Numerals and pictographs were now standardized across southern Mesopotamia and Sumerian began to be written. Independent city-states governed their relationships by diplomatic means, perhaps in a 'League of Cities' (Matthews, R.J. 1993), which included interregional cooperation with labour as state formation emerged. This movement to full urbanization and political identity resting with the city, as demonstrated by 'city seals', increasingly resulted in military competition for access to resources and sovereignty. The Uruk community offices, held by members of the leading families, thus acquired the attributes of monarchies. Nonetheless, the Uruk emphasis on an urban environment was perpetuated: for Sumerians the city represented civilization in its literal sense.

Exceptionally, a short lived example of continuity with the Uruk world is found beyond the southern alluvium at Tell Brak. As one of the first local Chalcolithic sites to have connections with the Uruk it appears also to have been among the last, suggesting a strong stable society that had adopted aspects of the Uruk world and maintained them. In area TW, levels 9-10 a number of ceramic types were found identical to those from Jemdet Nasr in the south, including two polychrome sherds (contemporary with Warka Eanna III). Tall 'flower pots' also appear to be local developments on the standard fourth millennium mass-produced vessels (Oates 1993: 405). This thus extends the Uruk presence, or social ideology, at Tell Brak into the post-Uruk period.

## 7.8. Theoretical review

The available evidence does not suggest that the Uruk world was the result of southern Mesopotamian domination of long distance exchange networks. Such theories based on 'core-periphery' models with unequal exchange relations have increasingly been shown to be flawed (e.g., Lupton 1996). There is limited evidence for differences between northern and southern modes of production: textiles and ceramics important craft activities across the region. The emphasis on trade mechanisms in studies has tended to obscure essential relations within communities and how these effect many of the patterns visible in the archaeological record. Where they have been investigated it is often in terms of the ruling élite (a political ideology). The focus has tended to concentrate on such things as exotic materials which can be taken as evidence of status. Such symbols may then be exchanged between equal ranking individuals or offices. Inevitably this brings in the question of procurement of the rare materials and international relations.

What is ignored is the role of the wider population and their place in the ideology. Thus people are viewed as simply serving the élite and play no part in the generation of a political ideology. Work on more recent periods has demonstrated the importance of taking a wider view and appreciating the importance of a social ideology. For example, twentieth century Europe has been dominated by political ideologies: Fascism, Communism and liberal democracy. The latter has so far emerged as triumphant, but, as Mazower (1999) has pointed out, there was no inevitability in this. The other ideologies (particularly Fascism) were not processes "in which people were hoodwinked by powerful regimes through censorship and manipulation. It is rather, a story of values shared, and argued over jointly, by leadership and population alike. The fundamental utopian projects . . . projected positive images of a new, undivided nation and were far from unpopular" (Mazower 1999: 36). Thus social ideologies actually created and supported the ruling élite. It is true that the ideology was reinforced through leadership cults, monumental buildings, mass rallies and parades which offered ritual and projected a sense of power, but ultimately much "of Nazi domestic policy could be fitted smoothly into traditional German life" (Mazower 1999: 38). That social ideologies are a powerful force in creating forms of community relations can apply as much to ancient world as the modern. This is demonstrated by studies of the Harappan culture (chapter **2.2.**). The Uruk world consisted of a social ideology linked to opposition to nature. In the form it developed the ideology failed. However, if "the dogmas of the past no longer hold us in their grip, this does not mean that they were merely grand deceptions from the start" (Mazower 1999: xii.).

## 7.9. Future research

A variety of research questions have emerged from this study. The most important, inevitably, concern those periods where evidence is especially lacking. The Early Uruk is poorly known throughout Mesopotamia. What then were the reasons for the disappearance of many local Chalcolithic settlements at this time? Was it related to the dominance of centres like Tell Brak and can this be linked to growing complexity across Mesopotamia? What were the steps that led from the Ubaid farming communities of Babylonia to the structures which created the Uruk phenomenon? Only further field work can provide answers to these questions.

Equally important is to gain an understanding of what was happening in the Uruk villages of Babylonia. More evidence is required to understand the relationship between the rural economy and the emerging cities. Indications of production and distribution can only be provided by survey and excavation. Similarly, investigation is required to discover the nature of Uruk occupation at the large local Chalcolithic sites. How was the contact organised? What benefits did the local communities gain from the association? Again only further fieldwork can provide the answers.

In terms of social ideologies it would be possible to apply the approaches in this book to the material of north Mesopotamia. Did the distinct regions identified in chapter ***3.1.2.*** have distinct ideologies or were they linked in more subtle ways than the ceramic evidence suggests? The presence of 'eye idols' and 'hut symbols' at many local Chalcolithic sites might suggest evidence of a possible common belief system. How did the Uruk social ideology compare with those of north Mesopotamia and is there a relationship between these and earlier Ubaid and Halaf world views?

A more detailed investigation of the Uruk legacy than could be undertaken in this thesis would be useful. How does the imagery and ideology of the Early Dynastic and Proto-Elamite worlds reflect continuity or novelty in relation to the Uruk phenomenon? The Uruk phenomenon may have ultimately been a failure but it appears to have laid the foundations for future Mesopotamian cultural unity.

# REFERENCES

Adams, R. McC. 1962. 'Agriculture and Urban Life in Early Southwestern Iran.' *Science* **136**: 109-22.

Adams, R. McC. 1966. *The Evolution of Urban Society: Early Mesopotamian and Prehispanic Mexico.* Chicago: Aldine.

Adams, R. McC. 1974. 'The Mesopotamian social landscape: a view from the frontier.' In C.B. Moore, *Reconstructing complex societies: an archaeological colloquium.* pp. 1-12. Bulletin of the American Schools of Oriental Research supplement 20.

Adams, R. McC. 1981. *Heartland of Cities.* Chicago: University Of Chicago Press.

Adams, R. McC., and H.-J. Nissen. 1972. *The Uruk Countryside.* Chicago: University of Chicago Press.

Akkermans, P.P.M.G. 1988. 'An updated Chronology for the Northern Ubaid and the Late Chalcolithic Periods in Syria: New Evidence from Hammam et-Turkman.' *Iraq* **50**: 109-146.

Akkermans, P.P.M.G. 1989. 'Tradition and Social Change in Northern Mesopotamia during the Later Fifth and Fourth Millennium B.C.' In E. F. Henrickson and I. Thuesen, eds., *Upon This Foundation - The Ubaid Reconsidered*, pp. 339 - 368. Copenhagen: Museum Tusculanum Press.

Alden, J. 1982. 'Trade and Politics in Proto-Elamite Iran.' *Current Anthropology* **23**: 613 - 628.

Alden, J.R. 1988. 'Ceramic Ring Scrapers: An Uruk Period Pottery Production Tool.' *Paléorient* **14/1**: 143-150.

Alessio, J., L. Allegri, C. Azzi, F. Bella, G. Calderoni, C. Cortesi, S. Imptota, V. Petrone. 1988. 'C14 dating at Arslantepe.' *Origini* **XII /2**: 575-580.

Algaze, G. 1986. 'Habuba on the Tigris: archaic Nineveh reconsidered.' *Journal of Near Eastern Studies* **45**: 125-137.

Algaze, G. 1989. 'The Uruk Expansion, Cross-cultural Exchange in early Mesopotamian Civilization.' *Current Anthropology* **30**: 571-608.

Algaze, G. 1993. *The Uruk World System: the dynamics of early Mesopotamian civilization.* Chicago: University of Chicago Press.

Algaze, G., T. D'Altroy, M. Frangipane, H. Nissen, H. Pittman, S. Pollock, M. Rothman, G. Schwartz, G. Stein, and H. Wright. 1998. 'School of American Research Advanced Seminar: Mesopotamia in the Era of Sate Formation.' http://www.science.widener.edu/ssci/mesopotamia / accessed 3rd December.

Allchin, B and R. Allchin, 1982. *The Rise of Civilization in India and Pakistan.* Cambridge: Cambridge University Press.

al-Soof, B. 1969. 'Excavations at Tell Qalinj Agha (Erbil).' *Sumer* **25**: 3-42.

Amiet, P. 1972. *Glyptique susienne. Mémoires de la délégation archéologique française en iran 43.* Paris: Geuthner.

Amiet, P. 1977. *L'Art antique du Proche-Orient.* Paris.

Amiet. P. 1979. 'Archaeological discontinuity and ethnic duality in Elam.' *Antiquity* **53**: 195-204.

Amiet, P. 1980. *La glyptique Mésopotamienne archaïque*. Paris: Centre National de la Recherche Scientifique.

Amiet 1994. review of Algaze, G. 'The Uruk World System'. *Revue d'Assyriologie et d'archéologie orientale* 88: 1-4.

Andrae, W. 1922. *Die Archaischen Ischtar-Tempel in Assur*. Leipzig: Wissenschaftliche Veroffentlichung der Deutchen Orient-Gesellschaft.

Aron, R. 1954. *The Century of Total War*. London.

Asher-Greve, J.M., and W.B. Stern. 1983. 'A New Analytical Method and its Application to Cylinder Seals.' *Iraq* 45: 157-62.

Ashur-Greve, J.M. 1985. *Frauen in altsumerischer zeit*. Malibu: Undena Publications.

Atre, S. 1989. 'Toward an economico-religious model for Harappan urbanism.' *South Asian Studies* 5: 49-58.

Bader, N.O. 1993. Summary of 'The Earliest Agriculturalists of Northern Mesopotamia (1989).' In N. Yoffee and J.L. Clark (eds.), *Early Stages in the Evolution of Mesopotamian Civilization: Soviet Excavations in Northern Iraq*. pp. 63-72. Tucson and London: University of Arazona Press.

Badler, V.R. 1998. 'A Chronology of Uruk Artefacts from Godin Tepe, Central Western Iran.' Paper presented at Artefacts of Complexity: Tracking the Uruk in the Near East. University of Manchester 6-7th November 1998.

Badler, V.R., P. McGovern, and D.L. Glusker. 1996. 'Chemical evidence for a wine residue from Warka (Uruk) inside a Late Uruk period spouted jar.' *Baghdader Mitteilungen* 27: 39-43.

Baines, J., and N. Yoffee, 1998. 'Order, Legitimacy, and Wealth in Ancient Egypt and Mesopotamia.' In *Archaic States*. pp. 119-260. Santa Fe: School of American Research Press.

Bar-Adon, P. 1980. *The Cave of the Treasure, the finds from the caves at Nahal Mishmar*. Jerusalem: Israel Exploration Society.

Barley, N. 1994. *Smashing Pots*. London: British Museum Publications.

Barrelet, M.Th. 1968. *Figurines et reliefs en terre cuite de la Mesopotamie antique I*. Paris: Geuthner.

Barrelet, M.Th. 1974. 'Dispositifs à feu et cuisson des aliments à Ur, Nippur et Uruk.' *Paléorient* 2: 243-310.

Basmachi, F. 1947. 'The Votive Vase from Warka.' *Sumer* 3: 118-127.

Basmachi, F. 1950. 'Sculptured Stone Vases in the Iraq Museum.' *Sumer* 6: 165-76.

Baudot, P. 1979. 'Iconographic Study of the Vessels on Archaic Near Eastern seals.' *Orientalia Lovaniensia Periodica* 10: 5-67.

Beal, T.W. 1978. 'Bevelled rim bowls and their implications for change and economic organization in the later fourth millennium BC.' *Journal of Near Eastern Studies* 37: 289-313.

Beal, T.W. and S.M. Carter, 1983. 'On the Track of the Yahya Large Kuš: Evidence for Architectural Planning in the Period IV C complex at Tepe Yahya.' *Paléorient* 9/1: 81-89.

Behm-Blancke, M.R. 1979. *Das Tierbild in der Altmesopotamischen Rundplastik*. Mainz am Rhein.

Behm-Blancke, M.R. 1985. 'Die Ausgrabungen auf dem Hassek Höyük im Jahre 1984.' *Kazi Sonuçlari Toplantisi* VII. pp. 87- 102. Ankara: Eski Eserler ve Müzeler Genel Müdürlügü.

Behm-Blancke, M.R. 1986. 'Die Ausgrabungen auf dem Hassek Höyük im Jahre 1985.' *Kazi Sonuçlari Toplantisi* VIII. pp.139-148. Ankara: Eski Eserler ve Müzeler Genel Müdürlügü.

Behm-Blancke, M.R. 1989. 'Mosaikstifte am Oberen Euphrat-Wandschmuck aus der Uruk Zeit.' *Istanbuler Mitteilungen* 39: 73-83.

Behm-Blancke, M.R. 1991. 'Hassek Hoyuk. Eine Uruk Station im Grenzland zu Anatolien.' *Nurberger Blatter zur Archaologie* 8: 82-94.

Behm-Blancke, M.R., H. Becker, J. Boesneck, A. von der Driesch, M.R. Hoh, G. Wiegand. 1981. 'Hassek Höyük: Vorläufiger Bericht über die Ausgrabungen den Jareh 1978-1980.' *Istanbuler Mitteilungen* 31: 11-94.

Behm-Blancke, M.R., M.R. Hoh, N. Karg, L. Masch, F. Parsche, K.L. Winer, A. von Wickede, G. Ziegelmayer. 1984. 'Hassek Höyük: Vorlaüfiger Bericht über die Ausgrabungen den Jareh 1981-1983.' *Istanbuler Mitteilungen* 34: 31-150.

Binford, L.R. 1987. 'Data, relativism and archaeological science.' *Man* **22**: 391-404

Black, J. & Green, A. 1992. *Gods, Demons and Symbols of Ancient Mesopotamia: An Illustrated Dictionary.* London: British Museum Press.

Blanton, R.E. 1989. 'Continuity and Change in Public Architecture: Periods I through V of the Valley of Oaxaca, Mexico.' In S.A. Kowalewski, G.M. Feinman, L. Finsten, R.E. Blanton, and L.M. Nicholas (eds.), *Monte Albán's Hinterland, Part II: The Prehispanic Settlement Patterns in Tlacolula, Etla, and Ocotlán, the Valley of Oaxaca, Mexico.* pp. 409-47. memoirs 23. Museum of Anthropology, University of Michigan: Ann Arbor.

Boehmer, R.M. 1990. 'Zur Funktion des Steinstifttempels in Uruk.' *Baghdader Mitteilungen* **19**: 49-65.

Boehmer, R.M. 1991. 'Uruk 1980-1990: A Progress Report.' *Antiquity* **65**: 465-78.

Boese, J. 1989. 'Excavations at Tell Sheikh Hassan. Preliminary report on the 1987 campaign in the Euphrates valley.' *Annales Archéologiques Arabes Syriennes* **36-37**: 67-101.

Boese, J 1991a. 'Excavations at Tell Sheikh Hassan. Preliminary report on the 1988 campaign in the Euphrates valley.' *Annales Archéologiques Arabes Syriennes* **37-38**: 158-189.

Boese, J. 1991b. 'Tell Sheikh Hassan 1984-1986.' *Archiv für Orientforschung* **36-37**: 323-332.

Boese, J. 1995. *Ausgrabungen in Tell Sheikh Hassan, Vorläufiger Berichte über die Grabungskampagnen 1984-1990 und 1992-1994.* Saarbrücker: Saarbrücker Druckerei und verlag.

Bonatz, D., H. Köhune, and A. Mahmoud, 1998. *Rivers and Steppes: Cultural Heritage and Environment of the Syrian Jezireh. Catalogue of the Museum of Deir ez-Zor.* Damascus: Directorate-General of Antiquities and Museums.

Börker-Klähn, J. 1982. *Altvorderasiatische Bildstelen und Vergleichbare Felsreliefs.* Mainz: Philipp von Zabern.

Boulding, K.E. 1956. 'General System Theory- The Skeleton of Science.' *Management Science* April. pp. 197-208. Institute of management Science: University of Colorado.

Braidwood, R. J., and L. S. Braidwood. 1960. *Excavations in the Plain of Antioch I. Oriental Institute Publications 61.* Chicago: University of Chicago Press.

Brandes, M.A. 1979. *Siegelabrollungen aus den Archaischen Bauschichten in Uruk-Warka.* Wiesbaden: GMBH.

Breniquet, C. 1989. 'Les origines de la culture d'Obeid en Mésopotamie du nord.' In E. F. Henrickson and I. Thuesen, eds., *Upon This Foundation - The Ubaid Reconsidered.* pp. 325 -338. Copenhagen: Museum Tusculanum Press.

Breniquet, C. 1991. 'Tell es-Sawwan - realités et problèmes.' *Iraq* **53**: 75-90.

Breniquet, C. 1992. 'Rapport sur deux campagnes de fouilles à Tell Es-Sawwan, 1988-1989.' *Mesopotamia* **27**: 5-30.

Breniquet, C. 1996. *La Disparition de la Culture de halaf: Les origines de la culture d'Obeid dans le Nord de la Mésopotamie.* Paris: Editions Recherche sur les Civilisations.

Bridel, P., C. Krause, K. Schuler, and R. Stucky, 1974. *Tell al Hajj, Zweiter Vorläufiger Bericht.* Bern: Universität Bern.

Brüschweiler, F. 1983. 'La Ville dans les textes littéraires sumériens.' In Brüschweiler, F. (ed.), *La ville dans le proche-orient ancien: Actes du Colloque de Cartigny.* pp. 181-98. Leuven: Éditions Peeters.

Buccellati, G. 1990. 'Salt at the dawn of History: The case of the Bevelled-Rim Bowls.' In Matthiae, P. Van Loon, M, and Weiss, H. (eds.) *Resurrecting the Past: A joint tribute to Adnan Bounni.* pp. 17-40. Istanbul & Leiden: Nederlands Instituut vor het Nabije Oostern.

Calderoni, L., I. Caneva, A. Cazzella, M. Frangipane and V. Petrone. 1994. 'Department of Earth Sciences at the University of Rome Radiocarbon Dates III.' *Radiocarbon* **36** (1): 143-152.

Canal, D. 1978. 'La terrace de l'Acropole de Suse.' *Cahiers de la Délégation Archéologique Française en Iran* 9 : 11-55.

Carneiro, R.L. 1978. 'Political expansion as an expression of the principle of comparative exclusion.' in R. Cohen & E.R. Service (eds.), *Origins of the state: the anthropology of political evolution.* pp. 205-23. Philadelphia: Institute for the Study of Human Issues.

Carter, E. 1978. 'Suse, Ville Royale I.' *Paléorient* **4**: 197-211.

Carter, E., and M. W. Stolper 1984. *Elam: surveys of political history and archaeology.* Berkeley: University of California Press.

Cauvin, J., and D. Stordeur 1985. 'Une occupation d'époche Uruk en Palmyrène: Le niveau supérieur d'El Kowm 2-Caracol.' *Cahiers de l'Euphrate* **4** : 191 - 206.

Chagnon, N. 1990. 'On Yanomanö violence: Reply to Albert.' *Current Anthropology* **31**: 49-53.

Chakrabati, D.K. 1997. *The Archaeology of Ancient Indian Cities.* Delhi: Oxford India Paperbacks

Chapman, R., I. Kinnes, & K. Randsborg (eds.) 1981. *The Archaeology of Death.* Cambridge: Cambridge University Press.

Chazan, M. and Lehner, M. 1990. 'An Ancient Analogy: Pot baked bread in Ancient Egypt and Mesopotamia.' *Paléorient* **16/2**: 21-35.

Childe, G. 1936. *Man makes himself.* London: Watts.

Coe, M.D. 1989. 'The Olmec heartland: evolution of ideology.' In R.J. Sharer and D.C. Grove, *Regional perspectives on the Olmec.* pp. 68-84. Cambridge: Cambridge University Press.

Cohen, S. 1973. 'Enmerkar and the Lord of Aratta'. University of Pennsylvania Ph.D; Ann Arbor: University Microfilms.

Collingwood, R.G. 1993. *The Idea of History* (Revised edition). Oxford: Oxford University Press.

Collins, P. 1994. 'The Sumerian goddess Inanna (3400-2200 BC).' *Papers from the Institute of Archaeology* **5**: 103-118.

Collon, D. 1987. *First Impressions. Cylinder Seals in the Ancient Near East.* London: British Museum Press.

Collon, D. 1995. *Ancient Near Eastern Art.* London: British Museum.

Collon, D., and J. Reade 1983 'Archaic Nineveh.' *Baghdader Mitteilungen* **14** : 33 - 43.

Connan, J. and Deschene O. 1991. 'Le bitume dans l'antquité.' *La Recherche* **22**: 156

Connan, J. and Deschesne, O. 1996. *Le Bitume à Suse.* Paris: Éditions de la Réunion des musées nationaux.

Conrad, G.W. and Demarest, A.A. 1984. *Religion and Empire. The Dynamics of Aztec and Inca Expansion.* Cambridge: Cambridge University Press.

Cooper, J.S. 1983. *Reconstructing History from Ancient Inscriptions: the Lagash-Umma Border Conflict.* Malibu: Sources from the Ancient Near East 2/1.

Cooper, J.S. 1986. *Sumerian and Akkadian Royal Inscriptions Volume I: Presargonic Inscriptions.* New Haven: The American Oriental Society.

Crawford, H. E. W. 1973. 'Mesopotamia's Invisible Exports in the Third Millennium.' *World Archaeology* **5**: 232 - 241.

Crawford, H.E.W. 1978. 'The mechanics of the obsidian trade: a suggestion.' *Antiquity* **52**: 129 - 132.

Crawford, H.E.W. 1991. *Sumer and the Sumerians.* Cambridge: Cambridge University Press.

Crawford, H.E.W. 1992. 'An Early Dynastic Trading Network in North Mesopotamia.' *La circulation des biens, des personnes et des idees dans le Proche-Orient ancien, XXXVIII R.A.I.* Paris: Editions Recherche sur les Civilisations.

Crawford, V.E. 1959. 'Nippur, the Holy City.' *Archaeology* **12**: 75-83.

Curtis, J.E. 1986. 'A Basalt Sculpture Found at Warka.' *Baghdader Mitteilungen* **17**: 131-4.

Dalley, S. 1984. *Mari and Karana: Two Old Babylonian Cities.* Longman: London & New York.

D'Altroy, T., and T. Earle 1985. 'Staple Finance, Wealth Finance, and Storage in the Inka Political Economy.' *Current Anthropology* **26/2**: 187-206.

Darling, P.J. 1988. 'Emerging towns in Benin and Ichan (Nigeria) A.D. 500-1500.' In J. Gledhill, B. Bender, M.T. Larsen, eds., *State and Society. The emergence and Development of Social Hierarchy and Political Centralisation.* pp. 121-136. London: Unwin Hyman.

Dawkins, R. 1989. *The Selfish gene.* Oxord: Oxford University Press.

Dawkins, R. 1991. *The Blind Watchmaker.* Harmondsworth: Penguin.

de Jesus, P.S. 1980. *The Development of Prehistoric Mining and Metallurgy in Anatolia.* Oxford: BAR International Series, 74 (i and ii).

Deimal, A. 1931. *Šumerische Tempelwirtschaft zur Zeit Urukaginas und seiner Vorgänger.* Rome: Analecta Orientalia 2.

Delougaz, P. 1940. *The Temple Oval at Khafajeh*. Chicago: Oriental Institute Publications 53

Delougaz, P. 1952. *Pottery from the Diyala Region*. Chicago: Oriental Institute Publications 63

Delougaz, P. 1968. 'Animals emerging from a hut' *Journal of Near Eastern Studies* **27**: 186-7.

Delougaz, P. and H.J. Kantor, 1973. 'Choga Mish.' *Iran* **XI**: 189-191.

Delougaz, P. & H.J. Kantor, 1996. *Choga Mish volume I: the first five seasons of excavations 1961-1971*. OIP 601.

Dennett, D.C. 1995. *Darwin's Dangerous Idea: Evolution and the meanings of life*. Harmondsworth: Penguin.

Diakonoff, I.M. 1969. 'The rise of the despotic state in ancient Mesopotamia.' In I.M. Diakonoff (ed.), *Ancient Mesopotamia: A Socio-Economic History. A Collection of Studies by Soviet Scholars*. Moscow: Nauka Publishing House. pp. 173-203.

Diakonoff, I.M. 1974. *Structure of Society and State in Early Dynastic Sumer*. Malibu: Monographs of the Ancient Near East I/3.

Diakonoff, I.M. 1982. 'The structure of Near Eastern society before the middle of the 2nd millennium BC.' *Oikumene* **3** : 7-100.

Dittmann, R. 1986. 'Seals, Sealings and Tablets: Thoughts on the Changing Pattern of Administrative Control from the Late Uruk to the Proto-Elamite Period at Susa.' In U. Finkbeiner and W. Rollig (eds.), *Gamdat Nasr: Period or Regional Style?* pp. 332-366. Beihefte zum Tübinger Atlas des Vorderen Orients, Reiche B, Nr. 62. Weisbaden: Ludwig Reïchert.

Duly, C. 1979. *The houses of mankind*. London: Thames and Hudson.

Dunham, S. 1983. 'Notes on the Relative Chronology of Early Northern Mesopotamia.' *Journal of Ancient Near Eastern Society* **15**: 13-38

Durkheim, E. 1915. *The Elementary Forms of the Religious Life*. Trans. J.W. Swain. London: Unwin.

Durkheim, E. 1982. *The Rules of Sociological Method*. London: Macmillan. First published 1895.

Earle, T. 1987. 'Chiefdoms in archaeological and ethnohistorical perspective.' *Annual Review of Anthropology* **16**: 279-308.

Earle, T. 1991. 'Property rights and the evolution of chiefdoms.' In T. Earle, (ed.), *Chiefdoms: power, economy, and ideology*. pp. 71-99. Cambridge: Cambridge University Press.

Ehrich, R.W. (ed.), 1992. *Chronologies in Old World Archaeology*. (3rd. ed.) Chicago: University of Chicago Press.

Eldredge, N. 1995. *Reinventing Darwin: the great evolutionary debate*. London: Weidenfeld and Nicolson

Eldredge, N. and S.J. Gould. 1972. 'Punctuated equilibria: an alternative to phyletic gradualism.' In T.J.M. Schopf (ed.), *Models in Paleobiology*. pp. 82-115. San Francisco: Freeman, Cooper and Co.

Englund, R.K. 1991. 'Archaic dairy metrology.' *Iraq* **53**: 101-104.

Englund, R.K, and H.J. Nissen. 1993. *Die lexikalischen Listen der Archaischen Texte aus Uruk*. Berlin: ATU 3.

Esin, U. 1979. 'Tepecik Excavations 1973.' In *Keban Project 1973 Activities*. pp. 97-113. Ankara: METU.

Esin, U. 1982. 'Tepecik Excavations 1974.' In *Keban Project 1974 Activities*. pp. 95-118. Ankara: METU.

Fairservis, W.A., Jr. 1961. *The Harappan Civilization: New Evidence and More Thories*. New York: American Museum of Natural History.

Fairservis, W.A., Jr. 1971. *The Roots of Ancient India: The Archaeology of Early Indian Civilization*. New York: Macmillan.

Fairservis, W.A., Jr. 1986. 'Cattle and the Harappan Chiefdoms of the Indus Valley.' *Expedition* **28/2**: 43-50.

Falkenstein, A. 1966. *Die Inschriften Gudeas von Lagash*. I. Rome: Pontificium Institutum Biblicium.

Ferguson, Y. 1991. 'Chiefdoms to city-states: the Greek experience.' In T. Earle, (ed.), *Chiefdoms: power, economy, and ideology*. pp. 169-192. Cambridge: Cambridge University Press.

Finet, A. 1975. 'Les Temples Sumérians du Tell Kannâs.' *Syria* **52**: 157-174.

Finet, A. 1979. 'Bilan provisoire des fouilles belges du Tell Kannâs.' In D.N. Freedman, (ed.), *Archaeological Reports from the Tabqa Dam*

*Project - Euphrates Valley, Syria.* pp. 79-96. Cambridge, Mass.: Annual of the American Schools of Oriental Research 44.

Finet, A. 1982. *Les fouilles belges du Tell Kannas sur l'Euphrate en Syrie.* Musée Royal de Mariemont.

Finkbeiner, U. 1986. 'Uruk-Warka: Evidence of the Gamdet Nasr Period.' In U. Finkbeiner and W. Röllig, (eds.), *Gamdet Nasr: Period or Regional Style?* pp. 332-66. Beihefte zum Tübinger Atlas des Vorderen Orients, Reihe B, Nr. 62. Weisbaden: Ludwig Reichert.

Finkbeiner, U. 1991. *Uruk Kampagne 35-37 1982-84: die archäologische Oberflächenuntersuchung (Survey).* Ausgrabungen in Uruk-Warka Endberichte 4. Mainz: Philipp von Zabern.

Finkbeiner, U. 1993. *Uruk. Analytisches Register zu den Grabungsberichten Kampagnen 1912/13 bis 1976/77.* Deutches Archäologisches Institute Abteilung Baghdad. Berlin: Gebr. Mann Verlag.

Finkel, I.L. 1985. 'Inscriptions from Tell Brak 1984.' *Iraq* 47: 187-202.

Fischler, C. 1981. 'Food Preferences, Nutritional Wisdom and Sociocultural Evolution.' In D. Walcher, D and N. Kretchmer, (eds.), *Food, nutrition and evolution.* pp. 59-68. Massan: New York.

Flannery, K.V. 1968. 'The Olmec and the Valley of Oaxaca: A Model for Inter-Regional Interaction in Formative Times.' In E.P. Benson, (ed.), *Dumbarton Oaks Conference on the Olmec.* pp. 79-110. Washington: Dumbraton Oaks.

Flannery, K.V and J. Marcus, 1998. 'Cognitive Archaeology.' In Whitley, D.S. *Reader in Archaeological Theory: Post-Processual and Cognitive Approaches.* pp. 35-48. London and New York: Routledge.

Fletcher, R. 1995. *The limits of settlement growth: a theoretical outline.* Cambridge: Cambridge University Press.

Forest, J-D. 1983a. *Les Practiques funeraires en Mesopotamie du cinquieme millenaire au debut du troisieme; etude de cas.* Paris: Editions Recherche sur les Civilisations.

Forest, J-D. 1983b. 'Aux origines de l'architecture obéidienne: Les plans de type Samarra.' *Akkadica* 34: 1-47.

Forest, J-D. 1984. 'Kheit Qasim III - An Obeid settlement.' *Sumer* 40 (1/2): 119-121.

Forest, J.D. 1987. 'Les bevelled Rim Bowls. Nouvelle tentative d'interprétation.' *Akkadica* 53: 1-24.

Forest, J-D. 1991. 'Le système de mesures de longueur obeidien, sa mise en oeuvre, sa signification.' *Paléorient* 17/2: 161-172.

Forest, J-D. 1998. 'L'habitat urukien du Djebel Aruda: approche fonctionnelle et arrière-plans symboliques.' *Subartu* IV.1: 217-233. Brussels: Brépols.

Forest, J-D. 1999. *Les premiers temples de Mésopotamie (4e et 3e millénaires).* BAR International Series 765. Oxford: Archaeopress.

Fortes, M and E.E. Evans-Pritchard. 1940. *African Political Systems.* Oxford: Oxford University Press.

Foster, B. 1981. 'A new look at the Sumerian temple state.' *Journal of the Economic and Social History of the Orient* 24: 225-234.

Foucault, M. 1981. *The Will to Knowledge. The History of Sexuality: 1.* Harmondsworth: Pelican

Frangipane, M. 1985. 'Early Developments of Metallurgy in the Near East.' In M. Liverani *et al.* (eds.), *Studi di Palentologia in onore di Salvatore M. Puglisi.* pp. 215-228. Rome: Dipartmento di Scienze Storiche Archaologiche e Anthropologiche dell' Antichita Universita di Roma.

Frangipane, M. 1993a. 'Local Components in the Development of Centralized Societies in Syro-Anatolian regions.' In M. Frangipane, H. Hauptmann, M. Liverani, P. Matthiae, and M. Mellink (eds.), *Between the Rivers and Over the Hills. Archaeologica Anatolica et Mesopotamica. Alba Palmieri dedicata.* pp. 133-162. Rome: Dipartmento di Scienze Storiche Archaologiche e Anthropologiche dell' Antichita Universita di Roma.

Frangipane, M. 1993b. 'Excavations at Arslantepe, Malatya. 1992.' *Kazi Sonuçlari Toplantisi* XV. pp. 211-228. Ankara: Eski Eserler ve Müzeler Genel Müdürlügü.

Frangipane, M. 1997. 'A 4th-Millennium Temple/Palace Complex at Arslantepe-Malatya. North-South Relations and the Formation of Early State Societies in the Northern Regions of Greater Mesopotamia.' *Paléorient* 23/1 : 45-73.

Frangipane, M. and A. Palmieri, 1990. 'Excavations at Arslantepe, Malatya. The 1989 Campaign.' *Kazi Sonuçlari Toplantisi* XII. pp. 209-224. Ankara: Eski Eserler ve Müzeler Genel Müdürlügü.

Frangipane M. and A. Palmieri, 1988. 'Cultural Developments at Arslantepe at the Beginning of the Third Millennium.' *Origini* **XII**: 287-455.

Frangipane, M. and A. Palmieri, 1991. 'The 1990 Season at Arslantepe.' *Kazi Sonuçlari Toplantisi* **XIII**. pp. 177-195. Ankara: Eski Eserler ve Müzeler Genel Müdürlügü.

Frank, D.R. 1975. *Versuch zur Rekonstruktion von Bauregeln und Massordnung einer nordsyrischen Stadt des vierten Jahrtausends - Untersucht anhand von Grabungsergebnissen der Deutschen Orient-Gessellschaft in Habuba Kabira.* **107**: 7-16. Berlin: Mitteilungen der Deutschen Orient-Gesellschaft zu Berlin.

Frankfort, H. 1936. *Progress of the work of the Oriental Institute in Iraq, 1934/35: fifth preliminary report of the Iraq Expedition*. Chicago: University of Chicago Press.

Frankfort, H. 1939a. *Cylinder Seals*. London: Macmillan

Frankfort, H. 1939b. *Sculpture of the Third Millennium from Tell Asmar and Khafajah*. Chicago: Oriental Institute Publications 44.

Frankfort, H. 1948. *Kinship and the Gods. A study of ancient Near Eastern religion as the integration of society and nature*. Chicago: Chicago University Press.

Frankfort, H. 1970. *The art and architecture of the ancient Orient*. Harmondsworth: Penguin.

Frazer, J.G. 1922. *The Golden Bough* (abridged edition) London: Macmillan.

Freud, S. 1918. *Totem and Taboo*. New York.

Gelb, I.J. 1979. 'Household and family in early Mesopotamia.' In E. Lipinski, (ed.), *State and Temple Economy in the Ancient Near East* I. pp. 1-97. Leuven: Department of Oriëntalistiek.

Gelb, I.J., P. Steinkeller, and R.M. Whiting, Jr. 1991. *Earliest Land Tenure Systems in the Near East: Ancient Kudurrus*. Chicago: Oriental Institute Publications No. 104.

George, A. 1999. *The Epic of Gilgamesh: A new translation*. Harmondsworth: Penguin.

Giddens, A. 1989. *Sociology*. Oxford: Polity.

Golzio, K-H. 1983. *Der Tempel im Alten Mesopotamien und seine Parallelen in Indien*. Leiden: Brill.

Gonen, R. 1992. 'The Chalcolithic Period.' In A. Ben-Tor *The Archaeology of Ancient Israel*. pp. 40-80. New Haven: Yale University Press.

Goodenough, W. 1957. 'Cultural Anthropology and Linguistics.' In P.L. Garvin (ed.) *Report of the 7th Annual Round Table on Linguistics and Language Study*. Washington D.C.: Georgetown University Press.

Gould, S.J. 1996. *Life's Grandeur: The Spread of Excellence from Plato to Darwin*. London: Jonathan Cape.

Gould, S.J. 1997. *Dinosaur in a Haystack*. Harmondsworth: Penguin.

Green, M.W. and H.J. Nissen. 1987. *Zeichenliste der Archaischen Texte aus Uruk*. Archaische Texte aus Uruk, vol. 2. Berlin: Gebbüder Mann Verlag.

Gut, R.V. 1995. *Das Prähistorische Ninive: Zur relativen Chronologie der frühen Perioden Nordmesopotamiens*. Mainz: Verlag Philipp von Zabern.

Hall, H.R. and C.L.Woolley, 1927. *Ur Excavations I. Al-'Ubaid*. Oxford: Oxford University Press.

Hansen, D.P. 1992. 'The Relative Chronology of Mesopotamia, Part II: The Pottery Sequence at Nippur from the Middle Uruk to the Old Babylonian Period (3400-1600 B.C.).' In Ehrich, R.W. (ed.), *Chronologies in Old World Archaeology*. pp. 201-15. Chicago: University of Chicago Press.

Harloe, 1977. *Captive cities: studies in the political economy of cities and regions*. London: Wiley.

Harper, P.O., J. Aruz, and F. Tallon (eds.). 1992. *The Royal City of Susa: Ancient Near Eastern Treasures in the Louvre*. New York: Metropolitan Museum of Art.

Hassan, F.A. 1988. 'The Predynastic of Egypt.' *Journal of World Prehistory* **2**: 135-185.

Hassan, F.A. 1992. 'Primeval Goddess to Divine King. The Mythogenesis of Power in the Early Egyptian State.' In R. Friedman, and B. Adams (eds.). *The Followers of Horus. Studies dedicated to Michael Allen Hoffman*. pp. 307-321. Egyptian Studies Association Publication 2. Oxbow Monograph 20.

Hassan, F.A. 1996. Review of Fletcher 1995. *Antiquity* **70** (269): 722.

Hauptmann, H. 1972. 'Die Grabungen Auf Norsuntepe 1970.' In *Keban Project 1972 Activities*. pp. 103-117. Ankara: METU.

Hauptmann, H. 1976. 'Die Grabungen Auf Norsuntepe 1972.' In *Keban Project 1970 Activities*. pp. 71-100. Ankara: METU.

Hauptmann, H. 1987. 'Lidar Hoyuk, 1986.' *Anatolian Studies* **37**: 203-206

Heinrich, E. 1936. *Kleinfunde aus den archaischen Tempelschichten in Uruk*. Berlin

Heinrich, E. 1939. 'Grabungen im Gebiet des Anu-Zntum Tempels.' *X. Vorläufiger Bericht über die von dem Deutschen Archäologischen Institut und der Deutschen Orient-Gesellschaft aus Mitteln der Deutschen Forscgungsgemeinschaft unternommenen Ausgrabungen in Uruk-Warka*. **10**: 21-34. Berlin: Gebr. Mann.

Heinrich, E. 1982. *Die Tempel und Heiligtümer in Alten Mesopoamien*. Berlin: Walter de Gruyter.

Heusch, J.C. 1979. 'Tall Habuba Kabira im 3. und 2. Jahrtausend- Die Entwicklung der Baustruktuk.' In M.C. Marqueron, (ed.), *Le Moyen Euphrate. Zone de Contact et d'Exchanges*. Leiden: E.J. Brill.

Hillier, B. and J. Hanson 1984. *The social logic of space*. Cambridge: Cambridge University Press.

Hodder, I. 1982a. *Symbols in Action: Ethnoarchaeological studies of material culture*. Cambridge: Cambridge University Press.

Hodder, I. 1982b. *The Present Past*. London: Batsford.

Hodder, I. 1991. *Reading the Past: current approaches to interpretation in archaeology*. 2nd edn. Cambridge: Cambridge University Press.

Hoffman, M.A. 1980. *Egypt before the Pharaohs*. London: Ark.

Hole, F. 1978. 'The Early Prehistoric Periods.' *Proceedings of the 6th Annual Symposium on Archaeological Research in Iran*. Tehran: Iranian Centre for Archaeological Research.

Hole, F. 1983. 'Symbols of Religion and Social Organization at Susa.' In T. Cuyler Young Jr., P.E.L. Smith, and P. Mortensen, eds., *The Hilly Flanks and Beyond. Essays on the Prehistory of Southwestern Asia*. pp. 315-333. Studies in Ancient Oriental Civilization 36. Chicago: University of Chicago Oriental Institute.

Hole, F. 1987. 'Settlement and Society in the Village Period.' In F.Hole, (ed.). *The Archaeology of Western Iran. Settlement and Society from Prehistory to the Islamic Conquest*. pp. 79-106. Washington: Smithsonian Institution Press.

Hole, F. 1989. 'Patterns of Burial in the Fifth Millennium.' In E.F. Henrickson, and I. Thuesen (eds.), *Upon this Foundation: 'Ubiad Mesopotamia Reconsidered*. pp. 149-180. Cophenagen: Museum Tuscalum Press, Carsten Neibuhr Institute no. 10.

Hole, F. 1994. 'Environmental Instabilities and Urban Origin.' In G. Stein, and M.S. Rothman, eds., *Chiefdoms and Early States in the Near East. The Organizational Dynamics of Complexity*. Monographs in World Archaeology 18. pp. 121-151. Madison: Prehistory Press.

Hopkins, T.J. 1971. *The Hindu Religious Tradition*. Encino: Dickenson.

Hymes, D. 1977. *Foundations of Sociolinguistics: An Ethnographic Approach*. London: Tavistock.

Ingholt, H. 1940. *Rapport Préliminaire sur Sept Campagnes de Foulles à Hama en Syrie (1932-1938)*. Copenhagen: E. Munksgaard.

Jacobs, 1975. *War its Causes and Correlates*. The Hague: Moulton.

Jacobsen, T. 1946. 'Mesopotamia.' In H. Frankfort, H.A. Frankfort, J.A. Wilson, T. Jacobsen and W.A. Irwin, *The Intellectual Adventure of Ancient Man*. pp. 125-222. Chicago: University of Chicago Press.

Jacobsen, T. 1957. 'Early political development in Mesopotamia.' *Zeitschrift für Assyriologie* **52**: 91-140.

Jacobsen, T. 1976. *The Treasures of Darkness. A History of Mesopotamian Religion*. New Haven & London: Yale University Press.

Jansen, M.R.N. 1993. 'Mohenjo-daro: Type Site of the Earliest Urbanization Process in South Asia.' In H. Spodek, and D.M. Srinivasan (eds.), *Urban Form and Meaning in South Asia: The Shaping of Cities from Prehistoric to Precolonial Times*. Hanover and London: National Gallery of Art, Washington.

Jasim, S.A. 1985 *The 'Ubaid Period In Iraq. Recent Excavations in the Hamrin Region*. BAR International Series 267. Oxford: British Archaeological Reports.

Johnson, G.A. 1973. *Local Exchange and early State Development in Southwestern Iran*. Ann Arbor: University of Michigan, Museum of Anthropology Papers 51.

Johnson, G.A. 1987. 'The Changing Organization of Uruk Administration on the Susiana Plain.' In F.Hole, (ed.), *The Archaeology of Western Iran. Settlement and Society from Prehistory to the Islamic Conquest.* pp. 107-140. Washington: Smithsonian Institution Press.

Johnson, G. 1988-89. 'Late Uruk in Greater Mesopotamia: Expansion or collapse?' *Origini* 14: 595-613.

Johnson, A.W. and T. Earle, 1987. *The evolution of human societies: from foraging group to agrarian state.* Stanford: Stanford University Press.

Jones, S. 1997. *The Archaeology of Ethnicity: Constructing identities in the past and present.* London: Routledge.

Jordan, J. 1931. *II. Vorläufiger Bericht über die von dem Deutschen Archäologischen Institut und der Deutschen Orient-Gesellschaft aus Mitteln der Deutschen Forschungsgemeinschaft unternommenen Ausgrabungen in Uruk-Warka.* **2.** Berlin: Gebr. Mann.

Kalsbeck, J. 1981. 'La Céramique de Série du Djebel Aruda (a l'époque d'Uruk).' *Akkadica* 20: 1-11.

Kantor, H.J. 1976. 'The Excavations at Choga Mish, 1974-1975.' In F. Bagherzadeh, (ed.)., *Proceedings of the 4th Annual Symposium on Archaeological Research in Iran* 4. pp. 23-41. Tehran: Iranian Centre for Archaeological Research.

Kauffman, S. 1996. *At Home in the Universe: The Search for the Laws of Complexity.* Harmondsworth: Penguin.

Kemp, B.J. 1989. *Ancient Egypt. Anatomy of a Civilization.* London & New York: Routledge.

Kenoyer, J.M. 1994. *From Sumer to Meluhha: Contributions to the Archaeology of South and West Asia in Memory of George F. Dales, Jr. Wisconsin Archaeological Reports, Vol. 3.* Madison: Prehistory Press

Killick, R.G. and M.D. Roaf, 1979. 'Excavations at Tell Madhur.' *Sumer* 25: 534-42.

King, A.D. 1980. *Buildings and Society: essays on the social development of the built environment.* London: Routledge.

Krispijn, Th.J.H. 1991-92. 'The Early Mesopotamian Lexical Lists and the Dawn of Linguistics.' *Jaarbericht ex oriente lux* 32: 12-22.

Kristiansen, K. 1991. 'Chiefdoms, states, and systems of social evolution.' In T. Earle, ed., *Chiefdoms: power, economy, and ideology.* pp.16- 43. Cambridge: Cambridge University Press.

Kubba, S. 1990. 'The Ubaid Period: Evidence of architectural planning and the use of a standard unit of measurement - the 'Ubaid Cubit' of Mesopotamia.' *Paléorient* 16/1: 45-55.

Kubba, S. 1998. *Architecture and Linear Measurement during the Ubaid Period in Mesopotamia.* Oxford: BAR international S707.

Kuhrt, A. 1990. 'Nabonidus and the Babylonian priesthood.' In M. Beard and J. North, *Pagan Priests.* pp. 117-156. London: Duckworth.

Kuhrt, A. 1995. *The Ancient Near East c. 3000-330 BC*, vol I. London and New York: Routledge.

Lake, M. 1998. 'Digging for Memes: Where Should We Look for the Cultural Analogue of the Gene in the Archaeology of Change?' Paper delivered for seminar series 'The Archaeology of Change', 16 Oct. Institute of Archaeology, University College London.

Lamberg-Karlovsky, C.C. 1976. 'The Third Millennium at Teppeh Yahya: A Preliminary Statement.' *Proceedings of the IVth Annual Symposium on Archaeological Research in Iran, 1975.* Tehran: Iranian Centre for Archaeological Research.

Lamberg-Karlovsky, C.C. (ed.), 1989. *Archaeological Thought in America.* Cambridge: Cambridge University Press.

Lamberg-Karlovsky, C.C. and Tosi, M. 1973. 'Shar-i Sokhta and Tepe Yahya: Tracks on the Earliest History of the Iranian Plateau.' *East and West* 23: 21-58.

Lamberg-Karlovsky, C.C. 1996. 'The archaeological evidence for international commerce: Public and/or private enterprise in Mesopotamia?' in M. Hudson and B.A. Levine, (eds.), *Privatization in the Ancient Near East and Classical World.* Cambridge, Mass.: Peabody Museum Bulletin 5: 73-108.

Lambert, W.G. 1975. 'The historical development of the Mesopotamian Pantheon: A study in sophisticated polytheism.' In H. Goedicke & J.J.M. Roberts (eds.), *Unity and Diversity.* pp. 191-200. Baltimore: John Hopkins University Press.

Landsberger, B. 1944. 'Die Anfaenge der Zivilization in Mesopotamien.' *Journal of the Faculty of Languages, History and Geography of the University of Ankara.* **II** : 431-37.

Langdon, S. 1920. 'Sumerian Origins and Racial Characteristics.' *Archaeologia* **70**: 145-54.

Le Brun, A. 1978. 'Le niveau 17B de l'Aropole de Suse.' *Cahiers de la Délégation Archéologique Française en Iran* **9**: 57-154.

Le Breton, L. 1957. 'The Early Periods at Susa : Mesopotamian Relations.' *Iraq* **19**: 79 - 124.

Leick, G. 1991. *A Dictionary of Ancient Near Eastern Mythology*. London: Routledge.

Leick, G.1994. *Sex and Eroticism in Mesopotamian Literature.* London and New York: Routledge.

Lenzen, H. 1955. 'Mesopotamische Tempelanlagen von der Frühzeit bis zum zweiten Jahrtausend.' *Zeitschrift für Assyriologie* **17**: 1-36.

Lenzen, H. 1959. *XV. Vorläufiger Bericht über die von dem Deutschen Archäologischen Institut und der Deutschen Orient-Gesellschaft aus Mitteln der Deutschen Forschungsgemeinschaft unternommenen Ausgrabungen in Uruk-Warka.* **15**. Berlin: Gebr. Mann.

Lenzen, H. 1960. *XVI. Vorläufiger Bericht über die von dem Deutschen Archäologischen Institut und der Deutschen Orient-Gesellschaft aus Mitteln der Deutschen Forschungsgemeinschaft unternommenen Ausgrabungen in Uruk-Warka.* **16**. Berlin: Gebr. Mann.

Lenzen, H. 1961. *XVII. Vorläufiger Bericht über die von dem Deutschen Archäologischen Institut und der Deutschen Orient-Gesellschaft aus Mitteln der Deutschen Forschungsgemeinschaft unternommenen Ausgrabungen in Uruk-Warka.* **17**. Berlin: Gebr. Mann.

Lenzen, H. 1968. *XXIV. Vorläufiger Bericht über die von dem Deutschen Archäologischen Institut und der Deutschen Orient-Gesellschaft aus Mitteln der Deutschen Forschungsgemeinschaft unternommenen Ausgrabungen in Uruk-Warka.* **24**. Berlin: Gebr. Mann.

Lenzen, H. 1974. 'Die Architectur in Eanna der Uruk IV Periode.' *Iraq* **36**: 111-28.

Lindemeyer, E. and L. Martin. 1992. *Uruk. Kleinfunde II.* Deutches Archäologisches Institut Abteilung Baghdad 7. Verlag. Mainz am Rhein: Philipp von Zebern.

Lindemeyer, E. and L. Martin. 1993. *Uruk. Kleinfunde III.* Deutches Archäologisches Institut Abteilung Baghdad 9. Verlag. Mainz am Rhein: Philipp von Zebern.

Livingstone, A. 1986. *Mystical and Mythological Explanatory Works of Assyrian and Babylonian Scholars*. Oxford: Oxford University Press.

Lloyd, S. 1954. 'Building in Brick and Stone.' In C. Singer et al. (eds.), *A History of Technology* pp. 456-94. Oxford.

Lloyd, S. 1948. 'The Oldest City of Sumeria: Establishing the origins of Eridu.' *Illustrated London News* Sept. 11: 303-5.

Lloyd, S. 1984. *The Archaeology of Mesopotamia* (revised ed.). London: Thames and Hudson.

Lloyd, S., and F. Safar, 1943. 'Tell Uqair: Excavations by the Iraq Government Directorate of Antiquities in 1940 and 1941.' *Journal of Near Eastern Studies* **2**: 131-58.

Loon, M.N. van (ed.), 1988. *Hammam et Turkman I: Report of the University of Amsterdam's 1981-1984 Excavations in Syria*. Leiden: Dutch Archaeological Institute in Istanbul.

Ludwig, W. 1979. 'Mass, sitte und Technik des Bauens in Habuba Kabira Sud.' In J.C. Margeron, (ed.), *Le Moyen Euphrate, zone de contacts et d'échanges.* pp. 63-74. Actes du Colloque de Strasbourg.

Lupton, A. 1996. *Stability and Change: Socio-political development in North Mesopotamia and South-East Anatolia 4000-2700 B.C.* Oxford: British Archaeological Reports S627.

Luth, F. 1989. 'Grabungen auf dem Tell B.' In W. Orthmann (ed.), *Saarbrüker Beiträge Zur.* pp. 85-110. Altertumskunde. Band 52.

Maisels, C.K. 1990. *The emergence of civilization: from hunting and gathering to agriculture*. London and New York: Routledge.

Maisels, C.K. 1991. 'Trajectory versus typology in social evolution.' *Cultural Dynamics* **4** (3): 251-269.

Maisels, C.K. 1999. *Early Civilizations of the Old World*. London and New York: Routledge.

Mallowan, M.E.L. 1947. 'Excavations at Brak and Chagar Bazar.' *Iraq* **9**: 1-259.

Mann, M. 1986. *The sources of social power*. volume 1. Cambridge: Cambridge University Press.

Marfoe, L., G. Algaze, K. Atamen, M. Ingraham, M. McDonald, N. Miller, C. Snow, G. Stein, B. Verharen, P. Wattenmaker, T. Wilkinson, A. Yener, 1986. 'The Chicago Euphrates

Archaeological Project 1980-1984: an interim report.' *Anatolica* 13: 37-147.

Martin, H.P. 1988. *Fara: A Reconstruction of the Ancient Mesopotamian City of Shuruppak*. Birmingham: Chris Martin and Associates.

Marx, K. 1963. 'Economic and philosophical manuscripts.' In T.B. Bottomore, (ed.), *Karl Marx: early Writings*. Harmonsdworth: Penguin.

Matthews, D.M. 1997. *The Early Glyptic of Tell Brak: Cylinder Seals of Third Millennium Syria*. Orbis biblicus et orientalis; Series archaeologica; 15. Fribourg: Fribourg University Press.

Matthews, R.J. 1992. 'Defining the style of the period: Jemdet Nasr 1926-28.' *Iraq* 54: 1-34.

Matthews, R.J. 1993. *Cities, Seals and Writing: Archaic seal impressions from Jemdet Nasr and Ur*. Berlin: Materialien zu den Frühen Schriftzeugnissen des Vorderen Orients, Gebr. Mann Verlag.

Matthews, R.J. 1995. 'Excavations at Tell Brak, 1995.' *Iraq* 57: 87-112.

Matthews, R.J. 1996. 'Excavations at Tell Brak, 1996.' *Iraq* 58: 65-78.

Matthews, R.J. and W. Wilkinson, 1991. 'Excavations in Iraq 1989-1990.' *Iraq* 53: 181-82.

Matthews, R.J., W. Matthews, and H. McDonald, H. 1994. 'Excavations at Tell Brak, 1994.' *Iraq* 56: 177-194.

Mazower, M. 1999. *Dark Continent: Europe's Twentieth Century*. Harmondsworth: Penguin.

Mead, G.H. 1934. *Mind, Self and Society*. Chicago: University of Chicago Press.

Meijer, D.J.W. 1988. 'Tell Hammam: Architecture and Stratigraphy.' In M.N. van Loon, (ed.), *Hammam et-Turkman. Report on the University of Amsterdam's 1981-1984 Excavations in Syria*. pp. 69-128. Leiden.

Mellink, M. 1989. 'Archaeology in Asia Minor, Samsat.' *American Journal of Archaeology* 93: 114.

Mellink, M. 1992. 'Archaeology in Anatolia.' *American Journal of Archaeology* 96: 119-150.

Merton, R.K. 1957. *Social Theory and Social Structure*. Glencoe: Free Press

Michel, R. P. McGovern, and V. Badler, 1993. 'The First Wine and Beer. Chemical Detection of Ancient Fermented Beverages.' *Analytical Chemistry* 65: 408-413.

Mieroop, M. van de 1989. 'Women in the economy of Sumer,' In B.S. Lesko (ed.), *Women's Earliest Records from Ancient Egypt and Western Asia*. Brown Judaic Studies 166. pp. 53-66. Atlanta: Scholars Press.

Mieroop, M. van de 1997. *The Ancient Mesopotamian City*. Oxford: Oxford University Press.

Millard, A.R. 1988. 'The Bevel Rim Bowls: Their Purpose and Significance.' *Iraq* 50: 49-57.

Miller, D. 1985. 'Ideology and the Harappan Civilization.' *Journal of Anthropological Archaeology* 4: 34-71.

Miller, D. and Tilley, C. (eds.) 1994. *Ideology, Power and Prehistory*. Cambridge: Cambridge University Press.

Miller, N.F. 1994. 'Appendix 1: Some Archaeological Remains from the 1992 Excavation Season at Hacinebi Tepe.' *Anatolica* 20: 168-72.

Montesqieu, C. de, 1989. *The Spirit of the Laws*. Cambridge (first published 1748)

Moore, H. 1996. *Space, text and Gender: an anthropological study of the Marakwet of Kenya*. Cambridge: Cambridge University Press.

Moorey, P.R.S. 1976. 'The Late Prehistoric Building at Jemdat Nasr.' *Iraq* 38: 95-106

Moorey, P.R.S. 1977. 'What do we know about the people buried in the Royal Cemetery?' *Expedition* 20 (1): 24-40

Moorey, P.R.S. 1982. 'The archaeological evidence for metallurgy and related technologies in Mesopotamia c.5500-2100 B.C..' *Iraq* 44: 13-38.

Moorey, P.R.S. 1987. 'On tracking cultural transfers in prehistory: the case of Egypt and lower Mesopotamia in the fourth millennium B.C.' In M. Rowlands *et al* (eds.), *Centre and Periphery in the Ancient World*. pp. 36-46. Cambridge: Cambridge University Press.

Moorey, P.R.S. 1990. 'From Gulf to Delta in the Fourth Millennium B.C.: The Syrian Connection.' *Eretz-Israel* 21: 62-69.

Moorey, P.R.S. 1993. 'Iran: A Sumerian El-Dorado?' In J. Curtis, (ed.), *Early Mesopotamia and Iran: Contact and Conflict c.3500-1600 B.C.*. Proceedings of a seminar in memory of Vladimir

G. Lukonin. pp. 31-43. London: British Museum Press.

Moorey, P.R.S. 1994. *Ancient Mesopotamian Materials and Industries: The Archaeological Evidence.* Oxford: Oxford University Press.

Moortgat, A. 1939. 'Ein fruhsumerisches Kultgefäss.' *Zeitschrift für Assyriologie* **11** (45): 1-7.

Moortgat, A. 1969. *The Art of Ancient Mesopotamia: the classical art of the Near East.* London: Phaidon.

Mumford, L. 1960. *The city in history: its origins, its transformation, and its prospects.* Harmondsworth: Penguin.

Murray, O. 1980. *Early Greece.* Glasgow: Fontana.

Nissen, H.J. 1972. 'The city wall of Uruk.' In P.J. Ucko, R. Tringham, and G.W. Dimbleby, (eds), *Man, settlement and urbanism.* pp. 793-798. London: Duckworth.

Nissen, H.J. 1986. 'The Archaic Texts from Uruk.' *World Archaeology* **17**: 317-34.

Nissen, H.J. 1988. *The early history of the ancient Near East 9000-2000 BC.* Chicago: Chicago University Press.

Nissen, H.J. 1993a. 'The Context of the Emergence of Writing in Mesopotamia and Iran.' In J. Curtis, (ed.), *Early Mesopotamia and Iran: Contact and Conflict c.3500-1600 B.C..* Proceedings of a seminar in memory of Vladimir G. Lukonin. pp. 54-71. London: British Museum Press.

Nissen, H.J. 1993b 'The Early Uruk Period - A Sketch..' In M. Fragipane, H. Hauptmann, M. Liverani, P. Matthiae, M. Mellick, (eds.), *Between the Rivers and Over the Mountains. Archaeologica Anatolica et Mesopotamica Alba Palmieri Dedicata.* Dipartmento di Scienze Storiche Archaeologiche e Anthropologiche dell' Antichita Universita di Roma. pp. 123-132. Rome: Università di Roma.

Nissen, H.J. 1998. 'Uruk: Key site of the period-key site of the problem.' Paper delivered at Artefacts of complexity: Tracking the Uruk in the Near East, British School of Archaeology in Iraq conference 6-7 November University of Manchester.

Nissen, H.J., P. Damerow, and R.K. Englund, 1993. *Archaic Bookkeeping: Writing and Technologies of Economic Administration in the Ancient Near East.* Chicago: University of Chicago Press.

Nöldeke, A. 1932 *IV. Vorläufiger Bericht über die von dem Deutschen Archäologischen Institut und der Deutschen Orient-Gesellschaft aus Mitteln der Deutschen Forschungsgemeinschaft unternommenen Ausgrabungen in Uruk-Warka.* **4**. Berlin: Gebr. Mann.

Nöldeke, A. 1934. *V. Vorläufiger Bericht über die von dem Deutschen Archäologischen Institut und der Deutschen Orient-Gesellschaft aus Mitteln der Deutschen Forschungsgemeinschaft unternommenen Ausgrabungen in Uruk-Warka.* **5**. Berlin: Gebr. Mann.

Nöldeke, A. 1937 *VIII. Vorläufiger Bericht über die von dem Deutschen Archäologischen Institut und der Deutschen Orient-Gesellschaft aus Mitteln der Deutschen Forschungsgemeinschaft unternommenen Ausgrabungen in Uruk-Warka.* **8**. Berlin: Gebr. Mann.

Nöldeke, A. 1938. *IX. Vorläufiger Bericht über die von dem Deutschen Archäologischen Institut und der Deutschen Orient-Gesellschaft aus Mitteln der Deutschen Forschungsgemeinschaft unternommenen Ausgrabungen in Uruk-Warka.* **9**. Berlin: Gebr. Mann.

Nunn, A. 1985. 'Die Wandmalereifragmente aus Uruk-Warka.' *Baghdader Mitteilungen* **16**: 7-16.

Nützel, W. 1976. 'The climatic changes of Mesopotamia and bordering areas.' *Sumer* **32**: 11-24.

Oakeshott, R.E. 1960. *The Archaeology of weapons.* London: Lutterworth Press.

Oates, D. 1968. *Studies in the Ancient History of Northern Iraq.* London: British Academy.

Oates, D. 1982a. 'The Excavations at Tell Brak, 1978-81.' *Iraq* **44**: 187-204.

Oates, D. 1982b. 'Tell Brak.' In Curtis, J.E. *Fifty Years of Mesopotamian Discovery.* pp. 62-71. London: The British School of Archaeology in Iraq.

Oates, D. 1987. 'Excavations at Tell Brak 1985-86.' *Iraq* **49**: 175-86.

Oates, J. 1982. 'Choga Mami.' In Curtis, J.E. *Fifty Years of Mesopotamian Discovery.* pp. 22-29. London: The British School of Archaeology in Iraq.

Oates, J. 1983. 'Ubaid Mesopotamia Reconsidered.' In T. Cuyler Young, Jr., *et al.*, (eds.), *The Hilly Flanks and Beyond.* Studies in Ancient Oriental Civilization 36. pp. 251-82. Chicago: Oriental Institute.

Oates, J. 1993 'Trade and power in the fifth and fourth millennium B.C.: new evidence from Northern

Mesopotamia.' *World Archaeology* **24/3**: 403-422.

Oates, J. 1998. 'Tell Brak: the 4th millennium sequence and its implications.' Abstract, Artefacts of complexity: Tracking the Uruk in the Near East, British School of Archaeology in Iraq conference 6-7 November University of Manchester.

Oates, D and J. Oates, 1991. 'Excavations at Tell Brak 1990-91.' *Iraq* **53** : 127-145.

Oates, D and J. Oates, 1993. 'Excavations at Tell Brak 1992-93.' *Iraq* **55** : 155-199.

Oates, D and J. Oates, 1994. 'Tell Brak: a stratigraphic summary.' *Iraq* **56** : 167-176.

Oppenheim, A.L. 1977. *Ancient Mesopotamia: Portrait of a dead civilization*. Chicago: Chicago University Press.

Orthmann, W. 1975. *Der Alte Orient*. Berlin: Propylaen Kuntstgeaschichte 14.

Ozdogan, M. 1977. *Lower Euphrates Basin Survey*. Istanbul: METU.

Palmieri, A. 1981. 'Excavations at Arslantepe (Malatya).' *Anatolian Studies* **31**: 101-119.

Palmieri, A. 1985a. 'Eastern Anatolia and Early Mesopotamian Urbanisation: Remarks on the Changing Relations.' In M. Liverani; A, Palmieri and R. Peroni, (eds.), *Studi di Palentologia in Onore di Salvatore Puglisi*. pp. 191-213. Rome: University of Rome.

Palmieri, A. 1985b. '1984 Excavations at Arslantepe.' *VII. Kazi Somiçlari Toplantisi* **VII**. pp. 29 - 36. Ankara: Eski Eserler ve Müzeler Genel Müdürlügü.

Palmieri, A. and M. Fragipane, 1987. 'The 1985 Campaign at Arslantepe.' *Kazi Sonuçlari Toplantisi* **VIII**. pp. 67-74. Ankara: Eski Eserler ve Müzeler Genel Müdürlügü.

Palmieri, A. and M. Fragipane, 1988. 'The 1986 Campaign at Arslantepe.' *Kazi Sonuçlari Toplantisi* **IX**. pp. 127-129. Ankara: Eski Eserler ve Müzeler Genel Müdürlügü.

Palmieri, A. and M. Frangipane, 1990. 'The 1988 Campaign at Arslantepe.' *Kazi Sonuçlari Topantisi* **XI**. pp. 191-201. Ankara: Eski Eserler ve Müzeler Genel Müdürlügü.

Parrot, A. 1968. 'Les Fouilles de Larsa: deuxième et troisième campagnes (1967).' *Syria* **45**: 205-39.

Parrot, A. 1948. *Tello, vingt campagnes de fouilles (1877-1933)* Paris: Albin Michel.

Peltenburg, E.J. 1999. 'The Jerablus-Tahtani Project, Syria.' http//www.geo.ed.ac.uk/jerablus/jerahome.htm/ accessed 13 August 1999.

Peltenburg, E.J. and F. Stephen, 1998. 'X-Ray Flourescence, X-Ray Diffusion and petrographic Analyses of Uruk Ceramics from Jerablus Tahtani and other Upper Euphrates Sites.' Abstract, Artefacts of complexity: Tracking the Uruk in the Near East, British School of Archaeology in Iraq conference 6-7 November University of Manchester.

Perkins, A.L. 1949. *The Comparative Archaeology of Mesopotamia*. O.I.P. 25. Chicago: Chicago University Press.

Piggott, S. 1950. *Prehistoric India*. Harmondsworth: Penguin.

Pittman, H. 1994. *The Glazed Steatite Glyptic Style: the Structure and Function of an Image System in the Administration of Protoliterate Mesopotamia.* Berlin: Berliner Beiträge zum Vorderen Orient 16.

Plotkin, H. 1994. *Darwin Machines and the Nature of Knowledge*. Harmondsworth: Penguin

Pollock, S. 1983. 'Style and Information: An Analysis of Susiana Ceramics.' *Journal of Anthropological Archaeology* **2**: 354-390.

Pollock, S. 1989. 'Power Politics in the Susa A Period' In E.F. Henrickson, and I. Thuesen (eds.), *Upon This Foundation: Ubaid Mesopotamia Reconsidered*. pp. 281-292. Copenhagen: Museum Tuscalum Press, Carsten Niebuhr Institute Publication no. 10.

Pollock, S. 1990. 'Archaeological Investigations on the Uruk Mound, Abu Salabikh, a Preliminary Report.' *Iraq* **52**: 85-94.

Pollock, S. 1999. *Ancient Mesopotamia*. Cambridge University Press.

Pollock, S., M. Pope, and C. Coursey. 1996. 'Household production at the Uruk Mound, Abu Salabikh, Iraq.' *American Journal of Archaeology* **100**: 683-98.

Pollock, S., C. Steele, and M. Pope, 1991. 'Investigations on the Uruk Mound, Abu Salabikh, 1990.' *Iraq* **53**: 59-68.

Possehl, G.L. 1993. 'The Date of Indus Urbanisation: A Proposed Chronology for the Pre-Urban and Urban Harappan Phases.' In A.J. Gail and G.J.R. Mevissen (eds.), *South Asian Archaeology 1991*. pp. 231-49. Stuttgart: Franz Steiner Verlag.

Possehl, G.L. 1998. 'Sociocultural Complexity Without the State: The Indus Civilization.' In G.M. Feinman and J. Marcus, (eds.), *Archaic States*. pp. 261-292. Santa Fe: School of American Research Press.

Postgate, J.N. 1972. 'The role of the temple in the Mesopotamian secular community.' In P.J. Ucko, R. Tringham, and G.W. Dimbleby, (eds.), *Man, Settlement and Urbanism*. pp. 811-25. London: Duckworth.

Postgate, J.N. 1983. *The West Mound surface clearance*. Abu Salabikh Excavations 1. London: British School of Archaeology in Iraq.

Postgate, J.N. 1984. 'Excavations at Abu Salabikh.' *Iraq* **46**: 95-114.

Postgate, J.N. 1986. 'The transition from Uruk to ED: continuities and discontinuities.' In U. Finkbeiner and W. Röllig, (eds.), *Gamdet Nasr: Period or Regional Style?* Beihefte zum Tübinger Atlas des Vorderen Orients, Reihe B, Nr. 62. pp. 90-106. Weisbaden: Ludwig Reichert.

Postgate, J.N. 1992. *Early Mesopotamia: society and economy at the dawn of history*. London & New York: Routledge.

Potts, D.T. 1997. *Mesopotamian Civilization: the material foundations*. London: The Athlone Press.

Potts, D.T. 1999. *The Archaeology of Elam: Formation and Transformation of an Ancient Iranian State*. Cambridge: Cambridge University Press.

Potts, T.F. 1994. *Mesopotamia and the East*. Oxford: Oxford University Committee for Archaeology Monograph 37.

Powell, M.A. 1990. 'Urban-Rural Interface: Movement of Goods and Sevices in a Third Millennium City-State.' In E. Aerts and H. Klengel (eds.), *The Town as Regional Economic Centre in the Ancient Near East (Proceedings Tenth International Economic History Congress Leuven, August 1990)*. pp. 7-14. Leuven: Leuven University Press.

Prag, K. 1978. 'Silver in the Levant in the Fourth Millennium B.C.' In P.R.S. Moorey and P.J. Parr, (eds.), *Archaeology in the Levant: Essays for Kathleen Kenyon*. pp. 36-45. Warminster: Aris and Phillips.

Quirke, S. and J. Spencer, 1992. *The British Museum Book of Ancient Egypt*. London: British Museum Press.

Rapoport, A. 1969. *House form and culture*. Englewood Cliffs: Prentice Hall.

Reade, J.E. 1991. *Mesopotamia*. London: British Museum Press.

Reade, J.E. 1998. *Assyrian Sculpture*. 2nd edition. London: British Museum Press.

Renfrew, C. 1972. *The Emergence of Civilisation*. London: Methuen.

Renfrew, C. 1984. *Approaches to Social Archaeology*. Cambridge, Mass.: Harvard University Press.

Renfrew, C. 1987. *Archaeology and Language: the puzzle of Indo-European origins*. London: Jonathan Cape.

Renfrew, C. 1994a. 'Towards a cognitive archaeology.' In C. Renfrew, and E.B.W. Zubrow, *The ancient mind. Elements of cognitive archaeology*. pp. 3-12. Cambridge: Cambridge University Press.

Renfrew, C. 1994b. 'The archaeology of religion.' In C. Renfrew, and E.B.W. Zubrow, *The ancient mind. Elements of cognitive archaeology*. pp. 47-54. Cambridge: Cambridge University Press.

Renfrew, C., and P. Bahn. 1991. *Archaeology: Theories, Methods and Practice*. New York: Thames & Hudson.

Rindos, D. 1985. 'Darwinian selection, symbolic variation, and the evolution of culture.' *Current Anthropology* **26**: 65-88.

Roaf, M. 1984. 'Ubaid houses and temples.' *Sumer* 43: 80-90.

Rothman, M.S. 1988. *Centralization, Administration and Function at Fourth Millennium B.C. Tepe Gawra, Northern Iraq*. Ph.D dissertation. Department of Anthropology, University of Pennsylvania.

Rothman, M.S. 1993. 'Another Look at the 'Uruk Expansion' from the Tigris Piedmont.' In M. Fragipane, H. Hauptmann, M. Liverani, P. Matthiae, M. Mellick, (eds.), *Between the Rivers and Over the Mountains. Archaeologica Anatolica et Mesopotamica Alba Palmieri Dedicata*. pp. 163-176. Rome: Università di Roma.

Rothman, M.S. 1994. 'Sealing as a Control Mechanism in Prehistory: Tepe Gawra XI, X and VIII.' In G. Stein and M.S. Rothman, (eds.), *Chiefdoms and Ealy States in the Near East*. The Organizational Dynamics of Complexity. Monographs in World

Archaeology 18. pp. 103-120. Madison: Prehistory Press.

Roux, G. 1980. (revised edition). *Ancient Iraq*. Harmondsworth: Penguin.

Rova, E. 1996. 'Ceramic provinces along the Middle and Upper Euphrates: Late Chalcolithic- Early Bronze Age, a diachronic view.' *Baghdader Mitteilungen* **27**: 13-38.

Rowland, G. 1995. 'Archetypes of Systems Design.' *Systems Practice* **8/3**: 277-288.

Rowton, M. 1973. 'Autonomy and nomadism in Western Asia.' *Orientalia* **42**: 247-58.

Safar, F., M.A. Mustafa, and S. Lloyd, 1981. *Eridu*. Baghdad: State Organisation of Antiquities and Heritage.

Sapir, E. 1949. *Selected writings*. D. Mandelbaum (ed.). Berkeley: University of California Press.

Sarcina, A. 1979. 'The private house at Mohenjo-daro.' In M. Taddei (ed.), *South Asian Archaeology 1977: vol. 1*. Seminario Di Studi Asiatici. pp. 433-447. Naples: Instituto Universitario Orientale.

Schele, L. and M.E. Miller, 1992. *The Blood of Kings: Dynasty and Ritual in Maya Art*. London: Thames and Hudson.

Schmandt-Besserat, D. 1992. *Before Writing. Vol. I. From counting to cuneiform*. Austin: University of Texas Press.

Schmidt, J. 1972. *XXVI/XXVII. Vorläufiger Bericht über die von dem Deutschen Archäologischen Institut und der Deutschen Orient-Gesellschaft aus Mitteln der Deutschen Forschungsgemeinschaft unternommenen Ausgrabungen in Uruk-Warka*. **26-27**. Berlin: Gebr. Mann.

Schmidt, J. 1974. 'Zwei Tempel der Obed-Zeit in Uruk.' *Baghdader Mitteilungen* **7**: 173-187.

Schmidt, J. 1978. *XXVIII Vorläufiger Bericht über die von dem Deutschen Archäologischen Institut und der Deutschen Orient-Gesellschaft aus Mitteln der Deutschen Forschungsgemeinschaft unternommenen Ausgrabungen in Uruk-Warka*. **28**. Berlin: Gebr. Mann.

Schwartz, G.M. 1989. 'Comments.' In Algaze, G. 1989. 'The Uruk Expansion, Cross-cultural Exchange in early Mesopotamian Civilization.' *Current Anthropology* **30**: 596-7.

Service, E.R. 1972. *Primitive social organization. An evolutionary perspective*. (2nd edn.) New York: Random House.

Service, E.R. 1975. *Origins of the State and Civilization*. New York: Norton.

Shaffer, J.G. 1982. 'Harappan Culture: A Reconsideration.' In G.L. Possehl, (ed.), *Harappan Civilization: A Contemporary Perspective*. pp. 41-40. Dehli: Oxford.

Shennan, S. 1993. 'After social evolution: a new archaeological agenda?' in N. Yoffee & A. Sherratt, *Archaeological theory: who sets the agenda?* pp. 53-59. Cambridge: Cambridge University Press.

Sherratt, A. 1981. Plough and pastoralism: Aspects of the secondary products revolution.' In I. Hodder, G. Isaac, and N. Hammond (eds.), *Patterns of the Past: Essays in Honour of David Clarke*. pp. 261-305. Cambridge: Cambridge University Press.

Sievertsen, U. 1998. *Untersuchungen zur Pfeiler-Nischen-Architektur in Mesopotamien und Syrien von ihren Anfängen im 6. Jahrtausend bis zum Ende der frühdynastischen Zeit: Form, Funktion und Kontext. Volumes 1 and 2*. Oxford: BAR International S743.

Smart, N. 1969. *The Religious Experience of Mankind*. Glasgow: Collins.

Smith, P.E.L., and T.C. Young, Jr., 1972. 'The Evolution of Early Agriculture and Culture in Greater Mesopotamia: A Trial Model.' In B. Spooner, (ed.), *Population Growth: Anthropological Implications*. pp. 1-59. Cambridge: MIT Press..

Sollberger, E. and J.R. Kupper, 1971. *Inscriptions royales sumeriennes et akkadiennes*. Paris: Cerf.

Spencer, A.J. 1993. *Early Egypt: The Rise of Civilization in the Nile Valley*. London: British Museum Press.

Spencer, C.S. 1987. 'Rethinking the chiefdom.' In R.D. Drennan, and C.A. Uribe, (eds.), *Chiefdoms in the Americas*. pp. 369-390. Lanham, M.D.: University Press of America.

Spycket, A. 1981. *La Statuaire du Proche-Orient ancien*. Leiden: Brill.

Stein, G. 1994. 'Economy, Ritual, and Power in 'Ubiad Mesopotamia.' In Stein, G. and M.S. Rothman, eds., *Chiefdoms and Early States in the Near East. The Organizational Dynamics of Complexity*. Monographs in World Archaeology 18. pp. 35-46. Madison: Prehistory Press.

Stein, G.J. and A. Misir, 1994 'Mesopotamian-Anatolian Interaction at Hacinebi, Turkey: Preliminary Report on the 1992 Excavations.' *Anatolica* **20**: 145-189

Stein, G.J., C. Edens, N. Miller, J. Özbal, J. Pearce, and H. Pittman, 1996a. 'Hacinebi, Turkey : preliminary report on the 1995 excavations.' *Anatolica* **22** : 85-128.

Stein, G.J., R. Bernbeck, C. Coursey, A. McMahon, N.F. Miller, A. Misir, J. Nicola, H. Pittman, S. Pollock, and H. Wright. 1996b. 'Uruk colonies and Anatolian communities : an interim report on the 1992-93 excavations at Hacinebi.' *American Journal of Archaeology* **100/2** : 205-260.

Stein, G.J., K. Boden, C. Edens, J. Pearce Edans, K. Keith, A. McMahon, and J. Özbal, J. 1997. 'Excavations at Hacinebi, Turkey - 1996: Preliminary Report.' *Anatolica* **23**: 111-172.

Steinkeller, P. 1993. 'Early Political Development in Mesopotamia and the Origins of the Sargonic Empire.' In M. Liverani, (ed.), *Akkad The first World Empire: structure, Ideology, Traditions*. pp. 107-129.   Sargon srl Padova: History of the Ancient Near East/Studies V.

Stève, M.-J., and H. Gasche. 1971. *L'Acropole de Suse. Mémoires de le délégation archéologique française en Iran* 46. Paris: Geuthner.

Stève, M.-J., and H. Gasche. 1990.'Le Tell de l'Apadana avant les Achemenides. Contribution à la topographie de Suse.' In F. Vallet (ed.), *Melanges Jean Parrot*. pp. 15-60. Paris: Editions Recherche sur les Civilisations.

Stolper, M.W. 1984. *Texts from Tall-i Malyan, I. Elamite Administrative Texts (1972-1974)*. Philadelphia: Occasional Publications of the Babylonian Fund 6.

Strommenger, E. 1979. 'Ausgrabungen der Deutschen Orient Gesellschaft in Habuba Kabira.' In D.N. Freedman, (ed.), *Excavation Reports from the Tabqa Dam Project-Euphrates Valley, Syria*. pp. 63-78. Annual of the American School of Oriental Research 44: Cambridge, Mass.

Strommenger, E. 1980a. *Habuba Kabira: Eine Stadt vor 5000 Jahren*. Mainz am Rhein: Phillip von Zabern.

Strommenger, E. 1980b. 'The Chronological Division of the Archaic Levels of Uruk-Eanna VI to III/II: Past to Present.' *American Journal of Archaeology* **84**: 477-87.

Sulloway, F.J. 1996. *Born to Rebel: birth order, family dynamics and creative lives*. New York: Vintage Books.

Sürenhagen, D. 1974/75. 'Untersuchungen zur Keramikproduction innerhalb der Spät-Uruklichen siedlung Habuba Kabira-süd in Nord Syrien.' *Acta Praehistorica et Archaeologica* **5/6**: 43-164.

Sürenhagen, D. 1985. 'Enige Kulturelle Kontakte Zwischen Arslantepe VIA und den Frusumerisch-Hochprotoelamischen Studtkulturen.' In M. Liverani, A. Palmieri and R. Peroni, (eds.), *Studi di Palentologia in Onore di Salvatore Puglisi*. pp. 229-236. Rome: University of Rome.

Sürenhagen, D. 1986a. 'The Dry-Farming Belt: The Uruk Period and Subsequent Developments.' In H.Weiss, ed., *The Origins of Cities in Dry-Farming Syria and Mesopotamia in the Third Millennium B.C.*. pp. 7-43. Guildford: Four Quarters Publishing.

Sürenhagen, D. 1986b. 'Archaische Keramik aus Uruk-Warka. Erster Teil: Die Keramik der Schichten XVI-VI aus den Sondagen 'Tiefschnitt' und 'Sagengraben' in Eanna.' *Baghdader Mitteilungen* **17**: 7-118.

Szarzynska, K. 1969. 'Céramique d'Uruk d'après l'écriture pictographique sumérienne.' *Travaux du Centre d'archéologie méditerranéenne de l'Académie Plonaise des Sciences* **6**: 16-24.

Tallon, F. 1987. *Metallurgie susienne*. Paris: Ministère de la culture et de la communication.

Taylor, J.E. 1855. 'Notes on Abu Shahrein and Tell el Lahm.' *Journal of the Royal Asiatic Society* **15**: 404-15.

Teissier, B. 1987. 'Glyptic evidence for a connection between Iran, Syro-Palestine and Egypt in the Fourth and Third Millennia.' *Iran* **25**: 27-49.

Thomsen, M-L. 1984. *The Sumerian Language: An introduction to its history and grammatical structure*. Mesopotamia vol. 10. Copenhagen: Academic Press.

Tobler, A.J. 1950 *Excavations at Tepe Gawra*, vol. 2. Philadelphia: The University Museum

Todd, E. 1985. *The Explanation of Ideology: family structures and social systems*. London: Basil Blackwell

Trigger, B. 1990. 'Monumental architecture: a thermodynamic explanation of symbolic behavior.' *World Archaeology* **22**: 119-32.

Tunça, Ö. 1998. comments in Forest 1998. pp. 233-34.

Tyler, E.B. 1871. *Primitive Culture*.

Upham, S. 1987. 'A theoretical consideration of Middle Range Societies.' In R.D. Drennan and C.A. Uribe, (eds.), *Chiefdoms in the Americas*. pp. 345-368. Lanham, M.D.: University Press of America.

UVB = *Vorläufiger Bericht über die von dem Deutschen Archäologischen Institut und der Deutschen Orient-Gesellschaft aus Mitteln der Deutschen Forschungsgemeinschaft unternommenen Ausgrabungen in Uruk-Warka*. Berlin: Gebr. Mann.

Vallet, R. 1996. 'Habuba Kebira ou las naissance de l'urbanisme.' *Paléorient* **22/2**: 45-76.

Vallet, R. 1998a. 'L'urbanisme colonial urukien: l'exemple de Djebel Aruda.' *Subartu IV*.1: 53-87. Brussels: Brépols.

Vallet, R. 1998b. 'Habuba Kébira sud, approche morphologique de l'habitat.' In C. Castel, M. al-Maqdissi, F. Villeneuve (eds.), *Les maisons dans la Syrie antique du IIIème millénaire au début de l'Islam: pratiques et représentations de l'espace domestique*. pp. 105-115. Acts du colloque de Damas, IFAPO, 27-30 June 1992.

van Buren, E.D. 1939. *The Fauna of Ancient Mesopotamia as Represented in Art*. Rome: Pontificium institutum biblicum.

van Driel, G. 1979. 'The Uruk Settlement on Jebel Aruda' In J.C. Marqueron, (ed.). *Le Moyen Euphrate. Zone de Contact et d'Exchanges*. pp. 75-93. Leiden: E.J. Brill.

van Driel, G. 1983. 'Seals and Sealings from Jebel Aruda 1974-1978.' *Akkadica* **33**: 34-62.

van Driel, G. 1998. 'Jebel Aruda: Collapsing Aspirations?' Abstract, Artefacts of complexity: Tracking the Uruk in the Near East, British School of Archaeology in Iraq conference 6-7 November University of Manchester.

van Driel, G. and C. van Driel-Murray, 1979. 'Jebel Aruda, 1977-1978.' *Akkadica* **12**: 2-28.

van Driel, G. and C. van Driel-Murray, 1983. 'Jebel Aruda, The 1982 Season of Excavation, Interim Report.' *Akkadica* 33: 1-26.

von der Way, T. 1992. 'Indications of Architecture with Niches at Buto.' In R. Friedman, and B. Adams (eds.). *The Followers of Horus. Studies dedicated to Michael Allen Hoffman*. pp. 218-226. Egyptian Studies Association Publication 2. Oxbow Monograph 20.

Voigt, M. and R.H. Dyson, 1992. 'The Chronology of Iran, ca. 8000-2000 BC.' In R.W. Ehrich (ed.), *Chronologies in Old World Archaeology* (3rd edition). pp. 121-35. Chicago: University of Chicago.

Wallerstein, I. 1974 & 1980. *The Modern World System*. 2 vols. Academic Press: New York & London

Watkins, T.F. 1983. 'Sumerian weapons, warfare and warriors.' *Sumer* **39**: 100-102.

Weber, M. 1978. *Economy and Society: An outline of interpretative sociology*. Berkeley: University of California Press.

Weiss, H. 1984. 'Prestate Political Formations.' In T. Earle, (ed.), *On the Evolution of Complex Societies: Essays in Honor of Harry Hoije*. pp. 41-78. Malibu: Undea.

Weiss, H. (ed.) 1985. *Ebla to Damascus: Art and Archaeology of Ancient Syria*. Washington DC: SITES.

Weiss, H. 1986. 'The Origins of Tell Leilan and the Conquest of Space in the Third Millennium North Mesopotamia.' In H. Weiss, (ed.), *The Origins of Cities in Dry-Farming Syria and Mesopotamia in the Third Millennium B.C.*. pp. 71-108. Connecticut: Four Quarters Publishing.

Weiss, H. 1989. 'Comments.' In G. Algaze, 'The Uruk Expansion, Cross Cultural Exchange in early Mesopotamian Civilization.' *Current Anthropology* **30**: 597-98.

Weiss, H., and T.C. Young, Jr. 1975. 'The Merchants of Susa: Godin V and Plateau-Lowland Relations in the Late Fourth Millennium B.C..' *Iran* **13**: 1-18.

Wheatley, P. 1971. *The Pivot of the Four Quarters: A preliminary enquiry into the origins and character of the ancient Chinese city*. Edinburgh: Edinburgh University Press.

Whorf, B. 1956. 'Language, thought and Reality.' In J.B. Carroll (ed.), *Language, thought and reality: selected writings of Benjamin Lee Whorf*. New York: Wiley.

Wilkinson, T.J. 1990. 'The Development of Settlement in the North Jazira Between the 7th and 1st Millennia B.C.' *Iraq* **52**: 49-62.

Williams, G. 1992. *Sociolinguistics: A sociological critique*. London and New York: Routledge.

Wilson, E.O. 1998. *Consilience: The Unity of Knowledge.* London: Little, Brown and Co.

Wittfogel, K. 1957. *Oriental despotism.* New Haven: Yale.

Woolley, C.L. 1939. *Ur Excavations V: The Ziggurat and its Surroundings.* London: The British Museum.

Woolley, C.L. 1955. *Ur Excavations IV: The Early Periods.* Philadelphia: The University Museum.

Woolley, C.L. 1956. *Ur Excavations IV: The Early Periods.* London: The British Museum.

Woolley, C.L. 1982 (Revised by P.R.S. Moorey). *'Ur 'of the Chaldees'.* London: Herbert Press.

Wright, H.T. 1977. 'Towards an explanation of the origin of the state.' In J. Hill (ed.), *Explanation in Prehistoric Change.* pp. 215-230. Albuquerque: University of New Mexico Press.

Wright, H.T. 1984. 'Prestate political formations.' In T. Earle, (ed.), *On the Evolution of Complex Societies.* pp. 47-77. Malibu, California: Undena.

Wright, H.T. 1987. 'The Susiana Hinterlands during the Era of Primary State Formation.' In F.Hole, (ed.). *The Archaeology of Western Iran. Settlement and Society from Prehistory to the Islamic Conquest.* pp. 141-156. Washington: Smithsonian Institution Press.

Wright, H.T. 1998. 'Uruk states in Southwestern Iran.' In G.M. Feinman and J. Marcus, (eds.), *Archaic States.* pp. 173-198. Santa Fe: School of American Research Press.

Wright, H.T., and G.A. Johnson. 1975. 'Population, Exchange, and Early State Formation in Southwestern Iran.' *American Anthropologist* 77: 267-89.

Wright, H.T., J.A. Neely, G.A. Johnson, and J. Speth. 1975. 'Early Fourth Millennium Developments in Southwestern Iran.' *Iran* 13: 129-48.

Wright, H.T., N. Miller and R. Redding. 1980. 'Time and Process in an Uruk Rural Center.' In M-T. Barrelet (ed.), *L'archéologie de l'Iraq du début de l'époque néolithique à 333 avant notre ère.* pp. 67-84. Paris: Centre Naional de la Recherche Scientifique.

Wright, H. and S. Pollock 1986. 'Regional Socio-Economic Organization in Southern Mesopotamia: The Middle and Later Fifth Millennium.' In J.L. Huot, (ed.), *Préhistoire de la Mesopotamie.* Paris: Editions de CNRS.

Yoffee, N. 1979. 'The decline and rise of Mesopotamian civilization: An ethnoarchaeological perspective on the evolution of social complexity.' *American Antiquity* **44/1**: 14-35.

Yoffee, N. 1993a. 'Too many chiefs? (or, Safe texts for the '90s).' In N. Yoffee & A. Sherratt, (eds.), *Archaeological theory: who sets the agenda?* pp. 60-78. Cambridge: Cambridge University Press.

Yoffee, N. 1993b. 'Mesopotamian Interaction Spheres.' In N. Yoffee, and J.J. Clark (eds.) *Early Stages in the Evolution of Mesopotamian Civilization: Soviet Excavations in Northern Iraq.* pp. 257-269. Tucson and London: University of Arizona Press.

Young, T.C. 1986. 'Godin Tepe VI/V and Central Western Iran at the End of the Fourth Millennium.' In U. Finkeiner and W. Röllig, eds., *Gamdat Nasr: Period or Regional Style?* Beihefte zum Tübinger Atlas des Vorderen Orients, Reiche B, Nr. 62. pp. 212-228. Weisbaden: Ludwig Reïchert.

Zaccagnini, C. 1993. 'Topography, Excavation, Stratigraphy and Chronology.' In G. Wilhelm and C. Zaccagnini, eds., *Tell Karrana 3, Tell Jikan, Tell Khirbet Salih.* pp.15-20. Bagdader.

Zagarell, A. 1986. 'Trade, Women, Class and Society in Ancient Western Asia.' *Current Anthropology* **27**: 415-30.

Zagarell, A. 1989. 'Comments.' In Algaze, G. 'The Uruk Expansion, Cross-cultural Exchange in early Mesopotamian Civilization.' *Current Anthropology* **30**: 600.

Zarins, J. 1990. 'Early pastoral nomadism and the settlement of lower Mesopotamia.' *Bulletin of the American School of Oriental Research* **280**: 31-65.

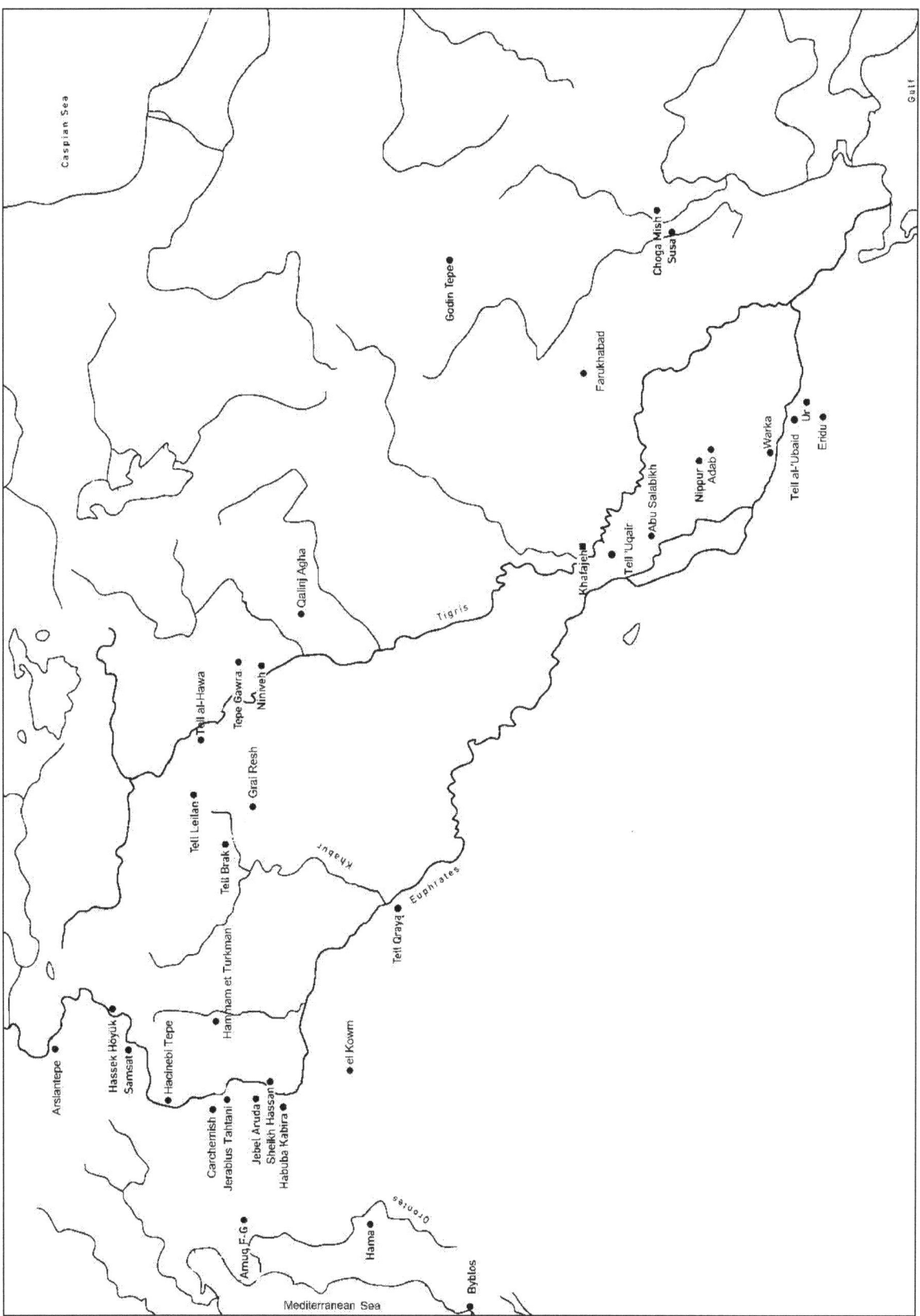

Fig. 1. Fourth millennium sites mentioned in the text.

Paul Collins

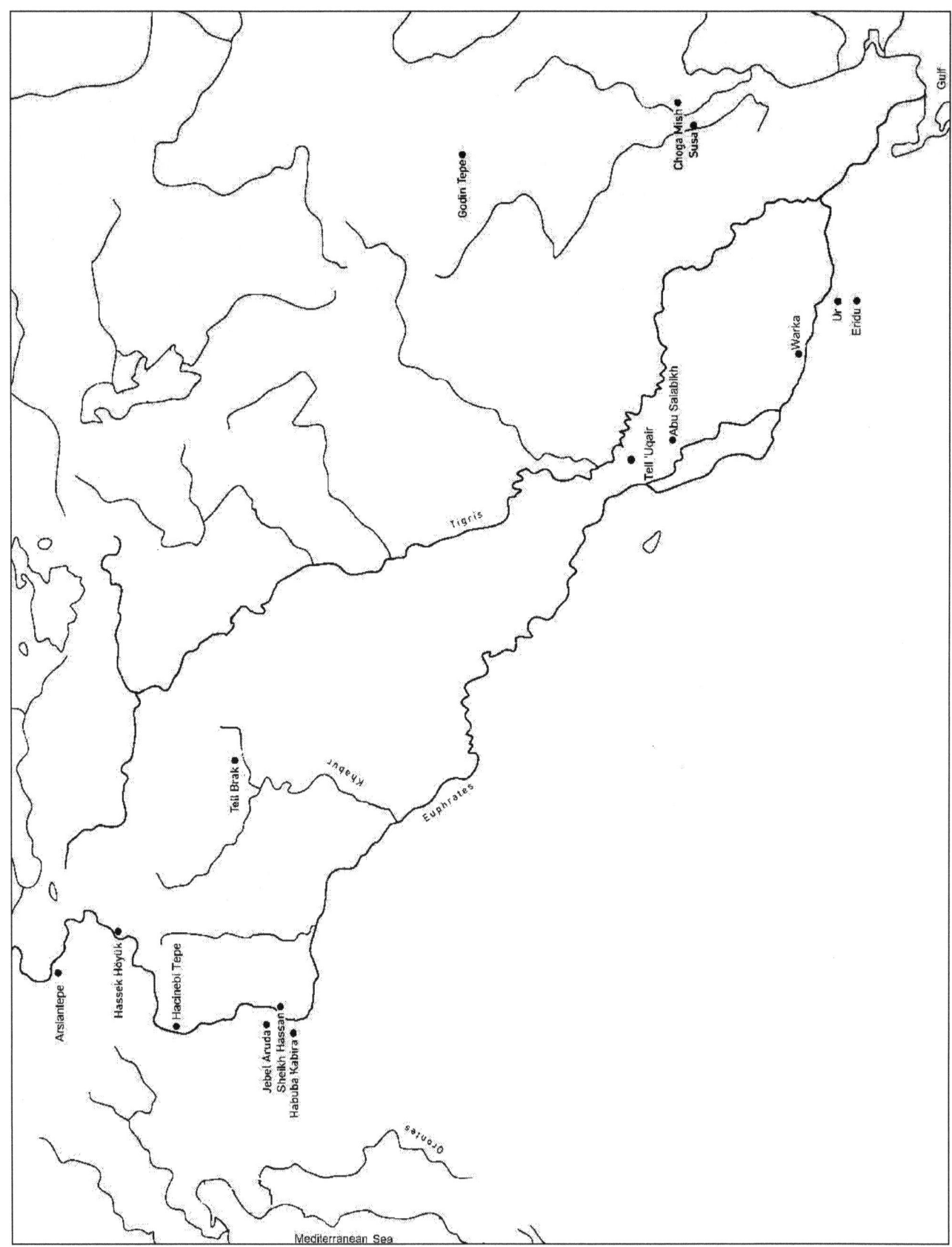

Fig. 2. Uruk sites of chapter 5

The Uruk Phenomenon

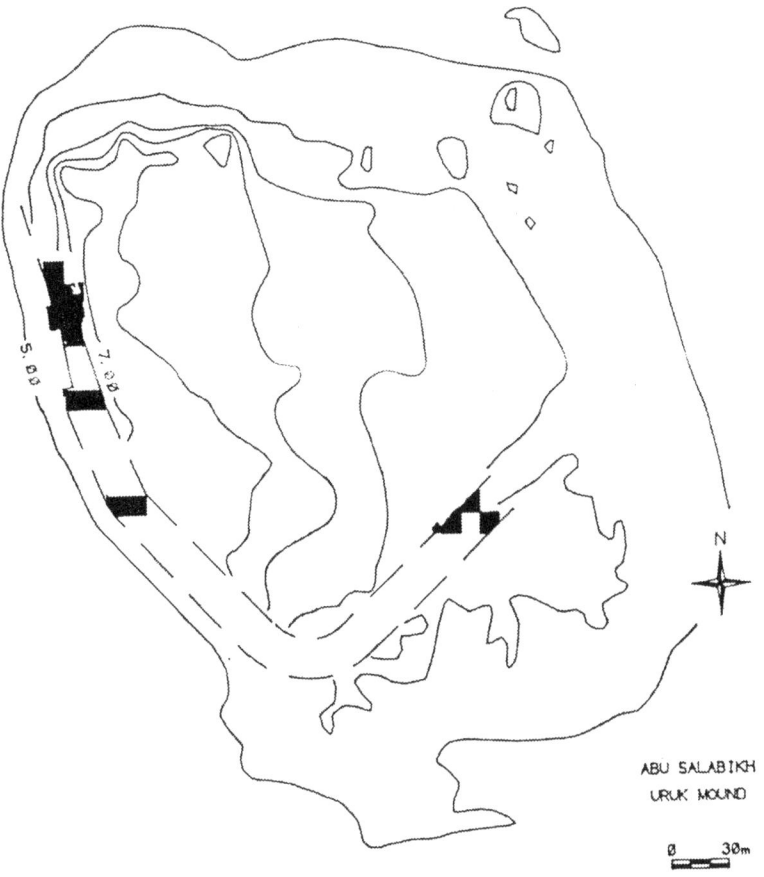

Fig. 3. The Uruk mound Abu Salabikh (Pollock et al 1991: fig. 4)

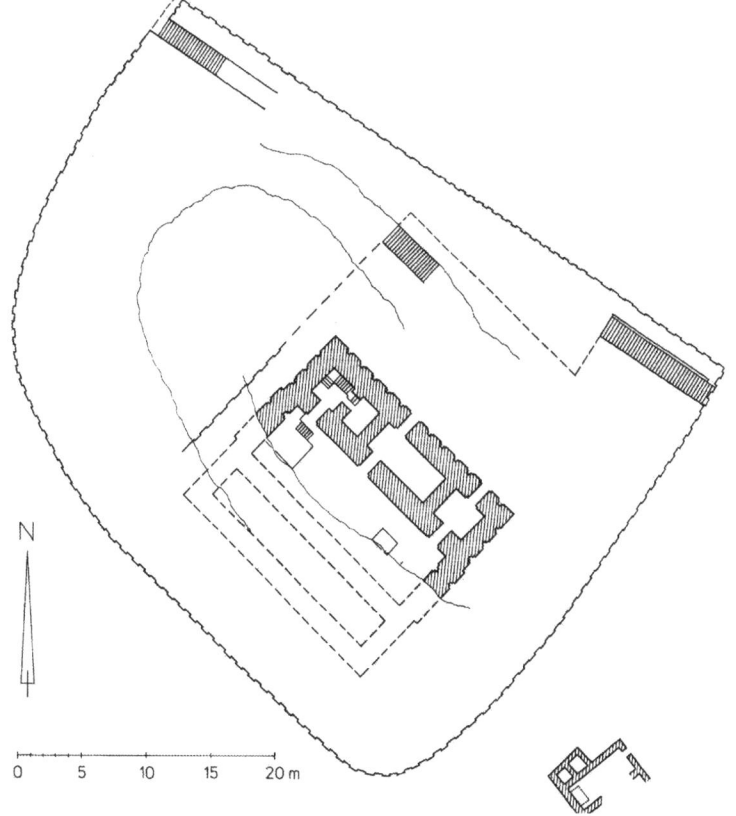

Fig. 4. Uqair platform (Heinrich 1982: Abb. 105)

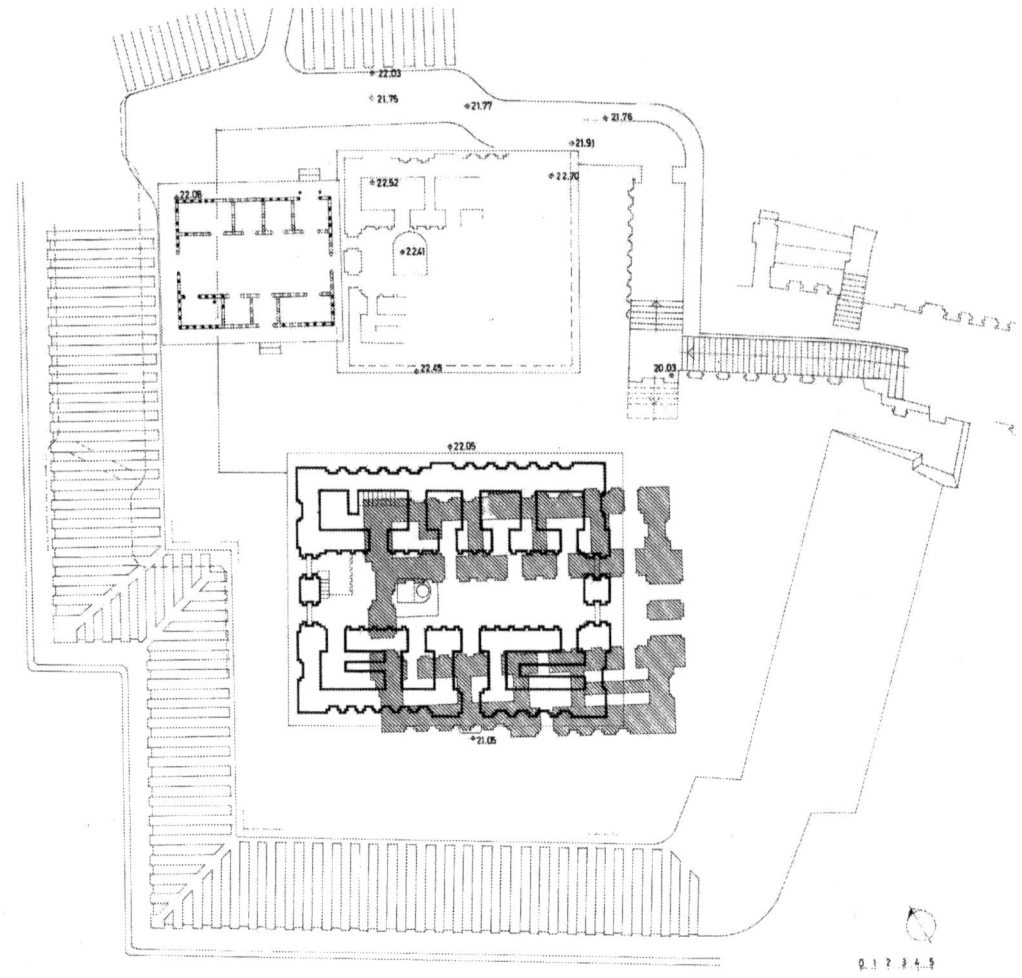

Fig. 5. White Temple B-D (Heinrich 1982: Abb 83)

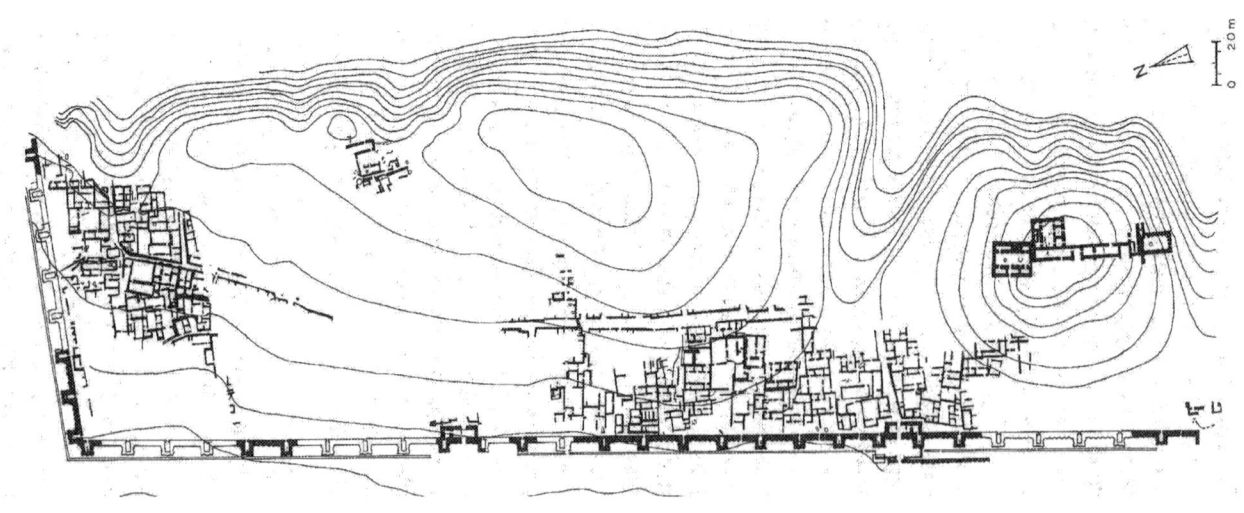

Fig. 6. Habuba Kabira Süd (Algaze 1993: Fig. 5B.)

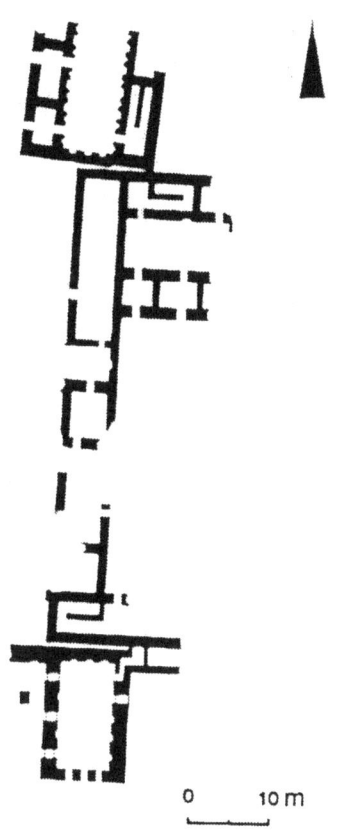

Fig. 7. Tell Qannas

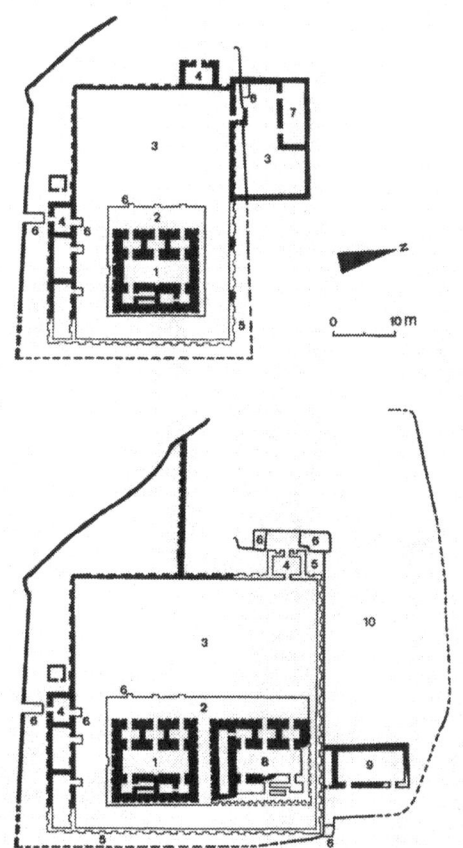

Fig. 8. Jebel Aruda Temple development (Vallet 1998a: Fig. 8)

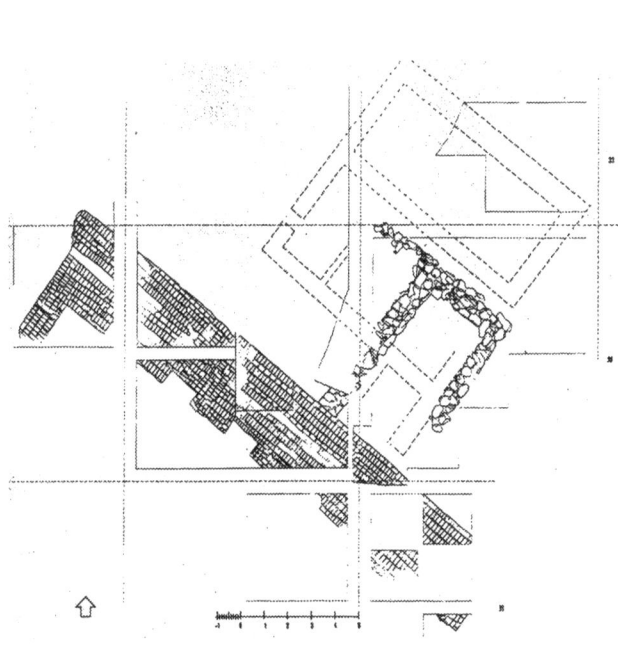

Fig. 9. City-wall, 'stone building' (level 6), reconstructed buildings (level 7) (Boese 1991: fig. 15)

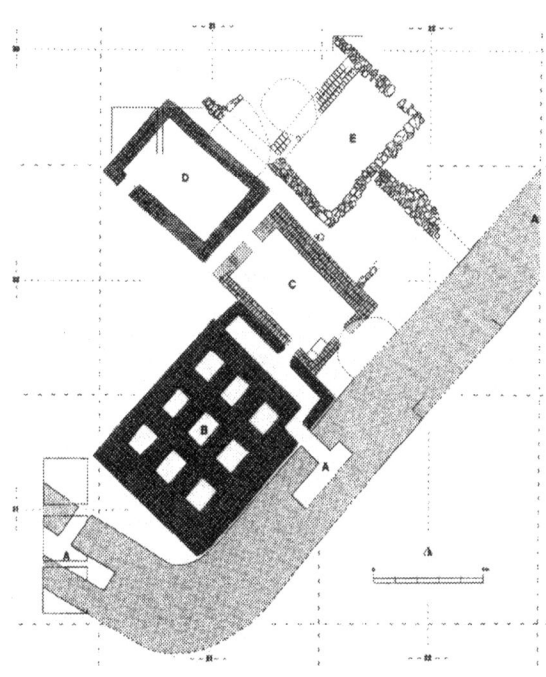

Fig. 10. Sheikh Hassan. (Boese 1995: Abb 5)

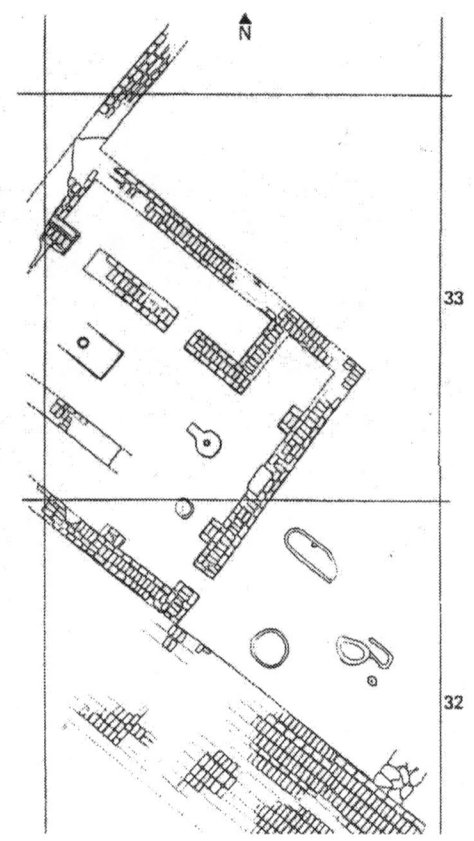

Fig. 11. 'temple' level 6 (Boese 1995: Abb. 6)

Fig. 12. 'temple' of level 6 (Boese 1995: Abb. 4.)

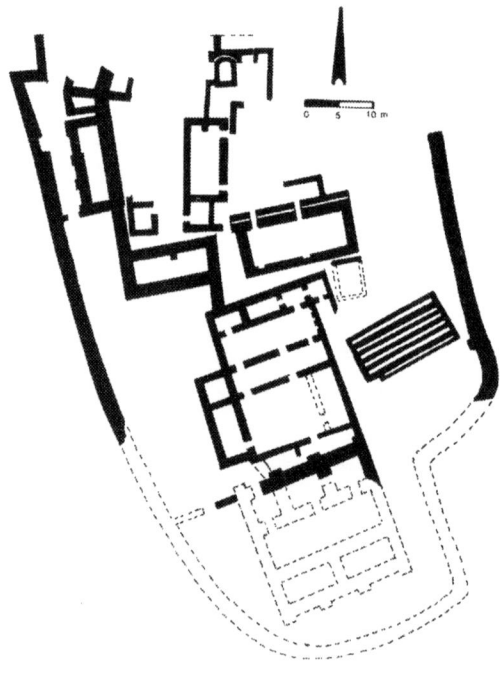

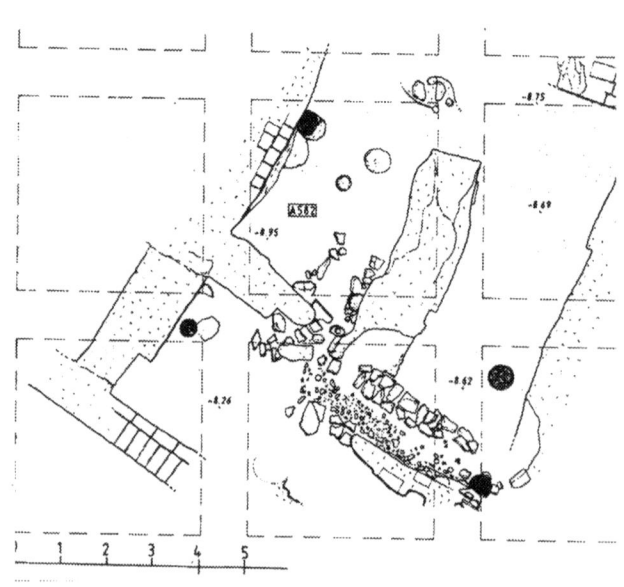

Fig. 13. Hassek Höyük (Algaze 1993: Fig. 23)

Fig. 14. Arslantepe Period VII (Frangipane 1997: Fig. 6)

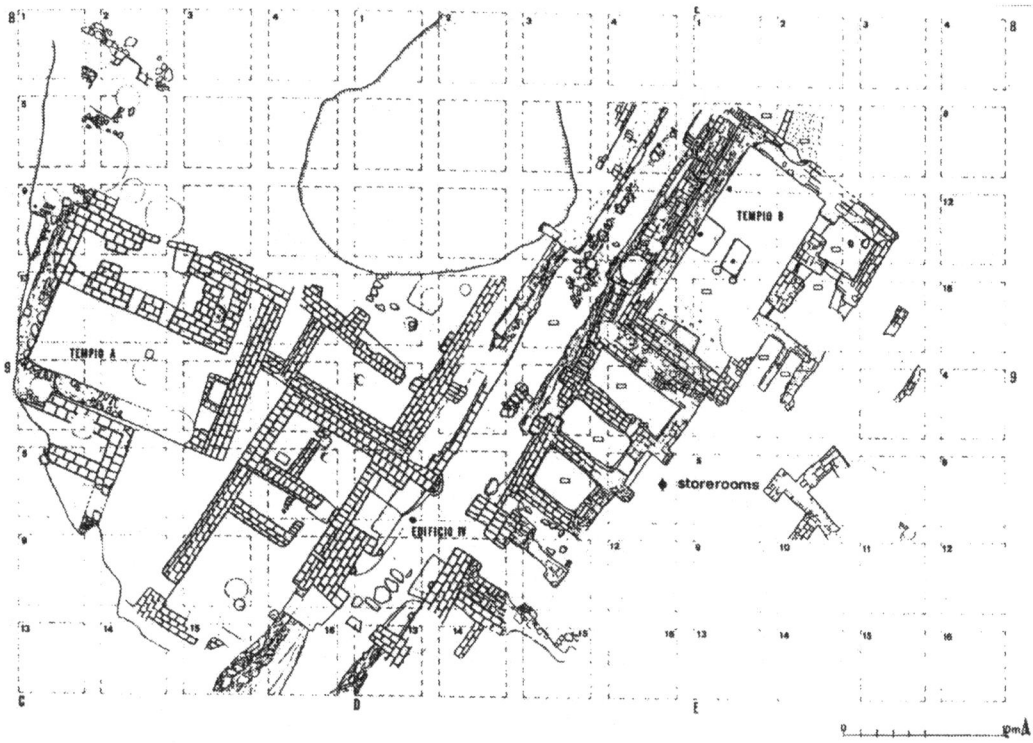

Fig. 15. Arslantepe Period VIA (Frangipane 1997: Fig. 2a).

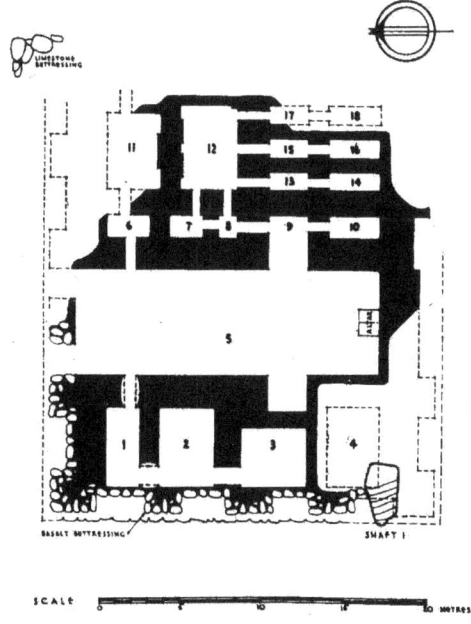

Fig. 16. Eye Temple (Oates, D. 1982: Fig. 49)

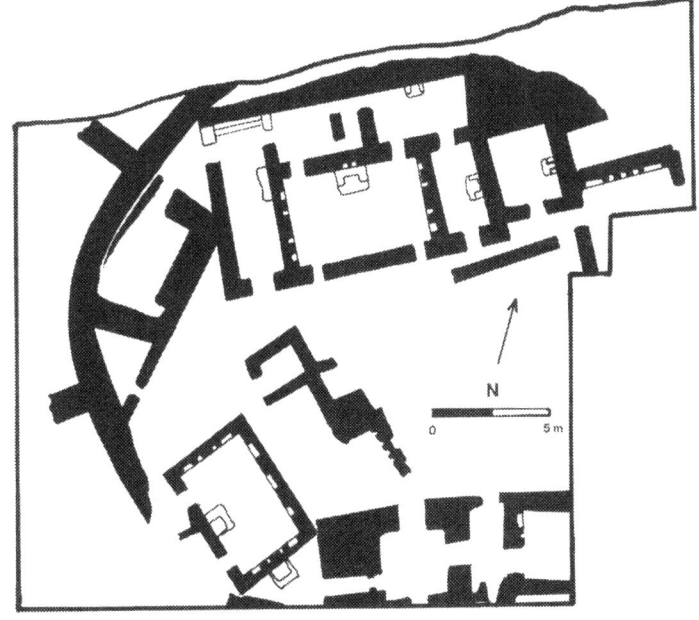

Fig. 17. Godin Tepe Level 5 (Algaze 1993: Fig. 25)

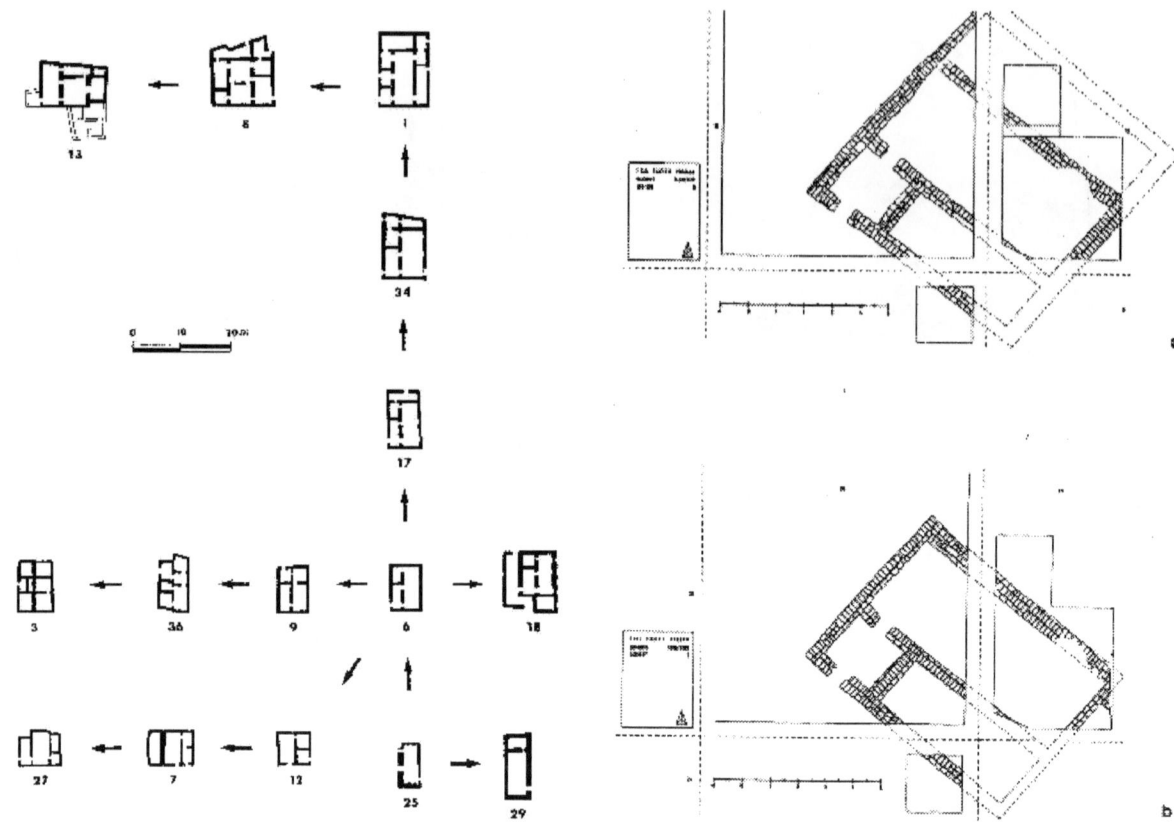

Fig. 18. Uruk architectural forms (Vallet 1998b: 119)

Fig. 19. 'Mittelsaalhaus' level 8 (top), level 9 (bottom) (Boese 1995: Abb. 5)

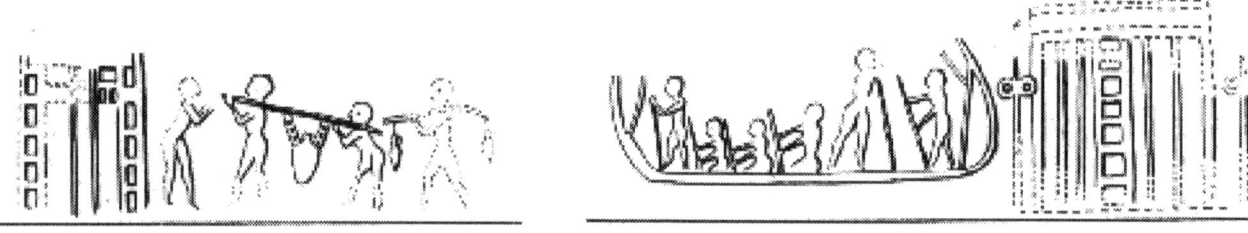

Fig. 20. Uruk glyptic (Amiet 1980: pl. 13, D & E)

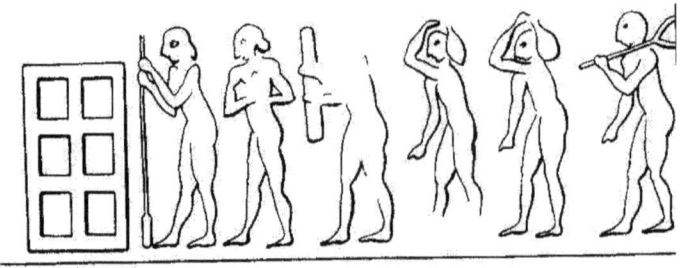

Fig. 21. Uruk glyptic. (Amiet 1980: pl. 11 no. 203 B)

Fig. 22. Uruk glyptic. (Amiet 1980: pl. 41, no. 621)

Fig. 23. Uruk glyptic. (Amiet 1980: pl. 44, nos. 642-3)

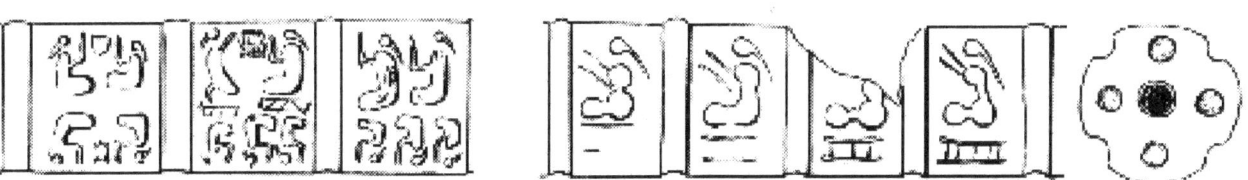

Fig. 24. Uruk glyptic. (Amiet 1980: pl. 20, nos. 322-3)

Paul Collins

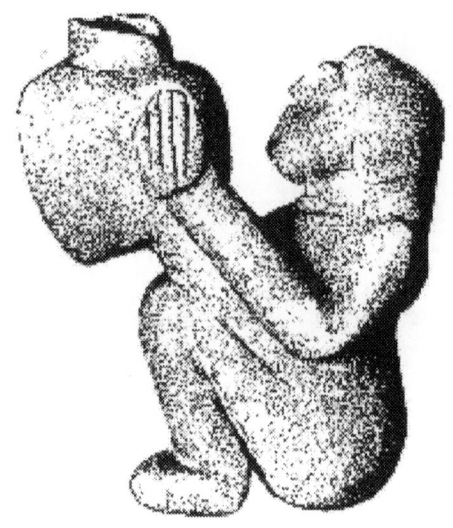 

Fig. 25. Uruk figure from Susa (Potts 1999: fig. 3.3)     Fig. 26. Uruk figure from Susa (Harper et al. 1992: no. 25)

Fig. 27. Uruk glyptic. (Amiet 1980: pl. 18, nos. 305-7)

Fig. 28. 'Priest-king' (Louvre Museum).

Fig. 29. The Warka Vase relief (Lindemeyer and Martin 1993: Tafel 25)

Fig. 30. Seal impression from Susa (Amiet 1980: pl. 46, no. 659)

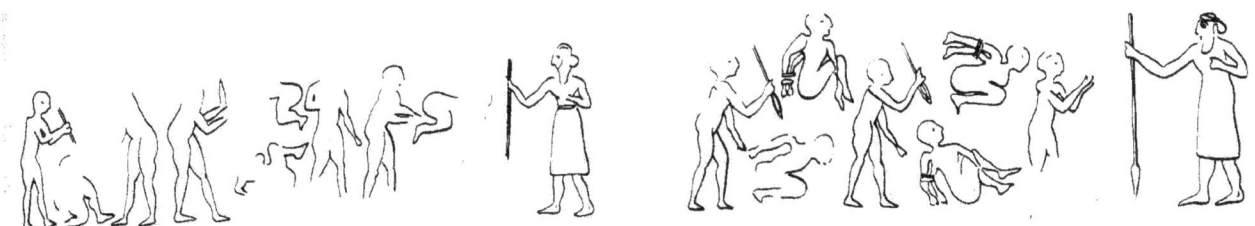

Fig. 31. Seal impressions from Warka (Amiet 1980: pl. 47, nos. 660-1)

www.ingramcontent.com/pod-product-compliance
Lightning Source LLC
Chambersburg PA
CBHW061544010526
44113CB00023B/2799